Gavin Boyter is an Edinburgh-born writer and film-maker whose first feature film *Sparks and Embers* was released in December 2015. A keen runner since his thirties, Gavin once ran 102 miles in a single day. His running superfood is chocolate cake. He lives in London but pines for Scottish mountains.

DOWNHILL
FROM HERE

Running from John O'Groats to Land's End

GAVIN BOYTER

SANDSTONEPRESS
HIGHLAND | SCOTLAND

Published in Great Britain by
Sandstone Press Ltd
Dochcarty Road
Dingwall
Ross-shire
IV15 9UG
Scotland.

www.sandstonepress.com

The publisher acknowledges support from Creative Scotland
towards publication of this volume.

ISBN: 978-1-910985-62-5
ISBNe: 978-1-910985-63-2

Cover design by Two Associates
Typeset by Iolaire Typesetting, Newtonmore
Printed and bound by CPI Group (UK) Ltd., Croydon, CR0 4YY

To Ian and Kath, my parents,
for their unflagging support and belief in me

ACKNOWLEDGEMENTS

First and foremost, huge credit must be given to my tireless support drivers / camera people Ian Boyter, Carol Hodge and Sorrell Kerrison, without whom I wouldn't have made it 1,174 miles without collapse. Thanks to my fellow ultra-runners Dave 'Stan' Stanning, Richard Durance and Chris Thrall, who joined me and spurred me on along the way. I owe a great debt of gratitude to Davey Henderson, Lol and the digger crew, the gentlemen at Bellingham and especially Sheila Lumm, who went out of their way to save us from car calamity, exhaustion and misery. For helping me at times of crisis: the forest rangers of Rowardennan, the hunters at Hetherhope and Thomas by Kielder Water. In appreciation of their efficiency, sympathy and diagnostic skills, the staff at the Livingston A&E department. Mum, Fiona and Katy proved staunch supporters with their families (and dogs) and, in Fiona's case, suggested the wryly fitting title. To the patient hoteliers and bed and breakfast owners who stayed open late, made home-cooked meals and washed my disgusting laundry, I salute you. With gratitude for their generosity and an excellent meal at The Old Bakehouse, Iain and Carol. For listening to early excerpts and helping me believe in what I was writing I must single out Guy Ducker, Sara Lodge and Yiannis Hayiannis (may my travails prove therapeutic). For inadvertently showing me the way through Dartmoor, Tracy D'Cruz. For the excellent coffee, free Wi-Fi and convivial surroundings in which I wrote much of the book, gratitude must be shown to the staff of C'est

Ici café at Barons Court. Special thanks to Lygeri Dimitriou and the team at the Middlesex University Sports Science labs for putting me through my paces and dunking me in ice-cold water. For key advice and warnings, too few of which I heeded (sorry) I must thank Monique Palmer, James Cattermole, Lucja Leonard and Andrea Havill. Essential last-minute ultrasound therapy was kindly donated by Geraldine Fergusson at Optimum Physiotherapy. Huge respect is owed to my charities, Whizz-Kidz and Limbpower for providing inspiration by example and a reality check when I was feeling sorry for myself. At Sandstone, I'm hugely grateful to Moira Forsyth for recognising something universal in my very personal journey, to Keara Donnachie for sterling publicity support, the typographers at Iolaire Typography Ltd and Roger Smith for proofreading. Helen Stirling provided excellent maps and David Eldridge at Two Associates Design turned my tatty old trainers into a striking cover design. And last but never least, to those I met along the way (including Kevin, Libby and Jesse), whether walking, running, cycling or driving – you made the arduous journey an unpredictable delight. Here's hoping this will inspire others to step out onto the trail or the tarmac in search of adventure.

CONTENTS

SECTION FOUR: The Last Leg

LIST OF ILLUSTRATIONS

1. With Dad at John O'Groats
2. Davey Henderson to the rescue, near Helmsdale
3. On the Great Glen Way
4. Lost, somewhere off the Great Glen Way
5. Carol Hodge enjoys a rare moment of respite near Gairlochy
6. With the Three Brethren on the Southern Upland Way
7. Receiving ultrasound therapy for my errant knee
8. My odd shin bulge examined in Livingstone A&E
9. On the Pennine Way with David 'Stan' Stanning
10. Helm Wind at Cross Fell
11. On the Pennine Way with Richard Durance
12. Alone on a wild, windy moor
13. The sun breaks through the mist
14. A spider's web by the roadside near Cowling
15. Blackstone Edge
16. A muddy trail in Somerset
17. Nearing Hebden Bridge
18. Kinder Scout
19. Planning at Edale
20. Sorrell Kerrison lines up a shot on the Yorkshire Dales

LIST OF MAPS

FOREWORD

It's just after ten o'clock in the morning and I have been running for twenty-two hours. The last three of those hours have been run in torrential rain, the kind that soaks to the skin in minutes and then pounds relentlessly into forehead, arms and legs, numbing them into submission. I've long ago lost sight of the ultimate reason I'm still running. Now I'm kept in motion by an arbitrary number: 100. I've decided to stop after I've run a hundred miles.

I say running, but at this point in the endeavour, I'm really just shuffling, like an extra from *The Walking Dead*, around the 9.1K circuit mapped out by the organisers of the inaugural Cotswold 24-Hour Challenge here on the Bathurst Estate near Cirencester. I'm barely managing 12-minute miles when my usual long run pace would be nearer eight minutes per mile. My right ankle has swollen badly and a ridge of livid flesh has thickened my shin to twice its normal circumference above my worn, waterlogged running shoes. My knees, always my weakness, have long given up their protestations as if to say 'He's not listening ... but at least we can say he was warned.' At this point in the day, teetering on the brink of delirium, it doesn't seem that irrational to attribute conscious thought to my rebellious joints and muscles.

Others shuffle round the well-marked course, zombielike or with cruel vigour, the latter group wearing the coloured wristbands of relay runners who have had breaks of several hours between circuits while awaiting their turn. No such luxury for us few yellow-banded solo runners in this 24-hour event. Where once the cheerful encouragements of the relay runners spurred us on, we're now digging deep and a badly timed 'good run, man' is as likely to break our spirits as lift them.

For those not in the know, let me explain. A 24-hour race, as its name might suggest, is a race run over the course of a whole day. Rather than the conventional system of seeing how quickly you can run a set distance, the 24-hour race takes time as the constant, and distance as the variable. The winner is the runner who completes the most circuits in the shortest time, within a 24-hour cut-off. Why take part in such a race? Why drive the body to such brutal limits for so many hours?

I think most casual runners and non-runners might understand the lure of a marathon, with its iconic distance, charity fundraising and cheering crowds. They might even see something worthwhile in the first ultra-race I'd run in May 2015 – the London to Brighton 100K Challenge. Certainly, the changing scenery and obvious end point of such an event fits with most people's understanding of what a race is, even though running more than two marathons in a day might seem somewhat extreme. In contrast, hobbling around the same, fairly unexciting, 9.1K course anything up to 22 times (in the case of that year's winner Paul Beechey) seems dangerously monomaniacal.

For me, it was as simple as finding out what I could achieve if pushed to my absolute limits. Although, it has to be said 'absolute limits' is a questionable concept amongst the really committed ultra-runner, ever looking for the next milestone to leap over. Ultra-running is more about pushing thresholds back than finding insurmountable limitations. But let's backtrack a bit.

My serious running began in 2004, when I decided to take the thrice-weekly fitness runs I'd been doing and put them to some use by attempting a marathon. I'd run occasionally at university in the late 1980s and early 1990s, tearing round Edinburgh's ¾ mile Meadows circuit, just minutes from my student flat, with fellow housemates Rob and Neil. We even got as competitive as recording our times on a wallchart we proudly displayed in the hallway, possibly with the hapless notion that female visitors would be in awe of our prowess. But this running was never with any end point in mind or any concrete goal. It was running for running's sake. Perhaps this was appropriate; the course we used to run included part of the Sri Chinmoy Mile, although it was much later in life that I read up on this guru of 'self-transcendence', meditation and running.

In my thirties, running for fitness took on a more urgent appeal but also begged the new question – 'What is all this running for?' Were he still with us, Sri Chinmoy would probably say that this question is essentially meaningless. We are, therefore we run. But for an average struggling Londoner (I moved from one capital to another in 1999), everything has to have a purpose, to contribute to a greater goal. Life is just too demanding for fripperies. By such simplistic logic, long-distance running can have only one aim – to prepare oneself for a race. In my comparatively youthful gung-ho manner, aged thirty-four, I decided that my first race had to be *the* London race, for how could I aim for anything less ambitious? And so it was that my first ever race (and the first time I'd alongside another person in twelve years) would be the 2005 London Marathon.

I trained pretty hard. Not 120 miles a week hard, like some hardcore marathon runners, but 50–60 miles a week, including short, fast runs and longer weekend slogs. I was not a member of a running club at that point. I don't think I was really aware that such groups existed or, at least, that they would be open to runners of all abilities. In my naiveté, I ran alone and untutored. I didn't read any books on marathon running (in any case, the boom in writing about running and racing technique came a decade or more later). I did no speed training, struggled repeatedly up no hills.

My only preparation was the one essential feature of marathon training – going the distance. After about eight weeks of sticking to my spreadsheeted plan, my weekend long runs had crept up to the teens in mileage and my weekly totals were hitting 50-plus miles. I'd identified favourite routes of different lengths and levels of difficulty and was using a basic running watch to record my times over various distances. It was gratifying seeing those times reduce; I felt motivated at the end of each run to put on one final sprint to beat my personal best. I'd done the requisite arithmetic, deciding that my goal would be a sub-3-hour marathon and I knew that this required an average speed of 6 minutes and 52 seconds per mile. Typically, I had no idea how much of a challenge I'd set myself (at London, you're in the 96th percentile if you run sub-3). But the goal, realistic or not, gave me something to work towards.

I stood at the front of the start line on a chilly April morning in 2005, terrifyingly close to the elite runners, shivering under the traditional pre-run garb of black plastic bin liner with torn-open arm holes. It was more than a little disconcerting to see the lithe, limber Kenyans and Ethiopians lined up, with a few token Europeans and Americans, just a few yards ahead of us. In the London Marathon, the fastest non-elite runners are typically herded into one small 'three hours and faster' pen at each of the three starting lines, which gives you an idea of how few people run that speed. I could probably have fitted all the runners in my projected time category into my flat at the time (and it was anything but palatial). Nevertheless, I tried my best to shake off any misgivings. After all, I could honestly say I'd done all I could. What would be, would be.

I ran a disappointing race. At least, in terms of

overshooting my goal by a full sixteen minutes, it disappointed me. It was of course a thrill to have completed a marathon at all, not to have resorted to walking at any point (this seemed vitally important to me in a way it simply doesn't now) and to have crossed that line with arms aloft and something approaching a sprint finish. However, I had failed to achieve the target I'd set myself and a pedantic little voice in my head kept telling me that 3 hours 16 minutes and 14 seconds was simply not good enough. The other voice in my head, the more animalistic cry of 'never again' as I hid, experiencing all-over pain and fatigue, in one of the Portaloos, was replaced by a background hum of 'you can do better' and so the cycle of ambition began all over again.

I did do better. The following year, my second London Marathon was completed in 3 hours 11 minutes and 43 seconds. Which was good ... except that it was by far my worst-judged performance strategically. Fired up with newfound zeal (this time I had something to prove) I'd blazed through the first half in a little over eighty-two minutes then died horribly over the last thirteen miles, losing an average of two minutes per mile by the end. To put it another way, that 82 minutes is still the fastest I've run a half-marathon distance *by over three minutes*.

Yet that 2006 result remained my best marathon time. My third attempt at the distance in 2008 produced my worst time (at that point) – 3 hours 17 minutes and 44 seconds. I'd paced myself, having learned the lessons of 2006, and it did me no good whatsoever. Subsequent marathons, albeit now in my late thirties and early forties, and run in hot conditions over different courses (Brighton and Edinburgh) added another twenty minutes to those London times. A sub-3-hour marathon became a distant fantasy. Perhaps the marathon wasn't my best distance after all. Half-hearted attempts to enter marathons subsequently always seemed to end with my forgetting to send off my application in time, failing to secure a charity sponsor (despite having run for Cancer Research and Shelter in previous years) or simply forgetting the deadline for entry. It appeared my heart was no longer in it.

I kept running through the late 'noughties' and beyond. I was a keen member of the Ealing, Southall and Middlesex AC from 2006 until 2012 when I moved away from the area. I found I had something of a talent as a middling cross-country runner and I enjoyed the mud, the chaos and the extremity of the sport, as well as the fact that it was impossible to measure myself against previous efforts since every course was different and every year brought new weather-related challenges – hard-packed soil, wet leaves, vicious hills and endless, relentless rain. Because I could only measure myself against fellow ESM runners at my approximate level of ability, and I could offer the catch-all excuse of having had 'a bad day', my running ambitions atrophied a little. Then I discovered ultra-running.

I think my first awareness of this discipline was when I was marathon training and doing my long runs up and down the Grand Union Canal between Brentford and Hayes. On one particularly long Sunday run, heading north out of London, dodging puddles and grumpy swans, I passed various runners wearing racing numbers and heading the other way. They seemed oddly unhurried, were largely in their forties or older and were sometimes running in chatting pairs. There were huge distances between the competitors. What sort of race was this? The front-runners hardly seemed to be breaking a sweat and were jogging along at a lackadaisical 8 or 9-minute mile pace.

I took a closer look at one of their bibs and the piece of paper pinned upon it read 'Town to Tring'. I'd never heard of Tring, although I assumed that 'town' meant Brentford, the southern extent of the Union Canal as it enters London. I'd previously run as far as ten miles up that stretch of canal with no whisper of a place called Tring, so it had to be a decent length race, not a 5K 'fun run'. That said, if it was Brentford to Tring, surely they were running the wrong way? When I reached the next road bridge over the canal I met a couple of high-vis clad marshals and asked them about the race. 'Oh, it's a 40-mile race from London to Tring. Some of the keen ones run back the next day,' came the blithe reply. Clearly I'd been passing those few participants who were running 'the double' – eighty miles – more in two days than I'd ever run in a week, by a considerable margin.

Forty miles – with some of them running another forty miles on the Sunday? I adjusted the parameters of my somewhat patronising assumptions about the runners I had passed. This race was as 'hardcore' as they come. Or so I naïvely thought.

Thus began my research into the then near-secret world of ultra-running. I found out about such events as the West Highland Way race (95 miles over terrain with a total ascent of 14,760 feet) and the South Downs Way 100 (one hundred miles, the record for the route being a little over fourteen hours). I ventured into the Piccadilly Waterstones' Sports section for the first time in my life (I'm not a big sports fan) and devoured books by US ultra legends Dean Karnazes, Scott Jurek and Rich Roll. It dawned on me that I was in the middle of something of a boom-time for this ludicrous sport of running until you drop (or cross the finish line, although the two can be skilfully combined for effect). It was adventurous, extreme and exciting, as all the YouTube race reports from the Badwater Ultra, Marathon des Sables, Spartathlon or Ultramarathon du Mont Blanc made clear. I became something of a theoretical ultra-running junkie.

Except I hadn't run one. Not yet.

If I was going to throw myself (is there any other way?) into this new world of extraordinary running, I needed a goal. And not just any goal – one in keeping with the superlative nature of the sport. What would be the ultimate UK-based ultramarathon?

All of it. Of course. There was already an established British tradition of John O'Groats to Land's End travel, generally by bicycle or by walking. So many people had in fact done this route that two miniature theme parks had sprung up at Land's End and John O'Groats, the somewhat arbitrary 'most Northern and Southern' outposts of the UK.[1] There is even a website devoted to the hiking and cycling 'End to Enders' co-created by commercial enterprises Natural Retreats and Heritage Great Britain.[2] Had anyone run it?

Of course they had. A quick bit of web surfing revealed that the record was a staggering 9 days and 2 hours. That's right – an average of over ninety miles a day. Several ultra-runners I've talked to have doubted the veracity of this achievement but the Guinness Book of Records, no slouch in terms of verifying outlandish claims, is adamant that Andrew Rivett managed it in the above extraordinary time.

Clearly, my run wouldn't be about breaking any records. Instead, what I would set out to do is to cover the entirety of the UK by foot, taking in as many off-road trails as possible, running 1,100 miles in total in under a month. How naïve that last clause feels now.

I wanted to get to know the country I'd lived in my whole life in an entirely new way, to see how its landscapes, peoples and climate changed as I proceeded south. And of course I wanted to test my mettle. But really, this was more than just something I *wanted* to do; it was something I *needed* to do. Let me explain.

It's not that I specifically had to run the length of the country. Nobody needs to run 1,100 miles in a month. It's more that I needed to do something grandiose and extraordinary because, if I'm honest, I felt like my life was rapidly going off the rails.

After almost twelve years in a dead-end administration job in the NHS, earning very little money, with no chance of promotion, no opportunity to innovate or use my creativity, I knew my office-based days were numbered. The work was boring and the atmosphere in the office often crackled with employees' frustration and sense of being pawns in a political game as a further round of restructuring and redundancies was mooted, greenlit and then dangled above us for over two years while Unison and NHS England battled it out. By the time voluntary redundancies were finally offered to those staff who wanted out, around half took up the offer, myself included. Having worked for over ten years as a permanent NHS employee, I was entitled to a generous payout and I decided to take the money and run. As it happened, literally.

My immediate problem was that, bar writing and film-making, I had nothing tangible with which to replace office work, in terms of a viable career. Eighteen years after leaving film school, I'd finally managed to complete a feature film, *Sparks and Embers*, which was due out in December, but I had a suspicion it would receive a rather limited release and I'd probably seen all the income I would from it.[3] Although I had another film in development, the psychological thriller *Nitrate*,[4] that was probably a year or more away from shooting. How would I earn a crust in the meantime? I had absolutely no idea.

I was living alone in a studio flat in west London, jobless and without a clear career plan and I knew I had a difficult choice – either use the redundancy money to fund a film project, or use it to live. If I had a wife or girlfriend, I'm sure she would have had a great deal to say about sinking this windfall into a film without any guarantee of distribution. I had no such partner, a fact that was making me increasingly unhappy. Recently, I'd found women I'd dated were not particularly impressed by me. London is an insanely expensive city to live in and I was barely scraping by, which made me feel inadequate when sitting across the table from successful female entrepreneurs, lawyers or executives. In all the aspects of life in which a man measures his worth (for right or wrong), I felt I was failing and this was making me more and more gloomy with each passing week.

I'd been down in the depths of depression before and had almost not made it back.[5] I couldn't afford to go there again. I had to do something desperate – something to make me feel powerful, to make me believe again that the best of life still lay ahead of me.

No job, no immediate career prospects, no partner, no kids. A pessimist could look at that set of circumstances and spiral into despair. I decided that, if I was going to save myself from what I used to call 'the black cloud', I had to be an optimist. I had to see this as an opportunity. I would combine my love of running with my desire to make films and finance an adventure with my redundancy money (topped up with some crowdfunding). I found that adventure in the notion of running the length of the UK and filming every step.

As soon as I had that exciting idea I was beset by doubts. How could I make the huge leap from occasional marathon runner to daily ultra-runner? I thought it likely that I'd be able to 'go ultra' if I slowed down and ran smarter but would I be able to do it for twenty-eight days straight, running all the daylight hours I could?

Making the film properly cinematic would also prove a challenge. As a film-maker, I had enjoyed the various short film clips and YouTube diaries about ultra-running, including interviews with Scott Jurek,[6] self-shot race reports by Michael Arnstein,[7] the self-styled 'fruitarian' and more aesthetically pleasing mini documentaries by Ethan Newberry,[8] 'the ginger runner'. But even the best of these seemed quite cursory and, at times, not particularly well made. I did not manage to find any filmed content about a John O'Groats to Land's End Run (until I heard about Sean Conway's Discovery Channel series,[9] by which time my documentary was long underway).

The production of *Sparks and Embers* had been troubled in terms of securing the finance and greenlighting the various stages of shooting and post-production, and at times it had felt like my film career was doomed to be an endless series of false starts and disappointments. I wanted my second film to be something entirely within my control. A documentary on ultra-running, and on JOGLE in particular, seemed ideal. I thought I'd probably only need to spend half of the redundancy cash; then I calculated the necessary budget and realised how unrealistic this estimate was. In the end, the film would eat up almost everything I had.

The second issue, how to film it, was partly a budgetary consideration and partly a creative choice. Given how much money I had at my disposal, I had to strip things down to the basics while trying to keep a variety of camera sources and cover as much of the preparation stages as well as the run itself as I could. I decided I couldn't afford a proper cinematographer but I could co-opt my support driver, whomever that would be, to leapfrog me and film shots of me running as well as general views and details of the environments through which I'd be passing. I bought the best 'compact systems' camera I could find, the new Panasonic G7 and muddled through most of its lengthy manual. I ordered two GoPro Hero 4 action cameras online (GoPro, like anyone else I contacted, had declined to sponsor me, so I paid full price) plus a number of accessories including head mounts and vehicle clamps.

My boldest purchase was a DJI Phantom 3 Pro quadcopter. My intention was to use this to capture the occasional 'God's eye view' of a landscape, with me as an inconsequential speck crawling along it. My support driver would also have to get to grips with this, of course. It became apparent that the tripartite role of support driver/cameraperson/production assistant would be a hugely challenging one. I began soliciting CVs and sifting through a lot of keen, experienced candidates. This would be a paid role, albeit at industry minimum, because I wanted a professional approach, given that I might literally be putting my health and well-being in their hands as well as delegating much of the most scenic cinematography to this individual.

Eventually the support role became something of a relay event, with my father, Ian, working the first week then handing over to Carol (whom I chose from the pile of CVs after a telephone interview) for two weeks and then to her experienced film-maker friend, Sorrell, for a further ten days, who handed back to my dad for a while and so on. This flexibility of approach allowed my one-person crew to work around the other commitments in their lives.

Meanwhile, I was training. I had no idea how to approach preparing physically for a challenge which would involve me running up to 280 miles per week. I couldn't risk that level of activity in training and nor was there time to put in anything like the hours necessary to experience what daily epic running would feel like. The closest I came was running two or three 20-mile-plus days in a row, which left me feeling drained and a little worried. I also started adding some big one-off practice runs, such as the thirty-five miles between Berkhampsted and Brentford along the Union Canal. Although a pretty level route, I found that this distance really challenged my energy reserves, no matter how many glucose gels I quaffed. How would I cope with making that a daily ordeal?

Ultramarathons were an important part of my preparation, as much about learning how to form mental coping strategies as anything physiological. I could have begun with one of the many 50K races around but that would only add eight kilometres to distances I'd run before and that didn't feel a significant enough step up. I could try for a 50-miler but those seemed a little thin on the ground and the timings of the few I found didn't suit my schedule. Instead, my first proper ultra was the London to Brighton 100K Challenge, which took place in May 2015. Hell, all I was doing was flipping the digits around on a standard marathon – sixty-two miles instead of twenty-six. How bad could that be?

The race could be walked, run as a relay or run solo. A surprising number of participants opted to go it alone. I was attracted by the organiser's positive, inclusive message on their website – that this, although undeniably challenging, was still a distance any able-bodied person could cover, were they sufficiently prepared and motivated. I hoped I was both. I brought along a GoPro and filmed some head-mounted POV footage of the race, although I didn't show my own face on camera much just yet. I found it by turns surprising (the friendliness of other competitors and comparatively slow pace), excruciating (I fell into a well of fatigue around 56k and suffered epic quad pains from all the hill-climbing and unexpected amount of tarmac-pounding the route required) and exhilarating (unexpected surge of power in my legs after the last two checkpoints). With something of a sprint finish at Brighton Racetrack, I crossed the line in 47th place in a time of 12 hours, 53 minutes and 7 seconds, which I thought was pretty good for a beginner. To put this into perspective, the winner's time was 09:32:00.[10]

An agonising (but effective) sports massage and ten days' rest later, I returned to training proper and then in July ran the aforementioned 24-hour event near Cirencester. My final practice race, an endlessly undulating 50-miler, took place just two weeks before the start of my challenge (perhaps unwisely close, in retrospect) around the small Scottish town of Strathaven. Again, this was an event with relay teams and solo runners (plus, unusually, many cyclists) and I was astonished to finish ninth in a time of 8 hours and 35 minutes. My satisfaction was only diminished a little when I found out later that there were only eighteen solo finishers (three other runners were timed out, which means they did not complete within an allowed cut-off).

When I limped through to Edinburgh and my parents' house to recuperate, taper off my training and make final logistical arrangements, I felt I was as ready as I'd ever be for the adventure to come. I had few concrete expectations, except to finish within the allotted time (how naïve that little assumption seems now) and still be able to walk. I was well-trained, mentally prepared, packed and eager to begin the adventure. I had decided to call the challenge and film *The Long Run*; the simplicity of this title pleased me.

What could possibly go wrong?

---

1.   The actual most northern and southern points on the UK mainland are, respectively, Dunnet Head and Lizard Point but, really, who's counting?

2.   www.endtoenders.com

3.   *Sparks and Embers* was released in the UK in one cinema on the very same day as *Star Wars: The Force Awakens*. Do I need to say any more? Well, perhaps a little. It was simultaneously released on various VOD platforms and on the 1st February 2016 was available on DVD. In the long run, it will probably do okay.

4.   With producer Christine Hartland and co-writer/co-director Guy Ducker.

5.   I may tell the full story later in this book. I'm not quite ready yet.

6.   Try this for instance: https://youtu.be/cpfacDbAltw

7.   www.thefruitarian.com

8.   http://gingerrunner.com/

9.   Sean's website: http://www.seanconway.com/

10.   Russell Tapping, whose 2015 London Marathon time was an impressive 2:42:07.

Section One

TOO FAR NORTH

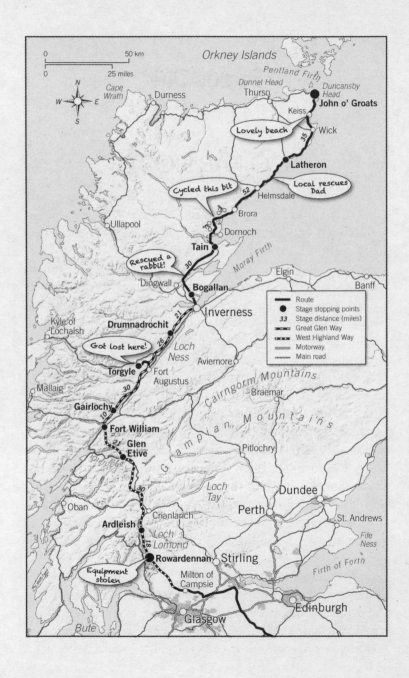

JOHN O'GROATS TO TAIN

'Fuck's sake . . . arrghhh . . . Fucking hell!'

With these prosaic words I double up, clutching my left knee. Something has twanged under the patella, like a large elastic band snapping against the joint. It comes from nowhere and is excruciatingly painful.

I'm on the grassy bank by the side of a small road in Colinton, a leafy Edinburgh suburb. I left my parents' house just minutes ago, wearing all the clothing and equipment I'd planned to use on The Long Run, with the intention of testing the GoPro camera on its gimbal device. It is two days before the event itself begins and I'm in agony, suddenly unable to walk. I hobble back to the house, shamefaced. My injury is captured in inglorious detail on camera and for the rest of that afternoon I continue to film images of myself prone, leg raised, ice-packed and immobile. Throughout the afternoon my mother fusses over me, giving me flashbacks to childhood. I'm forty-four years old but I'm pretty sure I've lain in the same position, in the same house, being ministered to with the same care and attention, almost forty years earlier. Comforting as it is, and helpful in terms of healing the injury, it increases my feeling of helplessness. The timing couldn't be worse.

In less than 48 hours I'm supposed to be embarking on a 28-day, 1,100-mile journey from one end of the country to the other. At the moment, it's a struggle even to get to the bathroom and I'm hopping everywhere, avoiding putting any unnecessary weight on the left leg. My knee has rebelled, seemingly for no reason and without warning. This could seriously jeopardise the challenge.

The pain is strange. It only seems to flare up when I bend my knee past a certain point (crouching is impossible) but remains a constant and throbbing low-level ache as I hobble around. It's a kind of 'background' pain and, with the instinctive insight of a runner who has injured himself countless times, I feel it's probably trauma caused by an unusual one-off event – something that happened when I was running. I put my foot down at an odd angle, something rubbed past something else and this pain is a residual reminder that my joints aren't supposed to work like that.

About ten years ago my mother watched a TV documentary that caused her to call me and insist I go and see my GP. The show had featured people with hypermobile joints, near-translucent and highly elastic skin, small lumps of hard subcutaneous tissue and heart defects. I always had the first three symptoms and thought of my hypermobility as little more than an opportunity for party tricks. I can bend my left arm right around my head and scratch my left ear, for instance. The skin on almost any part of my body can be stretched outward an inch or more without pain. As a child I used to put pegs or bulldog clips on my face to scare and entertain friends. I couldn't really feel the pegs or my awestruck friends pinching my skin. Apparently this was unusual.

The heart defect possibility was something new and worrying. After some persuading, I finally agreed to go and see my GP who, somewhat bemused, pored through a couple of books before deciding that I probably had Ehlers-Danlos Syndrome like the people in the documentary, albeit not the kind that came with a side-order of defective heart valve. With a mixture of relief and amusement I relayed this tentative diagnosis to my mother. I assured her that most symptoms of EDS, although weird, are benign. It's a result of a collagen deficiency, I reported, and nothing to worry about.

Lying in that comfortable Edinburgh sitting room, I began to wonder if this EDS had anything to do with the way my knee joint had moved, causing a tendon to rub past a muscle or knob of bone. Certainly that's what it felt like (although my knowledge of the anatomy of the knee has always been somewhat shaky compared with many ultra-runners). My mother remembered that my sister Fiona has a friend who was a physiotherapist. It was my best chance of getting an urgent appointment with a specialist who could give me a realistic prognosis. I called the physiotherapist, Geraldine Fergusson,[1] straight away and she was kind enough to agree to see me the following morning, just before we set off up north.

Nervous doesn't quite cover it. I was borderline terrified as I waited for my appointment in a small physiotherapy clinic in Loanhead the next day. Geraldine prodded and poked, stretched and massaged the region in question. After around twenty minutes of thorough examination she gave me the news I wanted to hear – the tissue was inflamed, having been through some trauma but she couldn't find any ongoing, underlying cause. My instincts were probably correct. It was an odd, one-off motion that had caused the painful event and the residual pain would fade.

'If you were a normal person, rather than a runner, I'd say rest it for a couple of weeks,' my saviour said, 'but I know you won't do that.' She then treated it with ultrasound and recommended a mixture of elevation, icing, support, anti-inflammatory medicines and lots of sleep in between days of running.

In summary, it wouldn't be easy, but nor would it be impossible to run.

Immense relief flooded me. Calling off or postponing the event now would have been difficult. We would have had to cancel twenty-eight hotels and my paid support drivers/ assistants would have been let down. A lot of money, training and time could have been wasted. That none of this would be necessary was the best news I could have received. I thanked Geraldine and we got back in the car and headed for the motorway.

Around seven hours later, we pulled into the car park of the Seaview Hotel, in the windy, rain-lashed northerly outpost that is John O'Groats. Tourism and farming are all that keep this remote, bleak place from returning to nature. It's battered by northerly winds and rain throughout the year. Now, on the last day of August, it was merely drizzling, overcast and cold. I couldn't imagine what it must be like living so far north in the middle of winter but then I am a lifelong 'townie'.

Sleep came relatively quickly and easily that night, despite my misgivings about the knee and the scale of the challenge ahead. In some ways it's difficult to really fear something you have absolutely no clear picture of. My trepidation was an abstract thing too non-specific to keep me awake. Nor did the rain, which grew heavier as it clattered down upon the corrugated metal roof of the hotel extension which contained our rooms.

The following morning Dad and I tucked into 'full Scottish breakfasts' while piped, synthesised version of folk songs assaulted our ears. We didn't talk much; I suppose there was little to say except 'good luck' and neither of us had much idea what the day ahead would entail. We studied our individual laminated map books – twenty-nine pages of B-roads, trails and tracks highlighted and annotated with stopping points and lunch breaks marked every ten miles. It all looked so logical, so finite and achievable. The rain had thinned out overnight and although it still fell intermittently, mostly the morning was just breezy and overcast – a blessing, in September.

At around 9.30 am, having had a little difficulty setting

up cameras and locating my fabric knee support, we started our mission at the iconic John O'Groats sign. Just as we arrived, a young man was setting off, alone, shouldering an immense khaki backpack. A sprinkling of anorak-clad tourists sprinted to and from the signpost to take photographs in the rain before dashing back to their vehicles. I shivered in my Long Run branded T-shirt and a thin jacket and shorts, while Dad set up the tripod for the first piece to camera. Once I got over my habitual awkwardness on the 'wrong' side of a lens, my opening spiel went relatively well and I jogged off, with a noticeable limp, at a fairly unimpressive velocity. With a month of running ahead of me, speed, for once, was not of the essence. The rain had stopped once more and held off for several hours and the traffic, although fast-moving on the comparatively straight, flat start of the A99, was fairly sparse. So far so good.

I caught up with the solo hiker after a few miles. His name was Dominic and he was walking the epic route partly for the charities he was representing (Cancer Research, Ghana Link, and Manx drink-driving awareness charity Isle Drive Safe) and partly because an old teacher of his had done it in his youth and recommended it as a life-changing experience. Dominic had the fervour and self-belief of a young man (he was only eighteen) and he knew his walk would stand him in good stead when he put in his Royal Marines application after finishing. He became the first interviewee for the film and I captured his energy and determination on my handheld GoPro camera.

Saying goodbye, I realised I'd found my inspiration for the day. As well as his positive example (Dominic was unsupported and mostly camping at night), there was the less laudatory thought that he must not pass me at any point. There must be no 'hare and tortoise' scenario. My speed increased as I made for the first rest stop, the start of the beach at Sinclair Bay, north of Wick. I'd hoped the A99 would remain a quiet A-road; of course that very notion was oxymoronic – they are denoted A-roads for a reason.

Trying not to get myself sideswiped by a wing mirror or surprised around a bend, I developed a technique which would stand me in good stead throughout the challenge. My default side was on the right, running into oncoming traffic. This is what the Highway Code recommends since it allows the pedestrian to react quicker to cars that might fail to see him or her in time. That said, on bends, I'd move over to whichever side was on the outside of the curve, in order to maximise the line of sight between me and the driver. And there were times when neither strategy would do, such as on blind summits, where I'd usually stay on whichever side of the road had the largest grass verge, so that I could take evasive action (i.e. leap aside) if required. There's no doubt this added miles and miles in total to my intended route. After all, there's a reason why the 'optimum' route in many marathons is spray-painted onto the tarmac – this allows the elite runners to run a proper 26.2 miles and gain precious seconds on each bend. The rest of us schmucks probably run closer to twenty-six and a half.

As I approached Keiss beach, around 10 miles in, I was in good spirits, enjoying myself and running around 9-minute miles, despite my worries about the knee. I passed the site of Scotland's first Baptist church, a humble house with a plaque dating it to 1750 and dedicated to the memory of Sir William Sinclair, who proselytised throughout the region to the extent that a local bishop dubbed him 'the preaching knight'. He conducted baptisms in the sea near Keiss Castle and published a book of sixty hymns. His home could probably have done with more than a carved eulogy, since it appeared to have fallen into a state of dilapidation.

I passed my father a little way down the road, standing on the verge with tripod and camera at the ready. He seemed to be getting into the rhythm of driving on ahead, locating a lay-by and leaping out to frame a shot before I got to him. His presence spurred me on; I'd soon memorise the number plate of his silver Mondeo and welcome its leapfrogging, hazard lights flashed in greeting.

My father waited for me, as planned, at Keiss Beach and I grabbed a ten-minute break in the car as a squally shower began. We could see the dark grey clouds passing overhead and were still hopeful it would clear by the time I set off again for Wick. I'd planned to run along the beach and we both thought it would be an excellent place to try out the quadcopter. These flying drone cameras were still fairly unregulated and it seemed an ideal time to get some aerial photography into my movie while it was still legal to do so. I admit, I'd taken a risk in deciding to use the quadcopter on the shoot. Neither I nor my dad had a licence for commercial aerial videography, which meant we couldn't get the project insured. Going ahead without insurance was a little reckless but, in my naïve ignorance, I believed it was a manageable risk. For reasons which will become apparent in chapters to come, that's not a mistake I'll ever repeat.

Our good fortune held and the shower passed over us, leaving clear skies for us to fly our 4K camera along the deserted sands. Like most remote Scottish beaches, Keiss was empty. As Dad drove away in the car and I promised to wait a while before setting off, I stood gazing down almost three miles of deserted, uninterrupted sand. I needn't have bothered waiting – the beach seemed to go on forever. There's a strange optical illusion involving long beaches – if they're a regular enough curve, their perspective confuses the eye and it becomes impossible to know exactly where you are along their length. After ten minutes of running, I couldn't say whether I was a quarter of the way along or halfway, or more. Another ten minutes later it felt like I was running along a slow-moving conveyor belt going in the opposite direction. Surely I must be nearing my father though, as he prepared our 'eye in the sky'.

We'd been training Dad up on the quadcopter for a couple

of weeks. Each of the two joysticks had eight possible directions, with eight basic operations in total. The left one made the copter either ascend or descent vertically, or rotate on its axis clockwise or anticlockwise. The right control sent it forward, backwards, left or right, relative to the direction of the lens. To further complicate matters, two knobs on the front of the controller could tilt the camera from straight down to horizontal (or anything in between) or adjust the aperture.

Relatively straightforward, one might think, until we discovered that by rotating the copter 180 degrees, the directions on the right joystick became reversed. Rotate it by 90 degrees and forward becomes left, left becomes reverse et cetera. Flying it with any finesse involved learning and internalising these highly non-intuitive moves. My dad I and would go daily to a disused quarry in Edinburgh, not far from my parents' house, where the secluded and empty bowl of rock would provide an ideal training ground for those early, erratic flights.

All in all, the drone was a tricky and stressful beast to master and by the time we left for John O'Groats, my dad had only just got to the stage of not panicking constantly while using it. As I ran along the beach towards him, I listened for the reassuring thrum of the copter's motor. I didn't hear it, despite seeing what looked like his familiar form in the distance, quadcopter case at his feet. I slowed down and then stopped, letting the hunched figure complete his tasks; the copter's GPS system has to be calibrated, which involves rotating the device (and hence your body) in two positions, like a strange tribal dance. I didn't see my father doing any of this as I stood straining my eyes to comprehend why he was suddenly striding towards and then into the sea.

It dawned on me that this was a random lone fisherman and not my father at all. The beach's false perspective had fooled me again. I ran on, passing the imposter and then wading up to my ankles through an icy stream that wormed its way across the sands.

About a mile further on, I saw my father in the dunes and heard the quadcopter's unmistakable hum. Self-consciously I kept going, no doubt gaining a little speed for the benefit of the imagined viewers. I didn't want to create a 'heroic' shot of someone jogging pathetically slowly. Despite my growing fatigue, I dug in, leaving a trail of deep footprints as I ran under the camera's gaze alongside the frothing breakers.

This felt good; this seemed cinematic; this was proper film-making. After a while, I doubled back to check my dad had got the desired shot and found him agitatedly claiming that he'd lost control of the camera and couldn't see me in the iPad's screen for most of the time. We got the quadcopter in the air again for another take and because time was running out, I was forced to leave him as the machine followed me, buzzing menacingly at my back. The pale golden sand eventually gave way to shingle and brick-sized rocks, impossible to run on. I picked my way along and then headed off the beach over a dishevelled barbed wire fence and through tough, spiky grasses before finding a path. As the drone's buzzing dwindled away, I had no idea if my father had anything 'in the can'.

Later that night I discovered that my dad needn't have worried. Accidentally or otherwise he'd captured some great aerial images of sand, surf and a tiny figure loping determinedly along.

Having enjoyed my off-road excursion, I decided to keep following the coastline round towards distant castles and a lighthouse. What seemed like a trail quickly gave way to farmers' fields. Not willing to be so readily dissuaded (I knew there would be some sort of footpath down to such obvious places of interest) I climbed my second barbed wire fence that day. There would be many more over the course of The Long Run. After struggling through long, wiry tufts of grass and alarming the first of many flocks of sheep, I emerged at the remains of a footpath to the impressively ruined Castle Sinclair Girnigoe, which dates back to the late fifteenth century and is probably one of the least frequented of Scotland's many ancestral piles. Only three miles North of Wick, it's worth a visit though, as are the horizontally striated cliffs upon which it perches. Clan Sinclair certainly had a sense of the dramatic when they built this edifice.

Further on, I passed a country pile in somewhat better condition – Ackergill Tower. Also fifteenth century in origin, it has become a five-star hotel. I worried a little about trespassing on its grounds as I picked my way along crumbled stone flagstones between the sea and its walls, until I remembered that Scotland has very different access laws than England.

Although the commonly held misconception is that Scotland has no trespass laws (The Criminal Justice and Public Orders Act 1994 specifies what is considered trespass in Scotland), it is true that much open land, including farmland is covered by a statutory right of access.[2] In layperson's terms this permits access to land and inland waters throughout Scotland, provided land users behave responsibly. These rights actually allow pedestrians to access grassy fields, even when they are walled or fenced.[3] I took much advantage of these freedoms during the Scottish part of my journey.

Exhausted from the slow progress I'd been making along the admittedly picturesque peninsula north of Wick, I was grateful to find an access road leading to and from the Noss Head lighthouse, which took me eventually to the Norse-named hamlets of Staxigoe and Papigoe. From there, I made it into Wick, got enough phone reception to call my support car and rendezvous in Wick for a late lunch. It was approaching three o'clock and the pretty but small town of Wick had little to offer but an enormous Wetherspoon. I didn't care, devouring a plate of chilli and a large slab of chocolate cake as torrential rain began to fall. I realised

I'd been usually fortunate with the weather so far. As it happened, the afternoon wouldn't be so kind.

Stiff-legged, I set off once more, reflecting that I'd made it nearly twenty miles already. Two days previously I'd have been in agony trying to run to the end of the street. The body's amazing healing abilities were surfacing, processing proteins and sugars, mending torn and inflamed tissues. In compensation for this good fortune, the heavens began to hurl down buckets of rain and the A99 south of Wick remained only just wide enough for two cars to pass, what little traffic it carried hurtling by. The rest of the afternoon would be a long, hard slog. My father kept leapfrogging me, filming from lay-bys and side roads, encouraging me through the seaside villages of Thrumster, Ulbster and Occumster. My legs began to rebel just after the town of Latheron, however, and I started to run out of daylight.

The nagging inner voices feared by every long-distance runner began to make themselves known.

You've done so well. Don't push it so hard on day one – there's a long way to go. Dunbeath is just an arbitrary stopping point along the route. Your support car can drive you to the bed and breakfast anyway.

Eventually I had to give in to the voices. They had a point. I'd managed around thirty-six miles with a decidedly dodgy left knee – that would do.

The owner of the unusually named The Blends B&B seemed to appreciate our exhaustion as my father and I stumbled in to the repurposed farmhouse a little after eight o'clock. Admitting that Latheron had little to offer in the way of pubs serving evening meals, she kindly whisked up a filling pasta dish and turned a blind eye to the boxes of equipment we lugged upstairs. My production assistant Carol, who would be joining us as support driver and camera operator later in the challenge, had booked two rooms but only the large family room had the en-suite bathroom, so my father and I decided to share. I grabbed the single bed and began what became a regular evening routine of charging equipment and transferring camera rushes to various hard drives.

That night I recorded my first video diary, after a few false starts, including beginning with the somewhat misleading words 'So, it's the end of day three.' I was exhausted in a way I hadn't experienced since my last ultra and, film tasks in hand, I decided to use the large, knobbly foam roller I'd bought for the purposes of self-massage. This was a fairly excruciating process but perhaps rolling my bodyweight over my quads and calves loosened them off a little. My sleep that first night was a little restless, not aided in part by my father's raucous snoring (we rarely shared thereafter), but chiefly due to the ache in my legs and the difficulty of finding a comfortable position. As a rule, I don't sleep well in unfamiliar beds and of course all beds for the next month would be unfamiliar. I could only hope fatigue would take over soon and wipe out consciousness. Eventually, it did.

Day two started where day one ended – by the side of the main road, which became the A9 just outside Latheron, on what turned out to be a potentially lethal blind summit, given the early morning traffic. I'd decided during my preparations that I'd be painstakingly accurate in terms of starting each day exactly where I left off the previous evening. I'd even bought some chalk with which to draw an 'X' on the tarmac but this seemed a step too far in practice. What my pedantry meant of course is that, if I didn't make it to a town or village big enough to deserve pavements, the next day I'd often be running the gauntlet of rush hour traffic along the verges of A-roads.

So it proved on day two which began, mercifully, in dry conditions. After a few miles of forcing traffic to arc around me, Dunbeath appeared and provided the respite of running along pavement for a while. Not for long, of course. I soon noticed a pattern – pavement would start about half a mile out of town and dwindle away to grass verge around the same distance beyond the last buildings. Even when the verge was wide enough to accommodate pedestrians on at least one side, no provision for walkers or runners (or cyclists) was made. I suppose there might not be much uptake for 8-mile walks between towns. Nor would there be many runners who weren't local enough to know whatever off-road routes might exist. Nevertheless, this constant feeling that the car was the only 'proper' method of transport between villages irked me.

That said, most drivers did give me a suitably wide berth and, once the school runs were over and the rush hour finished, the traffic lightened. Very occasionally a driver would seem to take umbrage at my very presence, grudgingly offering only a few inches of clearance. This seemed particularly odd to me – would they be so irritated by the presence of a cyclist? I was taking up no more room than a bicycle and my running towards oncoming traffic shouldn't make any difference (technically it meant they'd pass me quicker too). The inchoate rage of a small minority of motorists at anything that might hold them up for a minute or two was hard for me to fathom. Road rage is such a self-evidently optional modern malaise.

As the A9 wormed its way south-west towards Helmsdale, the traffic began to build again. Large lorries began to rumble by and, as the rain started mid-morning, sheets of spray were thrown up by the wheels of eighteen-wheelers transporting everything from fertiliser to washing machines. The far north of Scotland has only one A-road heading north–south, and we were all sharing it.

Meanwhile, my father was a little way ahead of me having his own vehicular drama. He'd got used to the rhythm of driving three or four miles ahead, pulling into a lay-by or bit of waste ground and setting up a shot as quickly as possible.

However, this time haste had got the better of him. Reversing up onto a small ramp by a disused shed, he'd misjudged the angle and managed to strand one front wheel off the side of the ramp. The car could get no traction on the damp gravelled concrete and was effectively stuck. Unfortunately, the car jack usually stowed in the boot was missing. Squeezing a pile of nearby planks under the stranded wheel proved ineffectual. It looked like a call to the recovery services might be required and potentially a long and shamefaced wait.

Salvation came unexpectedly in the wiry form of Davey Henderson, a local drystone wall builder who had seen my father's crisis while driving his daughter to school. Upon his return, he pulled over and set to work with his pneumatic jack, sliding a plank under the car's chassis and raising it sufficiently to wedge other planks under the stray wheel and level the vehicle.

'I do banger racing ... so I improvise, adapt and overcome,' Davey revealed, working the jack energetically. He was good-natured and full of rather off-putting insight into the nature of the journey ahead.

'Mind yourself on that bit of road ... Fecking lethal,' he warned, before describing a terrifying accident that had occurred on the next bend of the A9 and almost killed his wife. He didn't seem to mind at all while my father told him in unnecessary detail what The Long Run was all about and filmed his mechanical prowess, instead of assisting. Davey even offered a get-out clause for my father's bruised ego: 'You're not the first man to do this and you'll not be the last.'

A little later, I turned the corner to see my dad parked beside a yellow van and my heart sank – was the support vehicle out of commission? Davey was just preparing to leave and my dad explained the whole thing while his Good Samaritan offered some sage advice: 'There's no diversions around it, unless you go way up the hill and then you're adding hours ... just be very, very careful.' I vowed I would, hoping my father would take heed too, and set off again. Although a worrying incident at the time, the encounter with Davey was oddly encouraging – he was both interested in the project and had been proactively helpful. If other people we'd meet were this accommodating, we'd be fortunate indeed.

Precipitation. It's not something that serious long-distance runners can pay much heed to. There's no 'waterproof' jacket in the world that can keep out persistent, heavy Caledonian rain. Once you're wet, you're staying that way, so you had better get used to it, if running all day and every day is your aim. Actually, running in rain can be pleasant – it can cool the runner down, preventing overheating and dehydration. I find I often run faster in rain (admittedly sometimes just to get it over with quicker), and footpaths and pavements tend to be quieter and therefore easier to run. With soaked running shoes there's no longer any point in avoiding puddles. I tend to splash through them, enjoying the feeling of regressing to a childish pastime.

In really torrential rain, sometimes only we long-distance runners can be seen plodding along, nodding or smiling greetings to one another in mutual recognition of our shared lunacy. I've even run in a thunderstorm once or twice, wading through rivers that suddenly appeared in place of side streets, kicking through piles of wet leaves and leaping fallen tree branches. At night, flashes of lighting would rip open the darkness and reveal torrents of water swirling with fallen leaves and twigs, drains failing to cope with the sudden load. These memories are amongst the most vivid of the period when I would run hard and fast along dark Ealing streets, chasing that perpetually elusive sub-3-hour marathon time.

Road running on the wet A9 was a little different. Trucks would roll by incessantly, hurling sheets of spray over me. It mattered little – I was practically half-amphibious after the first hour. The roar and proximity of these monsters on slippery tarmac was what bothered me. As visibility diminished,

I hoped I stood out enough in my white cap and blue jacket to catch drivers' eyes through the wet windscreens and arcing wipers. I ducked my head against the slanting water and dug in. And this monotony of rain and running went on and on and on.

A brief bit of beauty flashed by in the form of Berrydale. Every bit as quaint as its name suggests, the village nestles in a knuckle of rock forming a sheltered bay at the mouth of a small river. The road up to Berrydale is steep and winding and I had to take great care to listen for traffic coming around corner after corner. I passed my father on a bend, tripod at the ready under his umbrella, before heading down into the town, with its picturesque waterfall and bridge. Leaving Berrydale, the road inevitably climbed again; I decided it was too steep to run and slowed to a stride.

One thing the layperson might not quite understand about ultra-running is how much of it isn't really running at all. For one thing, the terrain may make it simply impossible – footpaths comprising boulders or thick vegetation don't lend themselves to safe and speedy progress. Secondly, it is sometimes unwise or physically painful to run when the miles have taken their toll. There's little to be gained by running up a 12 per cent gradient for a mile if it means you're utterly drained of energy at the top. Walking breaks are a vital component of ultra-distance running, particularly on multi-day events.

When I ran my first ultra-race, I was disappointed to have to walk before I'd even reached marathon distance, let alone over the course of the thirty-six miles that remained. I felt a little ashamed, like I'd been defeated by my own limitations, even though these breaks seldom lasted more than a few minutes. Once I got a second wind and ran some of my fastest miles that race, I realised it was just my body's way of rationing its strength, a kind of bargaining strategy. If you let me rest now, I'll power you on to the finish line later, it seemed to be saying. Given the waves of exhaustion I was experiencing, I often had little choice but to submit to the deal but it proved to be a good one. Forty-seventh place at the finish line seemed like a reasonable result for a forty-four-year-old running a hundred kilometres for the first time.

That said, I did find that throughout The Long Run, whenever I recorded a piece to camera where I confessed to taking a 'walking break', I'd generally find myself abandoning it a little later and jogging then running a little further. It seemed that just giving myself the permission to walk sometimes removed the desire or need to do so.

Helmsdale came and went and I decided that Brora would be the place to stop for lunch. The monotony of that road began to get to me and the hours that followed were very difficult, even when the sun began to peep out from sheets of cloud overhead and throw sparkling patches of light over the slate-grey sea. Eventually, I'd had enough of the incessant roar of traffic and pounding of the tarmac on my aching feet and ankles. Outside of Brora, a branch railway line ran parallel to the road, beyond it a small, rocky beach. I decided to cross the tracks and use the beach to carry me into town. I phoned my support car to inform Dad of this change of plan. The new route proved challenging – slippery, rounded rocks the size of house bricks did not provide a sensible running surface. But I needed a break from the violence of the road and found the sound of the tide with its powerful undertow made a nice change from the angrier white noise of trucks and cars on wet tarmac.

Every silver lining has its cloud. At Brora it took me the best part of an hour and several strange encounters with costumed scarecrows (evidently a local tradition[4]) to locate the golf course where my father had apparently found us a cheap and cheerful place to eat. The peace of mind found wandering along the beach was rudely interrupted by the darkly surreal sight and sound of two Lancaster bombers blasting overhead, presumably on their way to an air show.

I was then further thwarted in my quest for calories by the golf course itself – a seemingly endless links with little sign of a route through to the town beyond. A Camping and Caravan Club site proved unwelcoming, reminding passers-by that its tracks and roads were for 'members only' with many red-lettered signs. Eventually I resorted to my usual strategy of climbing into a field and following the route taken by tractors and farmers back to the main road.

Sometime later I located the clubhouse a mile or so further on down the coast and my dad and I had a prosaic but welcome lunch and then a council of war. It was day two and my plan for The Long Run was already unravelling. By the time we finished eating it was almost 4 pm and with just three and a half hours of usable daylight and twenty-two miles to run, covering that distance on foot seemed a tall order, especially given the state of my legs. We'd have to do something drastic.

It seems outrageously optimistic in hindsight but in the planning stages it seemed quite reasonable to run forty miles a day. I was so confident that this was achievable that I had my production assistant Carol book guest houses and hotels along most of the route. Rescheduling in the light of my injury and fatigue would mean cancelling most of these bookings. I was reluctant to do so, not just for pragmatic reasons but because it would both symbolise a failure to achieve my targets and invite in a dangerous degree of freedom. Without bookings, there would be no specific reason to end each day at a particular place. I could just run on until I decided to stop for the day. That was fine, so long as my willpower held out and I really pushed myself. Not so helpful if obstacles, injuries and plain old weakness of will encouraged me to slack off. If I took that option, I'd have to rely upon my determination and resolve holding out for a month or more. On day two, I resisted this decision.

Plan B was logistically simpler and less problematic in

the long-term but felt morally questionable. My dad had brought his bicycle with him so that we could obtain the occasional 'tracking shot' along the route. Our plan was to clip a GoPro to the pannier rack to film me running along level bits of trail or canal towpath. Of course, a bicycle could have other uses too. I could theoretically use it to get to my Day Two destination before nightfall. If I was willing to cycle instead of running, that is. A big if. As I've already mentioned, walking is an acceptable part of ultra-running. Cycling really isn't. I wasn't planning a triathlon (cycling to Inverness and swimming the Great Glen?)

Furthermore, my project was called The Long Run,[5] not 'The Long Duathlon' or 'The Long, Compromised Run'. If I started cycling now, what would happen next? A spot of hitch-hiking? Maybe a jet-ski along Loch Lomond? It seemed farcical to have to admit my legs were not up to it after just over 7 per cent of the challenge was complete.

However, as I began to consider the scale of the task ahead (twenty-four miles on dead legs with only four hours of usable daylight left) it began to seem like the only acceptable solution. I certainly wasn't going to grab a lift in the support car. As ever, in situations where complex moral calculus is required, I began to rationalise. Cycling was still using my legs after all and there was nothing to say I had to cycle *slowly*. After sixty miles of running in two days, twenty-two miles of cycling would complete a pretty decent workout for most people!

The clincher was my decision to come clean about 'the cheating'. I would record my feelings on camera, as well as the thought process that led to the decision. I'd also attach a GoPro to the handlebars to record my thoughts as I cycled, as well as using my 'hatcam' to film the route I took. I could prove, at least, that this wouldn't be gentle cycle in the countryside. Committed to the idea now, we prepared the bike, which boasted twenty-one gears, and I got on and, after delivering my monologue to camera, cycled off. Ten seconds later, I fell off the bike. I hadn't even made it out of the car park.

I'd forgotten that, aside from one late-night, drunken trip on a Barclays hire bike in London, I'd not ridden a push-bike for over twenty years. I hadn't checked what gear the bicycle was in and the resistance was clearly set for whizzing downhill, not climbing out of a heavily cambered car park. My pratfall was captured on three high-definition cameras. Excellent start, I thought dolefully.

Things got better. Despite ludicrous rain and heavy traffic, I forced my aching quads to push as hard as possible and got used once more to manipulating the gears to keep the foot rotations high. There would be no freewheeling on this journey. While no Tour de France winning performance, around ninety minutes later I pulled into the quaint old market town of Tain, with plenty of daylight left, and found my support car waiting for me. I got off the bike, saddle-sore and vowing that it would be my only such lapse during the rest of the challenge. And so it proved.

MILES RUN: 65; MILES CYCLED: 22; MILES REMAINING: 1,013[6]

---

1. Of Optimum Physiotherapy: http://www.optimum-physiotherapy.co.uk – highly recommended.

2. As provided by The Land Reform Act (Scotland) 2003.

3. For more details, visit the Scottish Rights of Way and Access Society website: www.scotways.com

4. Or, rather, a new local festival: http://www.bbc.co.uk/news/uk-scotland-highlands-islands-34044817

5. The project was called 'The Long Run' but for the purposes of this book 'Downhill From Here' seemed a more fittingly ironic title, for reasons which will soon become apparent.

6. Of the original 1,100 mile estimate. As you'll see, this was far from accurate.

TAIN TO DRUMNADROCHIT

Something told me this was a more dangerous route than I'd imagined. First came the mangled remains of a small red hatchback, cordoned off with police tape, half-submerged in the large drainage ditch by the side of the road. Then later on I passed a miniature shrine created in memory of 'Keez', evidently an earlier victim of vehicular disaster. The shrine featured toy cars, a glove, a heart woven from twigs, the wheel off a car, a heavily carved nameplate and a harmonica. This person had been loved, evidently, by unusually creative and leftfield people. The tree that all of this was attached to had large sections of bark missing, a giant white gaping wound running down its front which, with the passing of years had cauterised without ever quite healing.

It was happening again. Sensible plans, involving runnable, quiet roads, were going awry. The traffic was tearing by, inches away, at lethal speed. The light was fading, predictably but irritatingly, with me still a few miles from my destination. Drivers had little or no time to adjust to my unexpected presence on *their* road as they veered around me, heading home for what we in Scotland confusingly call 'tea' (dinner). This all seemed drearily familiar. Day three was far too early to be experiencing runners' déjà vu. It had all started so well too.

My dad and I had chosen a route out of Tain that climbed a little way up into the hills and ran parallel to the fearsome A9, only rejoining it a couple of miles north of the Cromarty Firth. On my large-scale map-book (twenty-nine pages to cover the whole of the UK) this was an unmarked white road and seemed to lead nowhere in particular. That is, no towns were indicated along the ten-mile length between Tain and Alness, the next coastal town of any size.

As it transpired, that was because this was largely a farm and forestry access road. However, it did pass through a string of secluded houses called Lamington before skirting a forest and then opening out into fields. Although the rain fell pretty incessantly all morning, I felt much happier and more stress-free running these quiet, domesticated streets. My dad found it considerably easier to find places to pull over and film me (and more tree cover to hide under while it rained). All in all, it was a much more pleasant running experience. This was what I had signed up for.

A feeling of peace and relaxation descended (non-runners might question the concept of running as relaxation but believe me, it's possible) and I piled on the miles. My legs had endured pretty well from the previous day. Cycling for half the day's miles had limited repetitive strain and reduced impact injury to a minimum. Muscles ached and my knee injury reminded me of its presence now and again but there was nothing I couldn't easily deal with by basically ignoring it. I wore an elasticated knee support, which seemed to help by forcing the joint to move only in the directions nature intended. I thought I'd probably cope.

After a couple of hours, I jumped into the support car to hide from the rain, opposite a sign that informed us we were five and a half miles from Alness. My mood was buoyant and yesterday's painful decision to 'cheat' seemed justified. Hopefully nothing like that would be required again. The knee was aching a little more now, but still under the threshold of what I'd actually describe as 'pain'.

Alness appeared as scheduled and my father and I had a satisfying lunch and discussed options. The B-roads continued to loop alongside the main road as far as Evanton but if I wanted to hit the bridge over the Cromarty Firth, I'd have to rejoin my nemesis – the A9 – one more time. The alternative was a convoluted detour via Dingwall and Conon Bridge and that still involved A-roads (albeit smaller ones). I decided to go the former route, savouring the last few miles of farm roads and forest fringes I ran through, before descending to sea level at mile eighteen.

As I ran down the slip road towards the A9 and headed into a small tunnel, a coach swung round the corner round towards me. Traffic was flowing the other way, making it impossible for the coach to give me any room so I pressed myself into the hedgerow as it skimmed past, the driver making apologetic hand signals. Taking a deep breath, I sprinted the rest of the tunnel and emerged into the roar of commuter traffic. The shock of the rumbling vehicles was in stark contrast to the quietude I'd enjoyed all morning.

I availed myself of the unkempt grass verge and stony drainage dishes as I jogged or walked along the two-mile stretch of killer road. Speed would have to be sacrificed in favour of survival – the A9 was now the main artery south to Inverness and I was a flea on the side of a rampaging wildebeest. Fortunately, despite the discarded cigarette packets, water bottles and smashed-up hubcaps that littered the route, it was easy enough to make (slow) progress towards the bridge.

Half a mile from the sparkling Cromarty Firth, the rain having let up, I sat down at a lay-by and had a break for water, gel and a power bar. I was a little worried. Driving up, I'd not noticed a footpath over this particular bridge. What if there wasn't one? I'd not get far along a bridge thick with traffic, with one lane in each direction, if there was nowhere to jump off the roadway except into the Firth! I could only assume that it was probably not legal to design a road bridge in an area as remote as this without making some provision for pedestrians. I recorded these thoughts on camera as I got closer and closer to the busy roundabout that filtered several A-roads onto the bridge.

Then, as I quickly replaced the batteries on my headcam in preparation for the dash over the Firth, I heard a weird sound piercing the bassy rumble of traffic. It was a persistent high-pitched squeaking, the cartoonishly shrill sound of a small mammal in distress. I bent down to the verge and dug through dense grasses. There I saw a small rabbit, no more than adolescent, head and shoulders out of its burrow but seemingly stuck there, squealing in anguish. I put down my camera (after lining up a shot; I am nothing if not an opportunistic documentarian) and grabbed a sharp stone.

Not really having a clear idea what I was doing, I dug around the animal's hindquarters, removing as much soil as possible. Strangely, although it is perhaps fanciful to imagine that the rabbit knew I was trying to help, it fell quiet as I dug. I imagined that its burrow might have collapsed on its rear legs. Either that or it was entangled in something. Whatever was the case, after thirty seconds or so, the animal seemed to shiver itself free and bound away into the undergrowth. I felt a sense of relief and happiness – it was something of an unexpected bonus to be able to help. What were the chances of anything else, other than a fox or other predator, hearing the distressed creature on this noisy roadside, and coming to its aid, apart from me? Next to nil, I'd say. That was one lucky *lapin*.

Good karma thus banked, I played Frogger[1] with the cars at the roundabout and found, to my relief that the bridge did have a footpath along one side. It was strewn with shattered pieces of wing mirror and displaced gravel, yet navigable. As I ran, I got spectacular views of the sun doing impressive things with the silvery Firth, breaking through gaps in the cloud to throw slivers of metallic sheen on the wind-blown waves. It was with something like regret that I left the bridge, crossed the road once more and located the next set of B-roads.

It's probably about time I addressed the elephant in the room. Was all this effort, endurance and energy-depletion, by day three, bearing fruit? Was the adventure providing that feeling of renewed self-worth that I had sought?

Despite having fallen into my NHS job, my chosen career since 1997 at least had been film-making, specifically writing and directing independent movies. To say that this is an ambitious life plan is to push the limits of understatement. It is almost impossible to break into the world of independent film-making, as writer, director or producer.

To cut a long and tedious story short, my career in movie-making had not exactly proven a money-spinner so far. That said, having taken voluntary redundancy, I no longer had a futile nine-to-five to hold me back. One man's unemployment is another man's freedom. I'd committed to using this time without commitments to prove to myself that I could achieve amazing things if I utilised something my friends and family will confirm I have in spades – extraordinary, bloody-minded determination. All I had to do was be a little bit bonkers. I could do that. But was it working?

I didn't feel very extraordinary limping up a ridiculously steep rat run of a B-road towards a town called Culbokie at around 4 pm on the 3rd September. What had seemed like a quiet lane turned out to be a cut-through for locals wanting to avoid snarl-ups on the dual carriageway. My half-walk, half-limp up most of this road was interrupted by the need to jump up onto the grass verge every minute or three to let cars past. Eventually, however, the terrain levelled out and provided some spectacular views over the Forth and the landscape through which I'd travelled. It began to dawn on me how far I'd already come and yet, how little of my epic I'd completed. I quickly banished that unhelpful bit of perspective and ploughed on.

Occasionally the film-making side of the project would slow me down. Although I did most of my pieces to camera on the run (or limping walk) using the GoPro and gimbal stick, there were times when something caught my eye and I had to stop to admire a vista or an odd detail in the landscape and capture it on film. Approaching Munlochy along a high, flat road I looked down into an open expanse of field and saw that the clouds that had been hanging surprisingly low over the Forth had seemingly made landfall, a strange, angular column of mist linking one field with the sky. I had to film this impressive sight. Perhaps a meteorologist could explain the phenomenon to me later.

I tried to keep such static moments to a minimum but I also had to keep in mind the potential audience for the film I was making. If this trip was to cost me a substantial portion of my redundancy payout, I needed to secure worthwhile rushes to create a saleable product somewhere down the road. The realities of what my life might consist of upon my return were never far from my mind. So much for self-transcendence.

It was already early evening when I passed through Munlochy and paused to record a spectacular rainbow (about the third or fourth I'd seen so far on the trip).[2] Time, once again, was not on my side. At least I was managing a decent enough pace, running 9-minute miles whenever possible and navigating with relative ease. After the descent to Munlochy, the ground began to rise again, fields giving way to open moorland, the rugged asymmetry of Scots Pine and the spiky resilience of sporadically flowering gorse bushes.

The gorse reminded me of a childhood incident that's fondly remembered in family lore. I'd been about ten years old and we were on some sort of Highland family holiday. I seem to remember the weather being good as we stopped on our way somewhere for a break. My sister and I went for a wander around the gorse bushes and, amongst their unwelcoming spines I saw a wooden door lying flat against a rock. I stood on the rock and, for reasons that remain obscure, managed to lift the door into an upright position. I probably had some notion of leaving it propped upright as a sort of surreal exhibit. Sadly, this was not to be. With fateful inevitability, the door toppled backwards onto me, knocking me off my perch and right into the middle of the bush. The screams brought my parents running. My mother was picking gorse spines out of my legs and behind for half an hour as we drove away, my father trying not to laugh too much.

No such mishaps befell me as I made my way along the very straight, fast B-road across the high plateau north of Inverness. The traffic was relatively light but fast-moving, taking advantage of the ruler-straight line of the road. It was then that I passed the crashed hatchback and shrine that I described at the head of this chapter. I began to wonder if I'd make it safely to Inverness before nightfall and erred on the side of caution with oncoming traffic.

A couple of hours later, I had to admit to myself that I was, once again, not quite going to make it to my destination. I think it was somewhere in the region of Artafalie that I finally ran out of sensible daylight. Unusually, I found I had a flicker of phone reception so I stopped by the side of an especially murderous section of highway and made the call. A side road led to some sort of pottery and tourist attraction; I waited by the junction, knowing my father would be able to pull in there.

As it turned out, I was less than two miles from the bridge over the Beauly Firth to Inverness but stopping was very much the right decision. Even in broad daylight, that stretch of road could have killed me. It had no grass verge, just hedgerow and fences on both sides, was straight as an

arrow and full of traffic making for, or leaving, the biggest
town we'd encountered so far. There had to be another way.

The following day we made the sensible decision to ditch
that route and compromise my pedantic insistence of
starting in the literal spot where I finished the day before.
I decided to allow an amendment for impassable roads by
which it was allowable to retrace our steps to any parallel
road the same distance away from the eventual destination
(in this case Inverness). We scouted the alternatives by car
after breakfast and found a farm road which connected with
a B-road just before the junction with the A9. I'd seen a bike
track along the far side of the A9 heading into Inverness so I
could pick that up, although it meant somehow crossing the
flow of morning rush hour traffic.

It all went well and I tore across the A9, located the bicycle
path and followed it down, across the bridge and into Inverness, where it snaked along the side of industrial plots and
trading estates by the river before leading me towards the
city centre. I didn't want to get tangled up in city streets
because the trailhead of the Great Glen Way began north-
west of the city near a place called Leachkin. Passing a giant
plant constructing wind turbines, I used Google Maps on
my phone to navigate a route out of town and up steep
suburban streets towards the hills.

My ankle was unhappy from the very start on day four.
By the time I escaped Inverness, it was protesting loudly
with every impact. Then heavy rain began to fall, to add
to the morning's misery. Phone reception was intermittent
but I kept in contact with my support and eventually we
met up at a place called Great Glen House, where Scottish
Natural Heritage and other organisations seemed to have
their headquarters. I think we had missed the official starting
point of the Great Glen Way by a mile or so and this junction with a main road didn't seem to warrant an especially

visible sign. Luckily we encountered two young women out for a lunchtime jog (being hardy Scots, the rain didn't seem to bother them). My fellow runners directed me to the tiny wooden post carrying a blue emblem denoting the Way. I changed into my brand new Salomon trail shoes and did my usual piece to camera.

My father filmed me, from under the golf umbrella he'd tied to a stick and bungee-roped to his chest, as I set off on my first official trail which began, without ceremony, to circumnavigate a small building site. Minutes later, I was climbing steadily through beautiful natural forest, shaded from the worst of the weather and filling my lungs with oxygenated air. The feeling of relief was palpable and it was almost as if my troubled ankle and knee shared in that relief and decided to pause in their nagging. This felt more like it. It even felt familiar in a way. I'd been running and walking on forest trails since I can remember.

My first guide to such wild places was my dad, Ian, who took me with whatever dogs the family had at the time, to Dreghorn Woods. My mother, Kathleen, and sisters, Fiona and (later on) Katy, would sometimes join us. When I was around eleven or twelve it was often just me and my dad, primarily because my younger sister Katy was a toddler and the woods weren't exactly pushchair-friendly. A small patch of Ministry of Defence-owned forest near the army barracks in Dreghorn and Redford, these trees, through which wound a small tributary of the Water of Leith, constituted as big a forest as my pre-teen imagination could encompass. We would wander, run, scramble and explore our way through the mainly deciduous trees and, if we ever got temporarily lost, it was easy enough to locate one of the many criss-crossing footpaths to reach the perimeter fences. I climbed trees, swung on home-made rope-swings and learned how to make a bow and arrow. The latter seems an incredibly old-fashioned and analogue activity for a boy these days but it was a thrill at the time. I can still remember how to make such a weapon.

The technology was simple but specific. We'd first of all have to locate a recently fallen or broken tree branch about four feet long and at least half an inch thick. It had to be green because it needed to bend without breaking. My dad would cut off any extraneous twigs then level off and notch both ends of the branch. Then he'd take some thick string and, bending the branch with his bodyweight against the ground, string the bow, winding and tying off the ends so that they fitted into the notches and couldn't slip free. Taut as it needed to be, the bow had to have yet more bend in it for firing the arrows. These were made from drier, straighter and thinner branches with a two-inch nail gaffer-taped onto the end and home-made darts-styled flights created with cardboard we'd brought with us.

A well-made bow engendered a real sense of pride and accomplishment. They were lethal too – capable of shooting an arrow in a fifty-foot arc to lodge in the trunk of a tree. Parents would probably be arrested for helping their children create such weapons today.

After I reached my early teens I inevitably spent less time with my dad and more time with my close friend Richard, whose imagination was as lively, albeit a little darker, than my own. We were geeks with a love of such arcane delights as writing our own science fictional encyclopaedia and inventing our own somewhat sado-masochistic religion.[3] We were geeks when it wasn't yet a fashion choice or every hip kid's self-definition. One of our favourite activities was combining our love of maps with a child's more conventional desire to explore.

We'd walk from Richard's house down to the Water of Leith in Colinton, locate the beginning of a trail and follow it, whether it led anywhere or not. One of these paths, possibly created by generations of domestic dogs, would lead along a high, steep riverbank above the river and we particularly enjoyed mapping this route to its furthest extent (it emerged on a footpath by the neighbouring village of Juniper Green) and giving names to its various delights. Snake Pass, the High Trail, Wizard's Retreat. These aren't the actual names, which are long lost in the mists of memory, but they're in keeping with what we scribbled down on those now sadly lost sheets of graph paper back in the early 1980s.[4]

I offer these vignettes by way of explaining my affinity for forests but perhaps it's just a natural, human impulse to retreat to the safety of the trees – something primal buried deep in our ancestral memories. Whatever is the case, my favourite trails are forested ones. I hope one day to visit some of the great woodland trails in America and Canada. If there is ever to be a sequel to The Long Run, it's likely to take place on the Appalachian Way or the Pacific Crest Trail.

The Great Glen Way offered plenty of trees and, once I'd climbed as far as the tiny B-road between Easter Altouric and Woodend, amazing views down onto Loch Ness to the South and the valley of the Moniack Burn[5] to the north. My father managed to locate this road and got some great footage there. I even consented to rerun one small section when he didn't quite have the shot framed properly. At this stage in the project, we were both still willing to be perfectionists. I captured some beautiful views on my GoPros and my pieces to camera were full of renewed positivity. Even though my ankle began to pain me more than ever, I downed painkillers and pressed on, distracted by the scenery.

So distracted was I that I entirely missed the turn-off from the tarmac to the next bit of trail and ended up heading back down to the A9 at Abriachan. My father and I even gave directions to a local using our maps, blissfully unaware that we too were on the wrong road. Still, it was a mere three-mile detour so we drove back up the perilously steep road from the village and, after much head-scratching, met a couple of other runners who had just emerged from the next bit of the Way. It was signposted with perplexing subtlety, the tiny blue marker post dwarfed by a gleeful advertisement for a pottery and café, which I was recommended to visit but never found.

The Way shrank to something like a faerie trail, flowering shrubs and juvenile pine trees flanking a path barely a foot wide in places, which dripped with the moisture left from the omnipresent morning mist. I loved this stretch and filmed as much as I could. I even passed a few hikers, all coming the other way, which reassured me from time to time that I was going the right direction. I enjoyed every minute of my run as the trail broadened out, crossed a road and began to climb again.

At this point I started taking longer walking breaks to rest the ankle, which had begun to flare up again. The views of Loch Ness became more and more spectacular, particularly at one viewpoint I briefly stopped at. As well as a well-positioned bench, locals had created a small memorial dedicated to Andy, guitarist and regular walker in these hills. A little further on, as the sun blazed down, the mist having long dissipated, I enacted another mountain ritual. A fast-flowing stream plunged down from the high hillside over slabs of granite; I cupped my hands and drank deeply. It was cold and incredibly fresh, in the way that only rock-filtered mountain rainwater can be. They should bottle it . . . except they shouldn't.

For those considering drinking from streams, and in the interests of the omnipresent watchdogs of health and safety, you're recommended to follow the following rules. One: only drink from fast-flowing, very clear water. Two: Choose only water that has run through rocks, rather than surface water. Finally: try to avoid water that may have picked up run-off impurities from farmers' fields (fertilisers and manure, mainly). There are rarely dead sheep upstream but, yes, that's a possibility too. That said, I've never once fallen ill or even felt remotely unwell as a result of drinking from streams but caution and common sense should be exercised. In summary: At Your Own Risk.

As I ran the hilly trail, the Achilles tendon in my painful ankle began to feel the strain. This worried me more than the myriad other aches I'd enjoyed to date. If a runner's Achilles tendon snaps then it's game over, hence the figure of speech attributed to that body part. It's not an injury I could run off; it would effectively end my challenge. I began to monitor the pain closely and take shorter, faster steps to limit the stretch. It became evident I'd not make it much further than Drumnadrochit, a town some hikers had informed my father was over-touristy. I didn't particularly care how many 'Nessie' souvenirs were on sale, so long as it offered a comfortable bed and a plentiful dinner.

On the final stretch, the trail undulated in and out of forests, sections of it privately owned and protected from straying livestock with large metal gates that clanged loudly as I passed through them. Amidst the trees, I spotted strange square plastic panels, wired into the ground, facing one another across the pathway in pairs. I reasoned that these were some kind of sensor designed to measure trail usage. Research later revealed that my guess had been a good one. Between 2013 and 2014, these sensors showed that total annual usage increased from 36,305 to an all-time high of 49,880 walkers while the number of 'whole way' walkers on the Great Glen Way doubled, from just over 8,000 in 2013 to over 16,000 the following year.[6] Comparable data for 2015 is still being compiled but, clearly, word about this beautiful route is getting out.

I sped up as the path began to descend and wind its way circuitously towards the loch. I hadn't seen or heard from my father for some time and hoped he'd got the texts I'd sent him. When I reached the end of the trail and emerged onto the strip of pavement that accompanied the A9 into Drumnadrochit, I saw him walking out of town with camera and tripod. He'd waited at the trailhead for hours then headed into town in case he'd missed me. We'd downloaded a GPS tracking application to our iPhones to allow us to locate one another (when we had reception). However, even a plain GPS signal was hard to obtain on both our phones much of the time, a problem we never quite licked.

Still, dad had found me in the end. As we walked into town, pausing to film some of the more ludicrous 'Nessie World' signs and attractions, we reflected that the trail had been easy enough to follow so far. If the Great Glen Way was as well signposted throughout its length, the next couple of days would be nothing but pleasurable.

However, as Scotland's national poet once remarked, 'the best laid plans . . . '[7]

MILES RUN: 138[8] – MILES REMAINING: 962

---

1. For those too young to know, Frogger was an early home computer game in which a frog has to repeatedly cross a busy motorway. As in real life, this exercise usually doesn't end well.

2. My father and I had a running joke about becoming increasingly jaded with and angry about rainbows. But we still filmed them.

3. We called it Galaxianism and its two deities NIM and MONZO (with universal and local jurisdiction, respectively) required absolute craven worship. They even demanded their names be written in letters of a minimum height, under pain of various creatively unpleasant forms of death. We were big Douglas Adams fans.

4. I remained in contact with Richard after his family moved to Lincolnshire when we were both 14, in the form of long, partly encoded letters. He became a brilliant mathematician and was well on the way towards a Doctorate at the University of Manchester when, sadly, he developed schizophrenia. Richard's story is a depressing one – he got involved with drugs and became an alcoholic, spent years in and out of various institutions and was eventually arrested and incarcerated for five years for a minor firearms offence during a paranoid episode. He took his own life in HMP Manchester by means of suffocation using a plastic bag. Having finally lost contact with him, I only found out about his death several years later. I still feel guilty to this day that I wasn't a better friend to Richard in his darkest hours.

5. In Scots 'burn' denotes a small river or stream. Etymological coincidence, rather than irony, I suspect.

6. Data provided by the Great Glen Way Rangers and The Highland Council.

7. For those who are not as familiar with the work of Robert Burns as Scottish schoolchildren or American novelists, the full and proper quotation from To A Mouse (1785) is 'the best-laid schemes of mice and men / gang aft agley'. Only the third clause in this famous excerpt has not yet become the tile of a major motion picture. Maybe I should make it my mission to remedy this oversight?

8. From now on, I think it's better to fold the cycled miles into the running total – pedants may disagree.

DRUMNADROCHIT TO SOMEWHERE ELSE

I felt a strange sense of excitement as the water rose to my chest and then up to my neck. Excitement only turned to fear when the current, must stronger than it had seemed from the bank, began to pull my feet away from the rounded, slippery rocks on the riverbed. This could be serious; perhaps I should abandon filming if it meant capturing my own drowning on camera. I remember being amazed by the chasm of difference between my mood and circumstances now and the much more pleasant experiences I'd had that morning.

Thirteen hours earlier, I'd faced a challenge of a much more prosaic variety. Finding the next bit of the Way was proving challenging once more and my laminated map didn't seem to help. I began by climbing the steepest road I could find out of Drumnadrochit with no real conviction that this was the correct route. Even when I found the trailhead after a mile of fast uphill walking, doubts crept in. At one stage it seemed I had found a footpath leading to the dramatic-sounding Falls of Divach, which might produce impressive footage for my film, but would then entail backtracking for several miles to locate the correct turn-off, or crossing open country (rarely as easy as it should be) to intercept the proper route. No such waterfalls appeared, thankfully, and I pressed on.

The trail kept climbing through endless forestry

plantation, then followed a single-track tarmac road. Skittish roe deer leapt across my path and bounded ahead, looking for holes in the fence. I'd occasionally see a bird of prey, probably a kestrel, circling overhead. At one point, something like a ferret dashed across the path (if you're looking for more accurate zoological identification you're reading the wrong book). There were no humans on this route, which worried me. Wasn't this a National Trail, with all the funding, advertising and maintenance that implied?

The Great Glen Way was opened in 2002 by HRH Prince Andrew as one of Scotland's four long-distance trails. It follows the geological fault line that is responsible for the Highland's diagonal slash of lochs including Loch Ness and Loch Linnhe. It provides a 79-mile off-road route between Inverness and Fort William and is described on the internet as being suitable for 'all levels of walker'.[1] I would perhaps add, 'provided they have good maps'.

Eventually, the familiar blue marker posts and signs reappeared and reassured me I was on the right track. I could enjoy the solitude and mark it down to the 'Scotland Effect'. My home country is, to a large extent, devoid of people. I'm exaggerating of course but, at time of writing, the population of the whole of Scotland is around 5.3 million.[2] To put this into perspective, the population of London on census day in the same year[3] was 8.2 million.

As the single-track road climbed to around 250 metres, the trail ran parallel for a while before cutting through open moorland carpeted in a purple heather almost ludicrously livid. For the first time, 'proper' mountains were visible on the horizon, most noticeably the humped back of Meall Fuar-mhonaidh (the 'cold, round hill') at nearly 700 metres. There was something rather spooky about the quietude of the high moorland plains with their brooding backdrop of hills. From the top of Meall Fuar-mhonaidh I'd probably be able to see Boleskine House, on the opposite shore of

Loch Ness, once the home of legendary occultist Aleister Crowley and his acolytes, and later Led Zeppelin guitarist Jimmy Page. Perhaps it was the remoteness and quietude that appealed to Crowley (and Page). Certainly 'do what thou wilt' is a more workable credo when you have no nosy neighbours.

The pain in my ankle and knee meant I had to alternate periods of walking with running but, as the trail left the road once more and entered woodland, I found my awareness of the ache diminishing and it became easier to maintain a jogging pace over the level sections and downhill stretches. The woods were pretty and full of that incredible silence which is thrown into relief by the occasional creak of a branch, rustle of a small mammal in the fallen leaves or birdsong. I opened and closed more of the sturdy metal gates I'd encountered the previous day. The Way was well maintained – crushed gravel surfaced most of the trail and there was even a series of humps on one long straight, presumably to deter mountain bikers from dangerous displays of speed.

Although I was managing to run sections of the Way, it was at a pace considerably slower than I'd been planning – 10- or 12-minute miles instead of 8 or 9. Despite the pain and pace, I was heartened by the warm, sunny weather and easily navigable trail. The nagging realisation that dozens of hotel cancellations would probably be inevitable began to grow but I didn't let it get to me. For the first time, I began to make a list of 'good news' to balance these worries. I was injured, yet able-bodied and not suffering the privations and challenges faced by the recipients of the two charities I was raising money for, Whizz-Kidz[4] and Limbpower.[5] Compared to a child in a manual wheelchair or an ex-serviceman coming to terms with limb loss, I had it easy.

Considerations like this carried me on through Ruskich wood and on to a viewpoint on a high section of rocky trail that briefly broke the treeline, beyond which I'd face an important choice. I stopped by a map display and encountered Keith, a young hiker carrying his tent, food and clothing in an impressively heavy rucksack. Red-bearded like a proper Scottish mountain man, Keith was Edinburgh-born like myself and we chatted about the pleasures and trials of the Way and the swarming clouds of hell that are Scottish midges. These tiny beasts would congregate whenever I stopped to admire the view for any length of time. Keith told of black clouds of them waiting for him when he left his tent in the mornings, something I'd experienced myself on the West coast of Scotland as a youth. I believe Queen Victoria once called them 'Scotland's last line of defence'; the droll monarch was not exaggerating.

The decision both Keith and I faced (like me he was going against the grain by walking north to south) was whether to take the high road or low road ahead, with an altitude difference of 400 metres between them. Corny Scottish folk songs notwithstanding, we both opted not to wimp out and take the high trail, rather than descending to lochside. The vistas awaiting me at the top had better be worth it, I could imagine my knees protesting. I jogged away from Keith; it wouldn't do for a runner to be overtaken by a heavily laden hiker, no matter the twenty years between our ages. I soon had to reduce my speed to a steady yomp as the trail relentlessly climbed. A layer of sunscreen had the added benefit of dissuading the midges as I skirted the treeline and the path finally levelled off on the northern side of Mheall na Sroine (nose-like hill). The views down to the loch and distant mountains, predictably, were spectacular. I'd left a message on Dad's phone to tell him the new plan, knowing that, in any case, the twin routes joined one another before Invermoriston, my lunchtime destination. I wouldn't get lost and we'd end up in the same place.

After a very enjoyable section of well-marked mountainous trail, where I finally encountered a few other walkers, the Great Glen Way wound back into the trees and began to descend. It was on the way back into the woods that I realised I'd made a bit of a miscalculation. I'd only partly filled my water reservoir and the heat of the day and my thirst had emptied it hours ago. It hadn't even occurred to me to fill it back at the stream I'd drunk from. As I ran, dry-throated into the trees, I hoped I'd either locate another fast-flowing burn or my father soon. I began to fantasise about waterfalls and raindrops as the trees provided a welcome bit of cover from the unseasonably relentless sunshine.

Then, a minor miracle. I encountered Libby, a Californian hiker who was walking solo in the opposite direction (or so I thought). She had been warned of my imminent appearance by my father, whom she'd passed further down the trail. She stopped to talk to me and I interviewed her for the film. It turns out she was hiking nominally 'with' her father and brother but they had an unusual but practical family tradition of 'each hiking their own pace'. Abby was some way ahead of the menfolk, apparently. She asked me what my motivations were and I gave her the party line about combining my love of film and running (true, but not the whole story). She offered her water flask and I readily accepted. Her positivity and radiant smile cheered me considerably as I went on my way.

The rest of the route down to Invermoriston was relatively straightforward and my legs felt a renewed energy as wide forest track gave way to narrower, more winding trails. I slurped more stream water a mile further on and allowed myself to walk the brief uphill bits. My father had managed to get a message to me earlier in the day to say that he'd found a perfect spot to fly the quadcopter and so, when I finally ran out of the woods onto a hillside laid bare by logging, he was waiting for me. We took some photos and he managed to get a great, sweeping aerial shot of me running down the road towards the town, with Loch Ness sparkling in the background. Only during the last half mile did my knee pain return to plague me but I endured it, knowing I'd soon be stopping to eat.

When I hit Invermoriston, having completed sixteen miles over the hills, I sat in the sunshine waiting for my dad to drive back down the road and join me for lunch. Despite the aches and pains, I felt it had been a good morning. Whatever mileage I managed after lunch, the day would be worthwhile and I'd count it a success. Of course, I had no idea what lay ahead.

After a basic but filling meal of bacon rolls, cake and coffee, my dad and I thought to ask the proprietor of the café, Frank, about the next bit of trail. He pointed us in the right direction and told us that we'd find a low and a high path, the low path running alongside the river. It's possible we didn't listen clearly enough to Frank's directions.[6]

Wanting a bit of variety in terms of shooting methods, and to give my dad a bit of a change too, we decided to try our first 'bicycle tracking' sequence. I took the GoPro from my cap and clipped it to the pannier rack and we set off, exchanging good-natured banter along the way, enjoying the sunshine and evidently not paying enough attention. We saw the blue post marking the Great Glen Way but, assuming this indicated the entrance to the high route, we bypassed it and continued along the forestry track by the river. We thought this was the low path. We weren't even much concerned when, after an unmarked fork, the route we had chosen petered out at a clearing. My dad said he'd cycle to the junction a couple of miles back and scope out the left-hand fork. If it ascended to become the high path he might be able to wave down to me from the hillside, or shout and then I'd find a short cut and scramble up to meet him. It seemed a workable plan and I didn't even let the biblical swarms of midges dive-bombing my face dissuade me from waiting patiently for dad's signal.

When, twenty minutes later, it hadn't come, I began to retrace my footsteps and met Dad returning from his foray. The other fork had indeed led up the hill but he'd not been able to locate me down below and had struggled up a couple of miles of rocky forest path before deciding to turn back. Nevertheless, we both agreed that this must be the right route. Dad would cycle back to the car while I pressed on up the hillside. It hadn't dawned on either of us that none of this matched what the map showed or what Frank had told us. In a spirit of blithe optimism, we parted company and I began the schlep up the hillside.

Three miles later, a horrible feeling of déjà vu descended – the path seemed to peter out once more at a circular clearing, perhaps a turning circle for logging trucks. This left me, at almost 5 pm, with a dilemma – I could turn back three miles to the junction and then run a further couple of miles to the blue marker posts we'd ignored earlier, making a wasted journey of ten miles. Or I could press on. I could head off-trail over open country and try to find some way back to the Way proper. The latter seemed the preferable choice.

Beyond the clearing lay a patch of boggy moorland, with forest to the right and left and rolling hills straight ahead. I couldn't see any sign of a trail directly ahead of me and felt certain the high path must be somewhere up the hill to my left, beyond a small patch of scrubby woodland. However, there was no easy route through the bog or between those trees. There was what looked like a rocky path leading through the moorland, which I followed for a while until I realised it was probably the remains of a diverted stream which, in any case, lost itself amongst the marsh. I'd not seen any boot-prints on the muddy base of the old stream bed but there had been deer tracks. Perhaps the lack of signs of human life should have triggered alarm bells. Every mistaken action seems self-evidently foolish with the clarity of hindsight.

Stuck in the middle of a bog in the Highlands with no real notion of how to proceed, my thoughts began to cloud. I started to talk to the camera a lot, wry or ironic at first, although I'd lose my sense of humour later on. Without an obvious plan in mind, I decided to take a risk and strode off to my left, in the direction of the thinnest bit of forest and the closest peak. If I could get to higher ground I'd surely either locate the Great Glen Way or at least have a better vantage point from which to plan my next move.

Needless to say, there would be no more running for a while. For one thing, I'd made it my policy not to run unless I was certain I was going the right way. Secondly, it was just impossible. I could scarcely walk across the bog, which alternated deep, muddy pools with tufts of tall, wiry grass. I had to leap between these tufts and clumps of thick moss which often gave under my feet, sinking me ankle-deep into the water. Within moments my feet were soaked. It seemed unimportant. Eventually I reached the tree-fringe where there was more bad news.

The pine trees were incredibly close together – a couple of feet at most, with spiky branches running up their entire length. They were bedded into humps of convoluted, lumpy moss. The whole place dripped and was shrouded in a weird gloom. Although I love trees and enjoy being amongst forest generally, this was not an inviting place. I called my father, not expecting to get through. Voicemail; better than nothing. Abruptly, my foot plunged deep into a muddy pool and the frustrated message I was in the midst of leaving was comically truncated. That was the last flicker of phone reception I'd experience for several hours.

Meanwhile, my father had realised that we'd made a serious miscalculation. He'd looked at the map again and had seen the trail switch back on itself to head in the opposite direction around the range of hills I was skirting. I had been going in the right direction according to the compass but was on entirely the wrong side of the mountain. I should be able to see Loch Ness from the trail. I would probably have come to this realisation myself if I hadn't let my dad take *our only copy of the map*.

Of course, Dad couldn't get through to return my call, even after hearing my worrying message, which had ended with the black comedy of my 'Aarrghh!' as I plunged into the bog. He was left to fret and hope I'd somehow correct myself.

I seemed to have no choice. Perhaps it was my pride or dogged refusal to be defeated by mere geography but I knew I had to get through those trees. I decided to think like a deer, doubling over to follow the route animals would take. I actually found it easier, once I got lower to the ground, to force a path between the brittle, fibrous branches. As ludicrous as it might sound, thinking like a deer really worked – I started seeing droppings and places where animals had broken the lower twigs in passing. I zigzagged between the trees, passing the occasional clump of mushrooms, including a half-eaten fly agaric. For a moment I wondered whether a nibble at a hallucinogenic mushroom might improve my grim mood. Wisely, I decided against it.

Filming my experience in a continuous shot (by now my handheld GoPro was assuming the function of a confidante or therapist), I broke through the trees onto open hillside in about eight minutes. There was a wooden post ahead of me which I hoped was a trail marker. Getting closer, it turned out to be the remains of a long-dismantled fence. I surveyed the new terrain, hoping for a break.

Nothing obviously helpful lay in sight. Ahead of me was the rounded peak of a hill, perhaps a hundred or so metres of climb. To my left and right the forest stretched for miles. Maybe I could follow the line of the old fence, hoping it would take me down to a path of some sort. This was mere guesswork. I needed more information. I decided to climb the hill.

It was steep-sided, thick with heather and moss. I put the camera away and used my hands to pull myself up the most precipitous sections. Eventually I got to the top where, on a normal day, I would have admired the view, which was spectacular. Thick clouds glided quickly overhead, letting patches of sunlight roll over a landscape of endless hills. I couldn't see Loch Ness anywhere. This was a considerable worry. Where was the Great Glen? I couldn't lose one of the most significant landmarks in Scotland, could I?

By this time it was around 6.30 pm. I knew I had a couple of hours of sunlight left. Without any sign of a trail or road in sight, I made for a neighbouring summit, even higher than the one I'd climbed. I was now mountaineering; the ridiculousness of it struck me. My run had become a quest for survival. It was alarming how quickly the landscape had turned on me (or so it felt; the urge to anthropomorphise my plight grew as the sun slid ominously towards the horizon). On top of the second hill, I finally made out something that gave me a little hope. To the south-east (using the compass built in to my Garmin) was a thin strip of road, perhaps four or five miles away and not exactly buzzing with traffic. Still, it was a sign of human habitation. I'd make for the road, call my dad, from a payphone if necessary, and get him to pick me up.

Having some sort of goal in mind lifted my spirits a little. I was still frustrated but at least I had a target to aim for. As I began to descend the hillside, I sang to the camera a nonsensical ditty I dubbed the 'Fuckity Fuck Song'. It's only lyrics were expletives. I felt mildly deranged from exhaustion and stress and singing that stupid song did help considerably. Its full lyrics are reproduced for your delight in Appendix I.

Halfway down the hillside, as I negotiated ridges of craggy rock, tussocks of thick grass and patches of bracken, I could make out the river again, gleaming thinly between me and the road. I'd have to find a bridge, a weir or a rocky section to cross. It was too early to let this obstacle worry me. Quite literally, I'd cross that bridge when I came to it. First, there was the not inconsiderable matter of descending about half a kilometre through thick heather, ferns and tufty grasses concealing hidden marshy troughs. Nothing as helpful as a sheep path presented itself as I scrambled around the ruins of old cattle corrals, down steep hillsides and through waist-high bracken that scratched and entangled my legs. It took the best part of an hour to get down to level ground again.

Eventually I stumbled upon a service road that ran between electricity pylons. Unfortunately this seemed to lead away from the river and up through the hills, so I turned off it and into another strip of thankfully less dense forest. Climbing a high fence onto a more manageable route where the underbrush had been partially cleared (possibly to facilitate deerstalking), I followed its line down to the river.

The water was at least forty feet wide and seemed quite fast-flowing. I'd already waded through streams to get this far south but this was on a different scale altogether – this would entail swimming. With my cameras and mobile phone, this did not seem a sensible option. There had to be a bridge further upstream. In fact, looking to my left, I thought I could discern the surface of the water becoming choppier, near where it curved out of sight. Perhaps this indicated a weir. That would be better than nothing – I could carefully pick my way across the top of a weir – I'd done exactly that as a kid.

Unfortunately, it wouldn't prove that simple. For one thing, between me and the next bend of the river lay a mile or more of crazily undulating grassland. This grass extended up to my knees and seemed to have grown over a ploughed field, or equally awkward terrain. I could force my way through but it would not be fast progress. By now the sun was beginning to graze the horizon, a dramatic sunset forming beyond a distant line of trees. I forged on, briefly considering heading for some abandoned logging machinery. Maybe I could curl up and sleep in the cab of a vehicle if it came to that?

I refused to admit the possibility of sleeping rough, despite the fact that miles and miles of fields seemed to pass without any indication of a crossing over the river that glistened darkly through the trees to my right. My mood became bleak and I even cried in frustration and fear for a minute or so. It seemed to help. Ludicrously, I recorded my darkest thoughts to camera in case I 'didn't make it'. I realised how naïve I was to expect a bridge – this was not London or even Oxford, where every river is criss-crossed with roads. There might not be a sensible way of reaching the opposite bank for twenty, thirty, forty miles.

At least I wasn't in physical pain. Weirdly, although I felt deeply fatigued, the injuries in my knee and ankle had vanished as the adrenalin of fear flooded my system.

The road, it appeared, was my only rational idea for getting back to safety, warmth and my father, who by now must be in the throes of real panic. Every so often I checked my phone for a signal and each time it disappointed me. I noticed I'd somehow missed two calls but of course couldn't return them. Suddenly, a flock of sheep appeared and dashed away from me in mad panic, leaving one terrified animal lying on its side, in the process of giving birth. This was no time to learn animal husbandry and birth a lamb, however. We exchanged a look of shared distress and I left the poor creature to its own agonies and headed back down to the water's edge.

In the dim light, I saw that the river was just as wide here as it had been downstream and, although the surface was broken by little wavelets, these did not indicate a weir or anything man-made. By now I was desperate, so I decided to push aside my fears and wade into the icy water. I switched on the GoPro on the gimbal and hoisted it and my smartphone over my head. Everything else in my backpack was either waterproof or could survive a soaking.

As I stepped into the water, I stumbled over a submerged rock or tree root and briefly ducked the phone under the water, cursing violently. Fortunately, I regained my footing and continued. My plan was simple – to slowly wade across the river. As I stepped gingerly out, the water level rose to my waist, chest and then to my neck. Fortunately that's as far as it climbed; unfortunately, when I reached the middle of the stream, the current became unexpectedly fast-flowing.

The rocks beneath my feet were rounded and slippery. I tried to push against the current but, inevitably, I lost my footing and it began to carry me downstream. I desperately tried to keep my camera and phone out of the water as my legs shot out from under me. I began swimming in a peculiar stroke of my own invention, left arm circling while my feet kicked and my right arm stood rigidly out of the water. Had anyone been there to see me, I would have looked truly ridiculous. Slightly disingenuously, the camera was pointed away from me and the placid, floating nature of the resultant shot belies the struggle I was experiencing. For a moment I considered giving in to the current and letting it float me back downstream. Perhaps eventually it would take me back to where I'd started that afternoon. If I'd had a raft or dinghy, it would not have been a bad idea.

Instead, having floated downstream for only about fifty yards, I managed to get across to the other side and began grabbing desperately at branches, the first few of which were rotten and broke away in my hands, prompting more colourful Anglo-Saxon.

Eventually I hauled myself onto the land, shouting angrily 'I've beaten you!' My triumph was quickly accompanied by the realisation that it was now nightfall and I was soaking wet, cold and still had to clamber over a couple of fences and up some steep fields to reach the road. This took another ten minutes, by which time I was shivering and grimly determined to either thumb a lift back to the nearest town or knock on a local's door for help. It was late and no passing cars were in evidence as I wandered towards the tiny hamlet of Torgyle, not far from the town of Glenmoriston and, it later transpired with horrible irony, a bridge.

Blithely unaware of this, I walked dripping along the road, feeling grimly pleased that I'd succeeded in my desperate plan. More problems presented themselves at this point however – it was dark, there were no cars, I was wet and cold and had, as ever, no phone reception. A ramshackle barn appeared on my right, like a piece of set-dressing in a rural horror film. Then a telephone box and road signs promised some sort of civilisation (I couldn't make a call; stupidly I'd packed no coins). A light appeared on my left – a couple of houses on a small spur of road off the main one. I squelched up to the front steps of the first house, seeing the flickering illumination of a television inside. I decided to switch off my head-camera since it would be sending rather mixed messages to be carefully capturing documentary footage while pleading for rescue.

An elderly lady answered the door and stood there perturbed as I dripped on her front step. Not my ideal saviour, I thought, unkindly. I quickly explained as best I could the circumstances that had led to me swimming the river. Eventually Sheila resolved the conflict she must have been experiencing inwardly – whether to be afraid of me or sorry for me – and let me in. Providing a towel, she let me use the phone to call my father. Fortunately for my shaking fingers, she had a large-dial telephone, each button an inch across. I left a message on my dad's phone, as usual not being able to get through. I made a second call to the hotel where we were supposed to be staying that night to see if Dad had left a message there. He hadn't but I was at least able to explain why we'd be significantly late in arriving. It did not occur to me to call the police.

After that, I was a little stumped. Sheila offered to drive me back to Invermoriston and even on towards Fort Augustus, where I was supposed to have ended up that day. She was eighty-two years old and told me she didn't usually drive after dark but was willing to do so if we left soon. There seemed no other viable course of action. Other than me sleeping on her couch, which I'm sure neither of us wanted, I couldn't think of a better plan. Reluctantly I agreed, thanking her profusely.

Fortunately, the roads were devoid of traffic and Sheila drove at a surprisingly nimble pace back to Invermoriston. Something made me ask her to slow down as we approached the car park where my dad had stopped earlier in the day. There was a silver Mondeo waiting there with its headlights on. Remarkably, it was my dad. I thanked my rescuer profusely and let her go. I think Sheila was happy to be of service; I'm sure it was a diversion from the way she had expected her evening to develop.

My dad was hugely relieved of course. After providing me with a blanket and something to drink, he told me what he'd been doing in my absence. At around 6 pm, having realised it would be next to impossible for me to find the correct route over the mountains to the Great Glen Way, he'd called the police, who went into immediate action, having considerable experience with wayward Highland wanderers. At around 7.30, having sent out local officers to knock on doors in the neighbourhood, they had contacted the local mountain rescue team, based at Kintail, who said they could scramble a helicopter if I didn't show up soon on one of the neighbouring roads. It would be equipped with devices that could identify a human heat signature, even in the midst of the deepest forest.

When I did show up, mountain rescue were probably no

more than half an hour away from sending the helicopter out. Having driven with the police as far as possible up the rough track I'd initially taken in case I doubled back, my dad was instructed to wait in the Invermoriston car park while they canvassed the local villages and drove the streets in several vehicles. It must have been tough for my father having to remain alone in that freezing car park, powerless to assist further, in the hope that I'd eventually return to where I'd started my afternoon folly.

The police arrived in the car park a few minutes after I did and, surprisingly good-natured, took down my details. Jokingly, I said I had been prepared to bivouac before deciding to cross the river. Less humorously, one of them countered that this would have been 'a death sentence'. Given the sub-zero temperatures that could occur in September here and what I'd been wearing, he was probably right. I began to realise just how serious my misadventure could have been.

Having apologised profusely to the very understanding landlady at that night's bed and breakfast (many miles from Invermoriston) for our later arrival, and with a motorway service station takeaway as my evening meal, I quickly discharged the duties of saving the footage I'd recorded onto hard drive. I had a feeling that day's filming would provide the key to the film of the run. Cinematic structure notwithstanding, the events of the 5th September would remain vividly in the forefront of my mind throughout the rest of the trip.

I'd learned a valuable lesson the hard way – the Scottish Highlands are not a playground for the dilettante wanderer. They demand and require respect.

MILES RUN: 164;[7] MILES REMAINING: 936

1. http://www.outdoorhighlands.co.uk/

2. 2011 Census data available here: http://www.scotlandscensus.gov.uk/

3. Census taken as of the 27th March 2011: http://www.ons.gov.uk/ons/rel/mro/news-release/census-result-shows-increase-in-population-of-london-as-it-tops-8-million/censuslondonnr0712.html

4. www.whizz-kids.org.uk

5. www.limbpower.com

6. He also told us that the adventurer Sean Conway had also stopped by earlier in the year, while filming his Discovery Channel show about his own JOGLE run. I'd found out about Sean sometime after starting my own project but had decided not to let the similarity of our challenges bother me. Sean was something of a professional, having already cycled and, most incredibly of all, swum the route (the latter via the west coast). I was a rank amateur making a very different kind of film. I also hoped there was room for more than one book or film/show on the subject (time will tell). As it happens, we exchanged a few Tweets during my run and Sean was nothing but charming and encouraging.

7. Twelve of those miles in the wrong direction.

INVERMORISTON TO FORT WILLIAM

The next day, exhausted and aching, I decided, encouraged by Dad, to take a day off to recuperate and prepare for a second assault on the next section of the Great Glen Way. We set about cancelling all the hotels, with the assistance of Carol Hodge, Dad's 'relief' support car driver, who would be driving up from Manchester later on. The decision brought immense relief. There were just too many variables to stick to a predetermined schedule. Yesterday had proven that in a manner more emphatic than strictly necessary.

When I conceived the idea of The Long Run, I felt fairly confident that I could run forty miles a day. Although it seems wilfully naïve now, this was based on the fact that, having run several marathons and numerous half-marathons, I'd trained to the condition of being able to run ten miles with relative ease. I thought that if I broke each day into four chunks with breaks and meals in between, I'd rack up a sedately paced forty miles per day. Once the schedule began to slip, a decision had to be made about whether I somehow tried to regain the lost miles to get back on track or not. That would mean running even more than forty miles per day until I caught up. On injured and exhausted legs, that just didn't seem viable.

Accommodation plan altered, we settled on Fort William as an ideal locus for the next few days' running and drove into the busy but compact town to look for vacancies. At the tail end of summer, the place was still buzzing and every decent room was taken. We found basic rooms in a somewhat less than salubrious hotel and booked three nights. Comfort would have to give way to convenience. It was an easy trade-off.

Once we'd unpacked we had lunch and I did some urgent hand-washing of my running gear, filling my room with a deeply noxious smell that made me glad I was in a small prefabricated annex off the main hotel building, away from most of the guests. That done, there was still half an afternoon to kill before dinner. Dad and I decided to take a trip in the car. As well as the stiffness in my legs, my knees were aching badly and so it was all I could manage to limp up to the top of the hill at Glenfinnan where a coachload of Korean tourists were snapping photos of the two iconic views – viaduct and monument. It was an incredibly beautiful place and soothed away some residual tension.

Sightseeing done, we drove back to the hotel to await the arrival of the 'relief shift' in support car driving / second camera / production assistance. I'd found Carol Hodge by placing an advertisement in a low-budget film-makers' site called Shooting People.[1] When I'd first mentioned the notion of running the whole of the UK, my dad had volunteered to support me. However, when I revealed it would take a minimum of four weeks, he couldn't commit to the full project. At the age of seventy-two, still relying on twice-weekly gigs for much of his post-retirement income (he plays saxophone and clarinet in various New Orleans-style jazz bands) it was too big a favour to ask. For him to be away from home so long would also be unfair on my mother Kath who had (at that time undiagnosed) gall bladder problems and was looking after an energetic Labrador and two hyperactive and sometimes incontinent Lhasa Apsos, who she regularly took in while my sister Katy was away. Leaving Mum alone with health issues plus the hounds from hell for a month or more would have been cruel indeed.

Of course, the handover to Carol wouldn't be possible if my dad simply left the following morning. He had to talk her through the logistics of the task, the maps and other resources and the intricacies of the Panasonic G7 camera.

Fortunately, after some negotiation with my mother regarding the insane canines, my dad was able to do an additional day of handover before he left. We also agreed that he'd return to fly the quadcopter whenever that became possible later on in the run, possibly bringing my mother along too. As it happened, Carol proved a very capable replacement and the handover went without a hitch.

On the 7th September, having rested and recuperated as much as possible, I had to face the Great Glen once more and in particular the stretch from Invermoriston to Fort Augustus that had defeated me. We got an early start and by 8.30 am I was ready to run. We all walked up from the main road to the blue marker post where the Great Glen Way doubled back on itself and snaked through the trees along the shore of Loch Ness. With the clarity of hindsight, it seemed such an obvious route.

My dad and I had debated telling Carol the full horror of what had occurred on the 5th but in the end, we decided to be honest. She had to be prepared for the worst. And besides, I was now equipped with a detailed map, a compass and, most importantly, a clear sense of my own vulnerability in this sometimes hostile environment. So we showed her a few of the clips of me at my most desperate. Duly warned, she joined Dad for the day in operating the Panasonic and navigating to the next location where they might get a glimpse of me.

I started the day cautiously, alternating walking with running. My legs seemed to have benefitted from the day off and the sun was shining down on the trail, which made its way, in rather idyllic fashion, through woodland loud with birdsong. The contrast with 'the events of the 5th' as I'd come to euphemistically call my near-catastrophe, could not have been more marked.

I reached the place where the path split and one road skirted the edge of the loch while the high trail climbed to the top of the mountains. The climb was severe, making me wish I had a pair of hiking poles (although I've never used them). Sunscreen and sunglasses would be required before too long as the path weaved in and out of tree cover. I knew I'd get through a lot of water once again.

The views of Loch Ness from the top of the well-maintained gravel trail were stunning – it was almost an alpine scene, with wisps of cloud garlanding the distant hills and the deep blue loch sparking below. As ever, the landscape's beauty spurred me on and kept my pace up, as well as the knowledge that I was getting some impressive footage. As on previous days, I scarcely passed a single soul all morning as I maintained a 9 to 10-minute mile pace along the flatter sections and downhill stretches.

I'd been hoping the day would prove relaxing and help banish the demons of two days prior and the Way did not disappoint. Looking at the crystal blue waters down below, I even had a daydream about kayaking the length of the Great Glen, including all its lochs and canals, from east to west coast. Perhaps another year I'd accept that challenge. The task at hand was to keep up a good speed, not get lost and avoid additional injuries as I made my way to Fort Augustus.

From the south-western end of Loch Ness and the top of the trail, I could see the town appear four miles distant. From this high vantage point, it was literally downhill all the way. As I ran, I recorded some of my thoughts about how landscapes can turn from fun playgrounds to dangerous wildernesses as the result of one bad decision. Although the trail couldn't have been more conducive to a happy running experience and I even found myself managing 7-minute miles at one stage, I would carry this sense of the fragility of my own well-being in the 'great outdoors' throughout the remainder of my run.

Fort Augustus appeared, as scheduled, at lunchtime and I was still capable of a good pace as I searched for my support team amongst the tour parties and located the start of the Caledonian Canal. This would alternate with lochside paths as far as Fort William. I'd been running so fast that Dad and Carol hadn't realised I'd be arriving so soon. Once I caught up with them, we filmed a scenic shot of me climbing the flight of locks between Loch Ness and the canal's northern extent.

After a brief rest, I set off again at just after 1 pm, deciding to delay lunch for a little while. I knew that with seven hours of daylight and thirty-three miles between me and Fort William it was just possible I'd make it to the town, provided my various ailments didn't flare up. As ever, I was not lacking in optimism.

What I had a shortage of, however, was sunscreen, which I had forgotten to pack. A cloudless blue sky belied the clichés about Scotland's dreadful weather; this in the second week of September. I felt hot in my T-shirt and reluctantly put the shades on. I don't really like the barrier sunglasses place between me and passers-by. I find strangers respond in a less friendly manner when they can't see your eyes. There was absolutely no cover on this north-west to south-east strip of canal, however, which curved gently between Fort Augustus and Oich Bridge.

I'd done most of my marathon preparation on canals, specifically the Union Canal between Brentford and Hayes, and was used to the comparative monotony of level terrain. However, on urban canals there are always bridges, buildings, factories, narrowboats, canal-side pubs and locks to add variety. The Union Canal also varies underfoot from tarmac to cobbles to gravel to hard-packed mud interspersed with puddles. The feet have plenty of variety and the repetitive strain of endless footfalls is tempered.

This was less true of this stretch of the Caledonian Canal, the towpath of which seemed to have been recently widened, flattened and surfaced with hard, sharp gravel to facilitate access for motor vehicles of some sort. Its pristine whiteness hurt my eyes, reflecting the hot sun up above. The towpath was proving quite popular with cyclists but, apparently less popular with runners. I passed one or two but, on a day like today, might have anticipated dozens. I had to remind myself, once again, how far north I was. I'd have to find other diversions to limit the monotony and distract me from my aches and pains. Swans, moorhen and ducks, kayakers, cyclists and hikers (whose number had suddenly increased tenfold) provided some diversion for the eyes as I plodded on under the blazing sun.

Winding south-west in blinding daylight, the canal became a giant strip of mirror for the trees and bushes along its banks and the hills that provided a scenic backdrop. Although protesting, my knee was holding up well as I reached the remains of an old station from the Invergarry and Fort Augustus Railway, discontinued in 1947 and awaiting renovation as a local attraction. A little further on, at a 'water park', I met my support car and we had a basic but filling lunch in a café overlooked by wooden holiday chalets.

Along the side of Loch Oich there was further evidence of the railway as a ruler-straight section of path ran alongside the calm, deceptively inviting waters. I enjoyed the cool shade of the trees and high embankments but the ground beneath my feet remained hard-packed gravel. A cloudless sky dazzled me as far as Laggan, where a narrowboat converted into a pub offered the tempting possibility of relaxation. On any other day, the thought of having a pint and sitting in the sunshine listening to the birds chirping amongst the trees would have proven irresistible. Instead, I crossed over Laggan Locks and headed for the north side of Loch Lochy (had they run out of possibilities when they named that one, I wondered?) There I had my now daily dose of confusion trying to locate the next stretch of the Great Glen Way and found myself turning back from a mountain trail to Ben Tee and Sron A'choir Ghairbh ('the nose of the rough corrie'). Intriguing, but not where I should be heading.

Once I was back on track, a smoothly surfaced forest trail skirted the northern side of Loch Lochy and allowed me to make decent speed as the sun began its relentless descent. I'd hoped to make it to Fort William that day but the miles and concomitant fatigue were getting the better of me. Still, I enjoyed what was by now becoming a regular late afternoon spurt of energy (presumably my gut had finished processing the calories from my late lunch). I tore round a snaking lochside path in 8-minute miles, pleasantly distracted by the small, gnarly pine trees which projected into the water in places, losing their leaves and resembling bony fingers pointing skywards.

A few miles out of my revised destination I met Peter, a lanky Inverness postman who had decided to take a hiking holiday up the Great Glen Way. I commented that it seemed odd for a man with such a peripatetic profession to choose walking as a leisure pursuit but Peter replied that he felt strange when not on his feet all day. He seemed pleased to be filmed doing something he loved and was planning to defy the rather pointless 'no camping' signs by the side of the loch and pitch his tent by the lapping waters. Our conversation was a pleasant but brief pause in what had now become a mini-mission: to get to Gairlochy by the 'magic hour'. I loped off with renewed vigour and enjoyed spectacular views out over the loch; some bodies of water seem more majestic from water level than from a high vantage point.

For once, support and runner had co-ordinated well and I arrived in time for Carol to film me coming to a halt against a backdrop of golden sunset and mirroring water. Moments like these were what the project was all about – the serendipity of mood and weather. I'd been effectively living outdoors for a week now and it began to feel normal to see the sun rise and watch it fall while still on my feet. Banishing the horrors of the 5th September would be quite feasible if there were more days like this ahead.

The following day we returned to the more predictable charms of canal running. A longer stretch of Caledonian Canal would take me all the way to the small town of Caol (pronounced 'cool') to the north of Fort William and from there I'd skirt the shores of Loch Linnhe towards the city itself. Loch Linnhe is not really a loch, at least in the sense that it's not fully land-enclosed. After narrowing at Corran it opens out into the Atlantic Ocean between Oban and the Isle of Mull. I'd not be heading that far south-west though. Instead, my aim was to pursue the legendary West Highland Way, cutting south and south-east as far as Blaneford, just north of Glasgow.

As it was a lovely day, my father and I decided to try another sequence of bicycle tracking, leaving Carol to drive on to her next vantage point. The sunshine was less ferocious than it had been at Fort Augustus and this far south there were more runners, dog-walkers and cyclists out enjoying the unseasonable weather. I made reasonably good progress with the distraction of having someone to keep up with and talk to. My dad kept me going at a speed a little faster than I might have adopted if I was alone – nothing Olympian, mind you, probably 9-minute miles instead of 10.

We reached the Moy swing bridge, around three miles into the run, with relative ease, where an old steamer barge was chuffing along through the locks. Somewhat smaller than some of the paddle steamers that used to pass this way in the late nineteenth century, this relic of a bygone age was at once impressive and anachronistic as it vented huge gouts of white steam and one of its crew opened the bridge to let it glide majestically through.

At times during sections of The Long Run I began to feel like I was on holiday, a strange feeling when what I'd planned was a momentous feat of endurance. Pausing, however briefly, to watch and film that steamer pass exacerbated that odd sensation. We pressed on but it wasn't long before I suggested to my dad that we part company. I couldn't allow sightseeing to distract me from the fact that I was a man with a mission.

I can't remember the exact moment when I realised that the impressive mountain appearing between gaps in the trees to my left was Ben Nevis. I suppose I should have known its 4,409 feet would be visible from this low, flat vantage point. Its summit dipped in and out of low-lying cloud, Scotland's own mini-Alp. I re-evaluated the likelihood of running up and down it, something I'd considered at the planning stage, especially when I heard of the annual Ben Nevis Fell Race which takes place at around the time I'd be passing.[2] Fatigue and pain relegated this unlikely act of masochism. My ankle was beginning to throb with a persistence I could no longer ignore, although I deferred any drastic decision-making for as long as possible.

I next met up with support at Neptune's Staircase, an impressive flight of eight locks that allowed the canal to drop a final sixty-four feet to sea level, so that it could join Loch Linnhe at the Corpach sea lock. Unusually, we took several takes to get a decent shot of me running alongside these locks and through the village of Banavie. I sometimes wonder how many extra miles I ran as a result of the handful of 'multiple takes' we allowed ourselves.

Pressing on to Caol and Corpach, I got momentarily

confused finding the switchback that would head me along
Loch Linnhe's eastern beach. When eventually I found it, I
could no longer ignore the persistent agony of my left ankle.
It had swollen noticeably, retaining fluid, a soft doughnut
of flesh riding above my running shoe. Every step sent a
shock of pain up my calf as far as the knee, a wave of agony
tailing off only to be renewed with the next inevitable step.
Something had to give. I vowed to reach Fort William and
revisit the situation.

The route proved annoyingly indirect as it negotiated
suburban streets, a play park, the remains of Inverlochy
castle and the River Lochy's floodplain. Eventually, a more
urban environment emerged and I had a bathetic moment
trying to figure out if the end of the Great Glen Way really
was a supermarket car park (fortunately not). I crossed
a mini-roundabout, dodging weekend shopping traffic
and found the little green where the Way officially ended
(or began). My father and Carol were there and I'm sure
my pained expression told them all they needed to know.
Although it was halfway through the running day, I couldn't
face another step.

We had a picnic on the grass, while I pressed a bag of
crushed ice cubes around the traumatised ankle. Morrisons'
own brand sausage rolls and Irn Bru hardly constitute ideal
runner's fuel but they comforted me as I reclined, foot
elevated, enjoying the sunshine and debating what to do.
Given how hideous my ankle looked, I didn't have to argue
too vehemently with myself to stop for the day. Still, my
irrational inner voice, the secret whisperer that harangues all
long-distance runners, felt that I was malingering. It might
have been easier had it not been such excellent running
weather. I knew myself well enough by now to know that
to press on would be to risk significant, project-halting
injury. Discretion would have to be the better part of valour.
Tomorrow might offer more hope. Today had to be written

off. That's the way it goes sometimes in the wonderful world of ultra-running.

The afternoon wasn't wasted, however. When we got back to the hotel, my father and I made the long call to my mother that resulted in him being able to stay one more day and manage a longer handover to Carol. Later, unbeknownst to me, having heard our horror stories concerning the 'events of the 5th', Carol recorded an excellent and moving video interview with my father. It would be weeks later, viewing the rushes, that I would discover just how panic-stricken he had been.

MILES RUN: 204; MILES REMAINING: 896

---

1. www.shootingpeople.org – an excellent resource for crewing, funding or advertising film productions.
2. For a snapshot of this most agonising of fell-races, see Richard Askwith's excellent book *Feet in the Clouds* Chapter 27.

FORT WILLIAM TO ROWARDENNAN

I stood shivering in the pouring rain on the morning of the 12th September, dancing from one foot to another in my shorts, waiting for Carol to set up the shot. As she did, I ran over in my head the wording I'd use to explain my utter stupidity. With a day to savour the consequences of the previous afternoon's calamitous mistake, I still couldn't quite understand how I'd managed to lose over a thousand pounds' worth of film equipment. Nor did I know how the film would now proceed, shooting on the Panasonic, a camera-phone, an ancient handycam and a Canon Ixus compact camera.

Rewind to three days' prior and you'd see a huge contrast in both composure and self-confidence. Having had an enforced rest on the afternoon and evening of the 8th, I'd awoken the next day to more glorious weather with an entirely unjustified feeling that today would be kind of okay. I really have no idea how my subconscious plays this trick but my confidence level really does seem to change like the patterns of passing clouds – chaotically and unpredictably. Something had occurred in the dream-world to nocturnally process the worries and fears of the day. If I knew what it was I'd distil, bottle and sell it.

We'd made Fort William our home for two days and had one night more before we'd have to re-book accommodation. This gave us a secure base and a certain amount of relaxation against which to balance the uncertainties of the West Highland Way. Fort William is a massive tourist draw, being excellently suited for both explorations of the Great Glen and Ben Nevis and the surrounding mountains. Its vibrancy contrasted powerfully with the seclusion I felt as soon as I headed out of town towards the start of the Way. Although it was warm and sunny, a low-lying bank of mist lingered in the deepest valleys, with a higher band of cloud capping the huge mountain which loomed overhead.

I followed a B-road (thankfully provided with a generous strip of pavement) as far as a visitor centre near the start (or end) of the West Highland Way. Then, after a short briefing with Carol and my father, continued on to locate the typically downbeat signpost to the trail. Turning off the road onto a grassy pathway alongside fields, I saw thousands of miniature nets – the dew-flecked webs of spiders, aimed like satellite dishes at the sky. Everything seemed green, moist and thriving with life, even this late in the season. Coniferous forests dominate over deciduous in Scotland and so, at almost any time of year you can find yourself running through dark, verdant woodland, a soft carpet of needles cushioning each footfall.

Once again, the heavily oxygenated air, varied terrain and quietude of the forest path banished any lingering doubts about my injured ankle and my general fatigue. I'd been following Scott Jurek's tweets and Instagram posts about his own trailblazing experiences along the Appalachian Way and I could fully empathise with why he would spend forty-six days running through landscapes like these (albeit on a more immense American scale, of course). There is a kind of unspoken kinship between ultra-runners, even if they haven't met – we just 'get' one another. We don't need to ask one another 'Why?'

While my head was waxing lyrical, my feet were beginning

to climb. Inevitably, as the trail began to ascend the southern side of Glen Nevis, the incline increased. I began to hike, this time without any feeling of compromise. I was beyond that now – spells of walking were just part of my armoury of survival strategies. I knew I'd be back to running at each and every opportunity, my form improved by the rests in between.

One of the most enduringly beautiful stretches of countryside through which I ran over the whole journey, those fifteen miles from Fort William to Kinlochleven are a lasting memory. The valley stretched out before me with the iconic mountain its guardian, appearing and disappearing between ranks of arrow-straight pine trees. I stopped to take photos and film the views, each vista more and more impressive than the last as I rose above the treeline. After a short while the trail took a turn south and Ben Nevis vanished behind me, to be replaced by other mountains only a little less impressive. To my left, I could see five other Munros in the Nevis range; to my right the gentler, more rounded landscape north of Ballachulish. I felt no urge to go mountaineering anymore; just being able to run through this beautiful wilderness was privilege enough.

While raising seed money for The Long Run film on a crowd-funding website, I'd created something called 'Dedicate a Mile'. The intention was that I'd recite a short text chosen by a donor and dedicated to a loved one of their choice, then film the subsequent mile. Glen Nevis seemed the ideal place to recite the dedication my friend Sara had written for her baby Rosamund. Sara and her partner Guy (a talented film-maker who had also edited *Sparks and Embers*) had endured a terrible journey towards parenthood, their first attempt ending in the unimaginable heartbreak of stillbirth. Rosamund was the gift that made the memory of that pain endurable. The lines Sara, an academic and short-story writer, had composed, were moving and perfect for the landscape through which I was painlessly running.

How could I be feeling so little pain, given that my ankle was still swelling over the course of the day and it had been only eighteen hours since I last ran? I'm afraid I have no answer; all I can say is that there was so much to distract me, so much variety and sheer entertainment in the terrain through which I scampered, ambled and raced, that mere physical strife became unimportantly prosaic. I'm not a religious man and am sceptical of those who claim some species of agnostic spirituality, but there is something undeniably uplifting about being at large in a picturesque landscape, particularly one with as few indicators of human 'improvement' as possible.

When the West Highland Way was opened on the 6th October 1980, the intention was 'that [the Way] will offer the public between four and five days' walking, and provide them with a real sense of achievement.'[1] It was invented by rambler Tom Hunter and masterminded by geographer Fiona Rose, who spent a year traipsing over 1,000 miles, enduring the assaults of midges, the rigours of exhaustion and the hostility of local landowners to inform the proposals that the Countryside Commission for Scotland eventually approved.

The enthusiasm for this new long-distance walking route was not universal, however. My father, who worked for the National Trust for Scotland for almost thirty years, had a hillwalking colleague who was vehemently opposed to the Way on the grounds that it would gentrify and effectively 'tame' a rare and wild environment. He and others felt that the route could become a sort of 'walkers' motorway' and cause erosion and damage to an untainted landscape. Those fears proved largely groundless. The route is ninety-five miles long and can sustain a lot of traffic without significant erosion issues becoming apparent, primarily due to the ruggedness of the landscape and the resilience of the local flora and fauna (as well as human conservation efforts).

As I ran through rocky valleys and along hillside paths, chasing sheep out of my way, I considered on which side of the argument I might have fallen had I lived locally. The number of walkers increased towards midday and on into early afternoon, and the hikers I passed were international and often in large groups. Nevertheless, everyone I passed seemed friendly and respectful (at least over the first couple of days), most of them acknowledging my unexpectedly sudden appearance around the bend of the trail and stepping off the path to let me tear past. I didn't see much evidence of trailside litter, even on long stretches where there were no facilities to get rid of wrappers and empty drink containers. Most hikers are a self-selecting group, in terms of their attitude to the wildernesses they explore. They don't want to see rubbish and, for the most part, don't drop any.

On balance then, I'd rather see these incredible places opened up in this way than left accessible only to landowners and the privileged, Range Rover owning few. Most of the West Highland Way is unpaved, the signposts are minimal and there are few built facilities along its length. Then there's the economic argument – hillwalkers pay for accommodation, buy provisions and equipment, petrol for their vehicles and sundry other little expenditures that add up to a substantial contribution to the country's wealth. Tourism makes up 5 per cent of Scotland's GDP (approximately £6 billion in 2014)[2] and hiking is a substantial part of Scottish visitors' itineraries. That money makes its way, via taxation and conservation initiatives funded by public-private partnerships, back into the protection of those selfsame walking routes.

As I found out by cruel experience in the days to come, unused walking routes tend to return to nature and become all but impassable. Fundamentally, it comes down to this – walkers must use them or lose them.

Although the trail was well marked and I suffered no major mishaps, such as getting lost or injured, the rocky, hilly terrain slowed me down until I reached Kinlochleven at around 2pm. My support car wasn't far away and we had a hearty lunch in a local pub before I set off once more. Given the setbacks I'd already suffered, I felt reasonably confident and decided to start increasing the daily mileage again. That said, I'd realised that forty miles a day was unfeasible. That day I would try to make it as far as the Glencoe Ski Centre, the last landmark for many miles accessible by road.

A limitation of running trails when you've decided not to camp is that you need to apportion your mileage to coincide with pick-up points your support vehicle can actually access. Quite often on those off-road routes I'd reach a 'crisis point' in the middle of the afternoon where I had to make a best estimate of what was realistically achievable before sunset. I couldn't put my support crew through any more trauma by going AWOL. As far as the paltry phone reception on the West Highland Way would allow, we had to keep in touch and regularly reappraise the afternoon's progress.

The post-lunch section of day nine began with a bit of a schlep up the side of the hills south of Kinlochleven, following a set of enormous black hydro-electric pipes carrying water down from a high reservoir. In places, the joints between sections of these pipes were leaking, the pressure of all that plunging liquid sending large sprays of water into the air. In bright sunlight, these created miniature floating rainbows, a surreal distraction as I climbed. As it was afternoon, with Kinlochleven a key stopover on the Way, I found myself passing many groups of hikers, most of them equipped with poles. The contrast with the solitude of the Great Glen Way was again marked.

I was following the route of the Old Military Road. After the Jacobite rebellion of 1715 the British Government created a network of basic roadways across the Highland region, the Romans having thought twice about attempting any route-building this far north. Although General George Wade began the project, those designated simply as 'old military road' are usually those initiated by his less well-known successor Major William Caulfeild.[3] Since they pre-date motorised transport and that famous Scottish invention, tarmac, they are rudimentary at best. However, I found their width, relative straightness and visibility a definite boon as my tired afternoon legs struggled with the ascent to and beyond the small reservoir above the town.

When things finally levelled off, I was able to run again. A three-feet-wide strip of white gravel stretched out ahead of me, running along the side of the River Leven valley. Perfect for running, once I'd removed a few stray stones from my shoes. At times the gravel gave way to pointy chunks of flint and granite, well-weathered by the constant winds. Some of the GoPro gimbal shots I took over this section resembled moon lander footage, since the camera seemed to float eerily over inhospitable terrain. Nevertheless, it was great ground to battle across, requiring constant attention and therefore, paradoxically, taking the mind off such mundane concerns as exhaustion and ankle pain. I'd rather run a route that means I have to constantly think about each footfall than an endless pavement without variation. Too often we neglect the importance of mental effort in our running; for me the best exercise is that which utilises my proprioception and stamina equally. Trail-running and climbing are the simplest activities that engage both skills.[4] I'd have plenty of the former activity and (surprisingly) a bit of the latter in the days to come.

The landscape through which I now ran was amongst the most spectacular I'd encounter on the whole journey. Backlit by the blazing afternoon sun, a spine of craggy mountains formed a backdrop to the view ahead, including the iconic Buachaille Etive Mor (the big herdsman of Etive). The mountain comprises two Munros,[5] Stob Dearg (the red peak) and Stob na Broige (the peak of the shoe). Part of the joy of moving through these landscapes is learning their names and trying out the sounds of their pronunciation.[6] The mountain stood out like a blue-black shark's fin set against the azure skyline. The Way seemed to be determined to head directly towards the epic peaks on the horizon, none of them less than a thousand metres high. I knew I'd be winding between them, rather than over them, but it was an exciting prospect nonetheless.

I reached the top of the Aonach Eagach Ridge and took in the spectacular view of Glen Etive spread out behind me. As I ran down towards the A82, I allowed myself a bit of music to spur me on. In training, I'd often used music to help maintain a good pace and keep me motivated on long, and at times, monotonous canal or riverbank runs. When exhaustion sets in and the inner voices start urging you to stop, having that cinematic backdrop of sound can make all the difference. My favourite music to run to was either the rhythmic but many-textured sounds of Orbital[7] or the early instrumental albums of Mike Oldfield, some of which took me back to my lonely teenage years wandering through the Pentland Hills south of Edinburgh.

Oddly though, on The Long Run so far I'd hardly listened to music at all. Partly it was a practical thing – when I was running along roads, I needed my wits about me and had to be able to hear cars coming round corners or racing up behind me. Then there was the issue of filming – I'd have to keep turning the iPod off every time I wanted to film a clip for fear of noise leakage or interference. And finally, there were aesthetic considerations. It didn't feel right listening to The Strokes or John Coltrane while running through the Scottish Highlands.

That said, in this moment, blundering down twisting rocky paths towards Glen Etive, Icelandic 'sadcore' heroes Sigur Ros seemed appropriate, the keening tones of singer Jonsi and ambient soundscapes complimenting the vistas all around me. After all, Iceland is well known for its other-worldly landscapes and its quietude.

The music kept my pace up as I plunged past Carol, who was in position by the side of the trail, ready to capture an image of me running at my best (note to self – try to always be filmed at the end of a day running downhill). I reached the road, crossed carefully to the car park on the other side and slumped down on the grass, watching two teenagers take romantic selfies in the glorious early-evening sunlight. There were perhaps a couple of hours of runnable light left, but my legs had had enough. Ten days in, I'd begun to realise how important it was to listen to my agonised body. I'd start fresh and invigorated tomorrow. Hopefully.

That evening, my father joined us in the Falls of Dochert Inn, a restaurant and hotel by the eponymous falls situated, rather inconveniently, forty-three miles from Glen Etive. Carol had been phoning around for much of the day without much success and we'd had to resort to anything we could find on an A-road that linked up with the A82. Although all they had left was a twin room, at least the Falls would be good for two nights, in terms of relative proximity. It didn't make for a speedy journey from end point to rest point but when we arrived, the hotel and its location were beautiful and restful. The food in the restaurant was delicious and filling and the beds comfortable. I said goodbye to my father for a while (until he was due to return to shoot some quadcopter sequences) and fell asleep to the accompaniment of gently tumbling waterfalls.

Unfortunately, an early start the next morning meant that I probably managed around five and a half hours sleep and I didn't feel exactly buoyant with energy as I set off along the roadside path through the iconic Glen Etive valley. Mountaineers and hikers were already striding in both directions and, for once, I only barely kept pace with them. I tried to quash the pain throbbing around my shins and concentrate on the trail. I decided to alternate walking and running, even on level sections, at least for an hour or two. I couldn't keep cutting days short – the desire to get back on schedule or at least not fall too far behind had become an imperative.

I counted my blessings, by now a near-daily routine. It was another unseasonably sunny day and the trail, although climbing steadily, took a gradual incline as it rose, flirting with the contour lines at the side of Bheinn A' Chrulaiste (rocky hill). The mountains around me provided their usual distraction from the discomfort I was feeling. Fortunately, as the morning wore on and the trail rose through trees, under a small railway line and along the side of a sparkling river, the pain diminished to a low throb.

I was making for the Bridge of Orchy, the poetically named crossing point of road, river and rail which, for a well-signposted village, offers little more than a hotel, church and tiny railway station. Still, in this remote corner of Argyll and Bute, it is a welcome respite for travellers. First though, another, much less impressive bridge over a stream provided a resting point. My feet were hot with the constant pounding on rock, hard gravel and tarmac in the warm weather so I stopped, took off my shoes and socks and climbed a wall to dip my feet in the river. The Scots' word for this is 'plouter' and it is very specifically used for dabbling in a stream. The relief the icy water brought to my aching feet was immense as tiny fishes swam inquisitively around my toes. With typically unfortunate timing, I heard (but did not see) two female runners passing over the bridge above me, heading in the opposite direction. It would have been nice to ask them how far they were going. Something told me they might be ultra-runners, an ease of gait perhaps, as they loped towards a backdrop of cloud-swathed peaks. I dried my toes and squeezed the shoes back on. There were only about three miles between me and my midday meal and my stomach was already complaining.

After the customary epic lunch in the Bridge of Orchy hotel, I made off up a tiny track that led under the railway line and found myself following the course of the river for a mile or so. Something made me introspective and I confessed to the camera that I was at something of a crossroads in my life. For a multiplicity of reasons, I found myself single at forty-four. Call it commitment phobia, excessive choosiness or just plain bad luck but a 'life partner' still eluded me. I speculated that, on some unconscious level, this epic journey might be some sort of elaborate mating ritual. Absurd, but perhaps not so much. Other mammals have their dances, their displays of bravado. Why not us hairless apes? It clearly was not the sole reason why I'd attempt something so exhaustingly masochistic and time-consuming, but perhaps it was there in the mix.

As ridiculous as it seems, fondly imagining my future bride watching spurred me on and, although the aches and pains were increasing, so did a post-lunch vigour as I headed through the lead-mining village of Tyndrum and then skirted the gateway town of Crianlarich. I was a little over-eager I suppose, since I'd not told Carol that I intended to keep going after Tyndrum and she was expecting an update and a plan. In my eagerness, I was coasting along on a sudden jolt of energy and positivity and didn't think to stop for a confab. This would be my downfall later.

Near Crianlarich, the West Highland Way took a sudden turn south-west, following the course of the River Falloch and passing over and under the A82 towards the spike at the northern tip of Loch Lomond. Earlier, I'd hoped to get as far south as Balmaha or at least Rowardennan on the eastern shore of the loch before calling it a day. After all, the Way ran right along the side of the loch and would therefore be level and quick to run, or so I imagined. The Long Run was nothing if not a lesson in the foolishness of casual assumption.

During one hilly section, I bounded down the trail towards a crossroads between pathways. Forest lay ahead, a grassy slope to my left, a fence and trail to my right. At this crossroads I met a pair of Californian hikers – Michelle and her daughter Sarah – who had decided to walk a section of the Way having heard about it on Wikitravel's entry for Scotland.[8] They asked me about my adventure (an exhausted runner wearing a camera on his head seldom goes unquestioned) and I told them how well it was going in general and especially today. I was reminded of the dire warnings I'd heard about potential gastro-intestinal issues ultra-runners can face and said I felt lucky that nothing of this nature had troubled me so far. Michelle even gave me a book recommendation on this topic – *Gut* by Guilia Enders – an apparent best-seller which I haven't yet been brave enough to read.

At this junction, I also found a Post-it note left by Carol reading 'Gavin, not sure if I've missed you. I'm ½ mile this way' and then an arrow pointing down a grassy, muddy hill. I discovered later that Carol had waited a couple of hours and then gone back to the car, uncertain if I had already passed by. I called her and, surprisingly, got through. Once

I'd told her that I felt great and surmised that there were a couple of hours of viable daylight left, we decided I would continue on the West Highland Way. I suggested I'd either stop at Inverarnan or further on at Ardleish, locate the road and wait somewhere visible.

The latter part of the day's running was pleasurable and easy, apart from a slight hint of late afternoon delirium which involved me composing a puerile song which rhymed the words 'Cossacks' and 'Trossachs'. I tended to find my mind wandering into some very odd places at the end of each day's running. There was a section of the Way involving fields and I found myself speculating whether you could sell a coffee table book of photos of country stiles.

We'd been hoping the road and Way would cross somewhere helpful but the trail ducked under the A82 via a tiny tunnel and there was nowhere on the road above for a vehicle to stop. With the light fading beyond Inverarnan, which seemed to be a place name allocated to little more than a couple of farms, I decided to find the road and somewhere to wait. My decision was validated by a passing 4 x 4 full of hard-hatted men heading for a building site somewhere further on. They confirmed there was no place up ahead where the trail and road coincided. I retraced my steps past a farmhouse, headed up its driveway towards the A82, climbed a fence and waited by the roadside, cars flashing by carrying commuters to towns and cities.

Unfortunately, Carol had been driving up and down the road between Crianlarich and Ardlui for some time and must have missed me. When she finally pulled in to the driveway where I'd been shivering for half an hour, my support driver was not in the best of moods. I couldn't blame her. The lack of pre-planning and impossibility of communication was making her job extremely difficult, almost futile at times. She'd not been able to get any shots of me since Bridge of Orchy and I suppose her role may have seemed a little pointless if all it consisted of was dropping me off then hunting me down for a pick-up at the end of the day. I'd promised her something a lot more creative than being a taxi service.

I swore to keep in touch more regularly, whenever possible making an hourly call to assess progress and give her an idea of my pace. This proved especially vital the following day when the trail took on an altogether more challenging aspect than I'd anticipated.

After Ardleish, on the 11th September, I watched the River Falloch open out into a narrow strip of lake – Loch Lomond, another Scottish icon. The morning's run had felt pretty easy, a rocky path giving way to a gravelled access road for building works down by the river, then actual tarmac farm roads for a while before the Way reverted to its default setting of minimal muddy tracks, stiles and forested paths. Now and again there would be a small settlement with a few houses.

Outside one of these remote dwellings was a wonderful free resource – an 'honesty shop' selling tablet and cookies. It even had a glass punchbowl with a tap filled with water freshened with cucumber and citrus fruit. I dropped my spare coins into a petty cash tin and took the last slab of tablet wrapped in greaseproof paper. Tablet is a Scottish variant on fudge. Harder and sweeter than fudge, it snaps rather than bends. It's mostly condensed milk and sugar and insanely sweet. Being basically just fat and carbohydrates, tablet makes a perfect, albeit fairly unhealthy, running fuel. I love it and consumed an unreasonable quantity of it, along with Orkney Fudge[9] during my travels.

By the side of Loch Lomond I came across a tiny 'beach' of sand and gravel into which passing hikers had drawn their names and initialled declarations of love inside cartoon hearts (had many teenagers been dragged this way by zeal-ously outdoorsy parents?) Cheekily, I scrawled the web address for the film I hoped to make at the end of this (and for the blog I was already writing) and moved on.[10]

Carrying on down to the lochside I was looking forward to some good, picturesque waterside running. After all, given that there were several ultra races along the route, including the Highland Fling and West Highland Way Ultra, it must all be theoretically runnable. However, to slip into such a hope is to forget one of the key paradoxes of ultra-running – quite a lot of it does not involve running at all. There are stretches in every race over 26.2 miles where runners are reduced, either by exhaustion, injury or just the requirements of the terrain, to walking, shuffling, clambering and even rock-climbing.

For long sections of the run between Ardleish and the imposing Inversnaid Hotel, the West Highland Way became an obstacle course. Marshy sections that required hopping between stepping stones, overflowing streamlets you could either leap across or wade through and, most arduously, a mixture of giant, randomly arranged boulders and foot-tripping, exposed tree roots like those you'd expect in a mangrove swamp. While much of the Way had been accessible to a hardy walker of any age, this was borderline impassable. No sooner had I got up a bit of pace on hard-packed dirt, than a slab of granite or twisting maze of roots would stop me and necessitate use of hands and feet. It was a fantastic full-body workout but it slowed me to a pace that caused me to double-take whenever I looked at my Garmin. Did I really just take twenty-two minutes to cover that last mile? Apparently so – the next mile took twenty-five minutes.

About halfway along this section, I spied a small wooden sign reading 'Rob Roy's Cave', presumably where the Scottish rebel hero hid during his feud with the Duke of Montrose, who had evicted him from his home at Inversnaid and seized his cattle (Rob Roy had defaulted on a loan after having had his money stolen). Eager for a diversion from the frustrations of the Way, I followed a small track down to the lochside where an impressive jumble of car-sized boulders had to be cautiously navigated to locate a triangular opening, entirely hidden from the path (but visible from the loch). Helpfully, someone had daubed 'CAVE' in white on the grey rock with a large arrow pointing to its entrance. The opening could just accommodate an adult but I didn't fancy venturing inside on my tired legs so I took photographs and peered into the gloom instead. Whether the local lore is truth or fancy, the cave (which was actually a space beneath immense shards of fallen rock) would undoubtedly prove a good place to hide away from prying eyes while keeping dry and warm.

Returning to the Way, I passed quite a few teams of hikers heading in the other direction, all in stout boots, anoraked and armed with poles. There were no other runners. Later, when the ground finally levelled out for a relatively smooth section between scrubby pine trees, I met a group of mountain bikers. 'Do you know what's coming next?' I felt obliged to warn them. 'Oh yes,' one cheerfully replied, shouldering his vehicle over a boulder.

I burst out of the treeline at Inversnaid, finding a turn of speed which had been frustrated by the difficult section behind me. It was nearing lunchtime but I didn't want to stop. I couldn't see Carol or her vehicle in the hotel's car park so, after a brief shell-shocked rest on a bench with a lovely view of the deceptively placid loch, I set off again, through the manicured hotel grounds and around more of the convoluted shoreline. There was a small road leading around the campsite and ranger station at Rowardennan, at the Western edge of one of Scotland's largest forests. If I made for that, I felt sure that my support car and lunch would be waiting. A quick estimate put the distance remaining before lunch at ten miles.

It wasn't long until I passed Tarbet on the opposite shore and heard the buzzing of motorboats cruising the loch. The path became a gravelly forest track and started climbing, perhaps inevitably as I was now rounding the steep slopes of Ben Lomond (973 metres). The trees thinned out as the mountain rose to my left and I stomped downhill again. I began to pass hikers coming up who asked if I was Gavin and then cheered me on. This told me Carol couldn't be far down the trail. It was an ad hoc strategy she'd borrowed from my father – telling passers-by to look out for me meant I'd know the support car was close and it would encourage me to keep up the pace.

I passed Carol with tripod set up at the side of the trail and pressed on. Half a mile further on another surprise awaited – both my parents, with my sister's wayward Lhasa Apsos in tow, waving a Scottish flag and filming my approach on an old camcorder. After hugs and greetings they told me they'd made Carol keep their visit a secret. At a point in the day when my energy levels were at a low ebb, it really raised my spirits and after a brief chat, I agreed to wait for them by the Rowardennan car park and then we'd have lunch together.

Reinvigorated, I made good time and, after what still seemed an unnecessarily long and winding wooded trail around the campsite, I reached the parked cars and white-washed toilet block that meant I could stop. It was cold and a light drizzle was falling. With relief I stumbled into the toilet block. Depositing my GoPro cameras on the flat wooden top of the cistern behind me, I did what nature demanded. Then I left the toilet block to wait at a picnic table for my folks.

The others appeared about twenty minutes later and we had a generous lunch in a pub at the edge of the forest park. By this point in my adventure, eating had become something of an obsession, unusual for me (those who know me will know that I am anything but a 'foodie'). I was like a hungry horse with his head in the feed-bag. It was only after finishing my meal that I looked around for my cameras, didn't find them and remembered where I'd last seen them.

On top of the cistern, in the toilet block, where I'd left them over an hour and a half ago.

We drove back to the car park as fast as the rutted lanes would allow but it was to no avail. The cameras had gone. Checking in at the local ranger station and campsite turned up plenty of helpful people but no sightings of hikers dropping off forgotten camera equipment. Many fruitless calls were made to the Scottish Police lost property offices and the Forestry Commission, who owned and maintained much of the land. Nothing had been handed in or reported as found. The local National Trust for Scotland rangers were especially helpful, making calls on my behalf and letting me use their landline when our mobiles proved next to useless. But the quest proved fruitless. I was close to despair.

The frustration and anger I felt at my own incompetence could hardly be put into words. How could I have lost almost a thousand pounds' worth of vital gear by simply leaving it in a public lavatory? I could only imagine my exhaustion must have played a part in this mistake. I'm certainly absent-minded but this was taking my propensity for error to a whole new level.

We could only hope that some public-spirited person had found the equipment and, without any obvious recourse to hand it in to the police, had taken it with them on the trail. We all shared a belief that West Highland Way hikers were generally an honest and helpful group of people. It might take a couple of days but the cameras would surely be handed in.

Disappointingly, they never were.

MILES RUN: 273; MILES REMAINING: 827

1. Countryside Commission for Scotland report as quoted in *The Herald* online [http://www.heraldscotland.com/life_style/13124797. The_West_Highland_Way/]

2. According to the Scottish Government's own figures, available here: http://www.gov.scot/Topics/Business-Industry/Tourism

3. Yes, this is how his surname was spelt.

4. Parkour must, therefore, be its apotheosis.

5. Munros are Scottish peaks over 3,000ft, named after Sir Hugh Munro, who compiled the first table of them in 1891 – as of 2012 there were reckoned to be 282 Munros 'proper', although 227 subsidiary peaks complicate matters somewhat for the truly obsessive 'Munro bagger'.

6. Much-aided by the helpful pronunciation samples on www.walkhighlands.co.uk

7. Their 1996 album *In-Sides* is one of my favourite albums, not only for running to, but of all time.

8. Presumably here: http://wikitravel.org/en/Scotland

9. If you've never tried Orkney Fudge and have a sweet tooth, it is a revelation: http://www.argosbakery.co.uk/sweeties.html

10. It's www.longrunfilm.com and, as well as the blog of the run itself, should carry updates on the movie's completion and release dates, festival screenings et cetera.

Section Two

TRUE LOVE WAYS

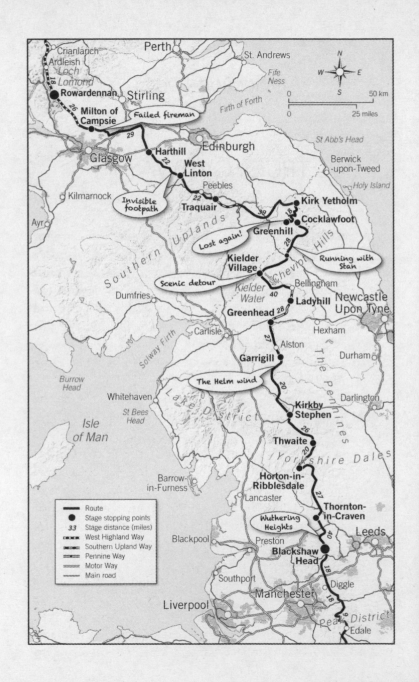

ROWARDENNAN TO FALKIRK

The theft of the cameras put paid to my running on the 11th. We spent hours trying to locate the lost equipment as my enthusiasm and the daylight ebbed away. However, the show had to go on. My father saved the day. Encouraged by my mother, he offered to replace the equipment. I didn't know what to say at first. This crisis was entirely my fault and the cameras were not going to be easy to source and replace in time. Plus, they were comparatively expensive and I'd not be in a position to repay him for a while. Having quit my job to fulfil this ambition and burning rapidly through my redundancy money as I was, things were already looking financially perilous.

However, we'd all committed to this project and to the act of filming it. I'd already shot dozens of hours of footage, mostly using the lost equipment. We decided that they had to be replaced. I gave my dad a list of the gear that was missing and within thirty-six hours he'd gone online and had managed to locate, purchase and arrange delivery of replacements. He'd even managed to create a new 'gimbal sling', a zipped, waterproof pouch worn around the shoulder big enough to take the GoPro and steadying device I used to record my pieces to camera.

The gear would take a day to arrive. This meant that for the 12th December, I'd have to rely on something a little more basic. When my parents had turned up at Rowardennan they'd been filming on a Panasonic camcorder. My dad also had a Canon Ixus compact camera, largely a stills camera

but which was also capable of 1080p[1] video clips. And then
I had my iPhone 6 which, for a phone, is about as good as
you're going to get (and also shoots 1080p). These would be
the emergency interim cameras.

It wasn't as if we'd lost everything from the previous
day's running either. I'd managed to exhaust one Micro SD
card in the head-worn GoPro and pocket it, so I had that
much to show for the morning's scrambling and clambering
(including the visit to Rob Roy's cave). Today's filming,
however, would require a patchwork of video sources to tide
us over until the replacement equipment arrived. I began, in
torrential rain, outside the toilet block where the theft had
taken place, shamefacedly explaining what had happened to
the main support camera. Already soaked by the time I left
the car park, I headed off along the trail, which ran parallel
to the road towards the small lochside village of Balmaha.

For long sections the path wound its way through dense
natural woodland, part of the Queen Elizabeth Forest Park
which extended south-east as far as the outskirts of Glasgow.
My plan was to exit the West Highland Way about ten miles
north of Milngavie and head towards the Forth and Clyde
Canal, which would take me east as far as Falkirk.

The rain was pretty relentless and I was glad of the tree
cover between Rowardennan and Balmaha. The latter town
seemed almost deserted, apart from a group of waddling
ducks who were enjoying the blurring of the usual distinc-
tion between water and dry land. I paused by the town's
statue of local conservationist, writer and broadcaster Tom
Weir[2] who, despite being immortalised in bronze, was still
much more appropriately dressed for the inclement weather
than I was.

After consulting with support, I headed off after a brief
rest under a tree, taking roads now (some even blessed with
a pavement) and confessing to camera the need to 'dig deep'
and 'keep in mind the greater goal'. I don't usually mind

running in rain but after three to four hours of constant precipitation, it gets wearying. There was something pleasingly ironic about the name of the town where I'd stop for lunch. Drymen (pronounced to rhyme with 'women', mind you) was only three miles further south-east.

Soon I passed the evocatively named Buchanan Smithy (a small hamlet proud of its community history) and then Drymen itself. I stopped gratefully on the bench outside the village shop as the sky poured its contents relentlessly down. Following lunch, ninety minutes later, it had still not stopped raining. The West Highland Way resumed on footpaths for a while and these were level and easy to run, allowing me to fall into the determined trancelike state that comes with perpetual rain running. Carol managed to catch me a couple of times as, head down, cap firmly pulled down over my ears, I totted up the miles. Sixteen miles to Drymen with, injuries allowing, fourteen more to Campsie Glen before sunset.

Not far from Campsie, I was briefly held up by a small fire left unattended and smouldering by the side of the footpath. For some inexplicable reason, someone had set light to a large pile of newspapers and absconded. Even Scottish rain had not extinguished the flames – the thickly layered paper had proved self-insulating and the breeze kept the embers lit. Being a generally public-spirited person, I decided to try to put the fire out ... by jumping on it. If anything, trying to stamp the flames out made matters worse. A switch of bracken proved just as ineffectual. Eventually I decided to call the local fire brigade. Civic duty done, I ran on. By the time Carol got there, the local brigade had already put the fire out, possibly by collectively spitting on it. Nevertheless, calling the proper authorities felt like the right thing to do.

Another obstacle awaited me a few miles further on and this time, I couldn't call for help even if there was such a thing as a 'Stray Bovine Helpline'. A herd of cows, smelling fresh weeds on the other side of a crumbling wall around their field, had broken out to investigate this smorgasbord. Around a dozen large heifers straddled the footpath, completely blocking it. I used my usual technique of shouting nonsense at them in a low 'farmer's voice' and waving my arms and they grudgingly gave way. Passing through them, I made reassuring noises, probably for my own benefit more than theirs, and put a gate between me and the herd. Unimpressed, the cows resumed denuding the verges.

The rain began to let up in mid-afternoon and the sky became an impressive palette of glowering greys backlit with golden evening light, Jacob's ladders slanting through fast-changing gaps in the cloud. I took several photos and, my iPhone battery becoming dangerously drained, switched to the Ixus for video. The running was going well and I began to look out for the trail to cross an A-road where I'd finally leave the West Highland Way. As it happened, I got a little bit confused at a junction with a half-dozen possible routes and headed further south than I'd planned.

The last bits of phone battery ran out as I was route-finding with the help of a local man. Eventually, I found my way back to the main road near Blanefield and took the A821 east to join the main road to Haughhead. Having no way of directly calling support now, I borrowed a phone from a local in the Blane Valley Inn and left a message on my parents' answering machine. Fortunately, luck proved on my side and support had sensibly staked out the road ahead of me, solving our communication difficulties.

At Strathblane, my parents turned up with replacement GoPro cameras for the next day's shooting and we met Carol and stopped for an uncharacteristic afternoon cuppa (and to charge my phone). This sustained me for a further run along a busy A-road towards Haughhead. At this point in the journey, my spirits were generally high, despite the change in the weather. I'd just about 'defeated' the West Highland

Way and was within a few days of leaving Scotland entirely. Psychologically, if not geographically, this made me feel I was approaching the halfway point. In reality, by the end of the day, I'd have covered less than 300 miles. It's funny the tricks the mind can play when you're in the middle of a battle between the inner armies of determination and exhaustion.

The fag end of that day brought a lot of pavement pounding in various species of rain (including the wonderfully evocative Scots variety, *smirr*, meaning a very fine, mist-like drizzle). A moment of mystery was presented by sign reading 'Schoenstatt', which didn't sound like a very Scottish place name. A little light googling reveals it to be a retreat and pilgrimage centre set in some rather lovely grounds.[3] Intriguing, but not for this atheist.

A sign mysteriously festooned with party balloons indicated Milton of Campsie was just a few miles further on. Those miles proved achingly long but by this stage in the endeavour, I was determined to try and end each day at some sort of recognisable landmark or town, rather than an anonymous stretch of road we'd have trouble recognising the following day.

Around 6 pm I arrived at the town of Milton, stopping by a floral verge where Carol was waiting with camera poised. I could hardly raise the energy to summarise the day. Everything was throbbing with an egalitarian ache. I wasn't even a third of the way through the journey and I felt utterly drained – would my body simply collapse before I got anywhere near the wilds of Cornwall?

The 13th September brought some relief in the form of a long, flat railway path and a bright and sometimes sunny day. Milton looked very different in sunlight and with relative ease I negotiated its side streets and found the Strathkelvin Railway Path, which forms part of the John Muir Way, a walkers' route running from Helensburgh in the west to Balloch at the southern tip of Loch Lomond.

John Muir is a legend amongst conservationists.[4] Born in Dunbar in East Lothian in 1838, his family relocated to America in 1849 where he became entranced by the country's epic wildernesses as well as studying botany and chemistry. He was something of a restless soul, rejecting his father's staunchly organised religion for what we would now recognise as a more amorphously 'spiritual' attraction to nature and the preservation of wild places. In September 1867 he undertook a 1,000-mile walk from Indiana to Florida, recounting this is his book *A Thousand Mile Walk to the Gulf*.

The more I read about Muir, the more I realise what a great companion he would have been for my own undertaking, except that he was mostly inclined to solo expeditions. Amongst his achievements are petitioning the US government to put in place a protection order over what would eventually be known as Yosemite National Park. Thousands of American hikers owe their own wilderness experiences in part to the conservation efforts of this obsessive and determined Scot. They have named a route of their own after him – the 210 mile John Muir Trail which runs from Yosemite Valley to Mount Whitney. The latter is of especial interest to ultra-runners, being the end point of the infamous Badwater Ultramarathon.[5]

Sadly, I am not a botanist, so my trailside discoveries remain largely unlabelled. This does not mean I don't appreciate the flora and fauna through which I run; far from it. However, I do have to use the internet to discover just what I've been squinting at during my much-needed rest breaks. The 'lore of the country' is no longer something commonly known and handed down the way it once was when a minority lived in cities and many more lived off the land and relied on its provender.

Following the railway path, I trotted along a tarmacked

footway between mixed deciduous trees, heading generally south towards Kirkintilloch. The sun was shining brightly and cinematic shafts of light broke through the thinning autumnal leaf canopy. In fact, the atmospherics looked a little overdone to me – could there still be that much morning mist around?

As I ran further into the woodland, I realised that a pall of white smoke was acting as a medium for the light. I heard myself grumble 'not again' as I found myself investigating another abandoned fire under a small footbridge. It was the dying remains of a campfire created by someone or other and seemingly abandoned. Several empty cans of super strength lager were strewn nearby. At least the fire had been made on a hard-packed earth and cement surface and wouldn't spread. Lacking any immediate way to put the fire out, this time I ran on. Someone else would have to play concerned citizen today. There were plenty of dog-walkers and cyclists about that fine morning. I admit that this is not a good excuse but we all rationalise away our laziness from time to time.

A couple of miles further on, I located Carol and we decided to try a bit of bicycle tracking to capture the start of the canal towpath, prosaically marked as NCR754 on maps. Climbing a flight of steps to the raised canal, we set off at a moderate pace. I realised after a while that, at some point the previous day I must have left the West Highland Way. I had not marked the occasion in any way, which seemed a shame. However, this was no time for sentiment – the towpath ahead wound for a level but sinuous seventeen miles and if I was to get to Falkirk before lunch, this would require concentration and a decent pace.

Once again, the canal reminded me of the earliest days of my thirty-something distance-running and I fell into a familiar lope on an unfamiliar trail. I began to pass occasional runners and exchanged the customary nod or 'hi there', which was all was required for us to acknowledge our shared exertion and determination. Fluffy white clouds drifted overhead, offering intermittent shade, which made the sometimes monotonous route more pleasurable. The towpath offered views of industrial yards, factories and countless back gardens (when did trampolines become so ubiquitous?) Tired but not as drained as I'd expected to be, I maintained a pace of around nine and a half minutes per mile as I let my eyes rove over the patios, flowerbeds, car parks and industrial estates of central Scotland.

Distraction is essential in multi-day running events. You can't think about the process of running for eight or nine hours per day. Instead, you let the little things divert you from sinking into fatigue – a family of swans, late-blooming sunflowers, an obsessive collection of garden gnomes or sometimes just the grim detritus of industry – rusty pipes, sheets of corrugated metal, stacks of pallets. I sometimes think myself into other people's occupations. A strangely banal thought often occurs to me – everything I see around me is designed and manufactured and people are employed doing those jobs. I often try a thought experiment, imagining what it would be like if I was 'parachuted in' to a random workplace and asked to muck in. I imagine myself in those factories, workshops and offices; I hope I'd be able to fit in amongst my fellow employees in these theoretical work placements. Such empathic daydreaming whiles away hours on an urban trail. Try it and you'll see what I mean.

Auchinstarry, with its abandoned quarry and compact marina of colourful narrowboats, provided a brief rest stop, although I couldn't see my support car anywhere. I'd carried some glucose gels and muesli bars with me and these would have to suffice for fuel until lunch. I was a little over halfway through the morning's running and it was going well. A little further on I heard the buzzing of light aircraft and saw small planes circling overhead – perhaps those belonging to the Leading Edge Flying Club?[6]

I found myself speeding up a little, running 9-minute miles now. My lunchtime target was the Falkirk Wheel,[7] an engineering marvel I'd visited for the first time only a couple of weeks prior to the start of The Long Run. The world's only rotating boat lift, as its guidebook proudly proclaims, the wheel provides a speedy link between the Forth & Clyde and Union Canals, which meet at Falkirk where the landscape necessitates a drop of twenty-four metres from east to west. Before the wheel was built in 2002, the descent from the high western canal to the stretch that ends at Edinburgh took several hours, via a system of eleven locks. Using the wheel, it lasts around fifteen minutes. It is also a rather beautiful object, even to those not of an engineering bent. Over 400,000 day trippers currently visit it per year and most of them take a narrowboat trip of less than a mile from one canal to the other just to experience it in operation. Falkirk also offers The Selkies[8] of course, two 30-metre-high metal sculptures of horses' heads but impressive as Andy Scott's artwork is, I think I prefer the practical grandeur of the wheel to the symbolic gigantism of the Selkies.

Anticipation of lunch at the wheel was magnetically pulling me along past hedgerows heavy with hawthorn berries, brambles and bulbous rosehips. As a child, I remember using the grainy pollen of these rosehips to create home-made itching powder. I can't quite remember if it was my father or a wayward teacher who directed us to this antisocial usage. Perhaps not all plant lore goes un-inherited in an urban upbringing.

Having overshot my support car more than once, I made it to the Falkirk Wheel in time for a decent lunch with Carol (I seem to remember a baked potato with passable chilli) and to stop and plan the next section of canal. The giant yin and yang shaped metal wheels rotated slowly above us as we ate in the no-frills canteen within the visitor centre. If I could just keep my own limbs rotating with as much energy-efficiency as the wheel, I'd complete The Long Run without further mishap. But where would the drama be in that?

MILES RUN: 328; MILES REMAINING: 772

---

1. At time of writing, 1080 pixels (vertically) is considered by many the lowest acceptable resolution for High Definition cinema. By contrast, my missing GoPro worn on the head mount had been shooting at 2.7K (2716 x 1524 pixels) and the camera on the gimbal at a data-slurping 4K resolution (3840 x 2160 pixels).

2. Weir is perhaps best known for his long-running travelogue series *Weir's Way*, which ran from 1976–1987 on Scottish Television and which was rerun, to great popularity, in the 1990s. He did much to popularise walking routes and celebrate the more remote regions of Scotland.

3. http://www.schoenstatt.co.uk/ – see for those into that sort of thing.

4. One of the better-written Wikipedia pages gives a good precis of his life and work: https://en.wikipedia.org/wiki/John_Muir#Explorer_of_nature

5. http://www.badwater.com/ – not for the faint-hearted!

6. http://www.flyleadingedge.co.uk/

7. https://www.scottishcanals.co.uk/falkirk-wheel/

8. http://www.thehelix.co.uk/things-to-do/the-kelpies/ – if enormous public art is your thing, this is a must-see.

FALKIRK TO TOWN YETHOLM

Having wolfed down my lunch at Falkirk, I climbed the hill alongside the raised viaduct that feeds the wheel at the Forth and Clyde canal's western extent. After watching three young Labradors playing in the water, I jogged through a concrete tunnel to emerge on the placid, sunlit canal towpath once more.

The plan wasn't to take the canal as far as Edinburgh (although in retrospect that might have been a good idea). Instead, running with the heavy weight of lunch in my gut, I was looking for a turn-off point which would send me through West Lothian towards the westernmost extent of the Pentland Hills and then on to the Scottish Borders. I found it at Falkirk Road, to the south of the city, but first the route had a final spooky surprise for me. The canal, it seems, passes under a large section of Falkirk. Completed in 1822, the tunnel is 630 metres long, dimly lit with archaic strip-lights that seem to dim or flicker on as you approach them. The roof, stippled with tiny stalactites, dripped worryingly. Sounds echoed bizarrely as my run became a cautious walk. A cyclist wheeled his bike fifty yards ahead as some pedestrians came my way – given the darkness, it seemed prudent not to try to dash towards them. Impressively, despite the low light conditions, my GoPro captured the whole eerie experience until I burst out into sunlight again on the other side.

Back on the B-roads heading south, I was soon climbing again, gently, up through arable farmland and onto an unexpected patch of what looked almost like Highland moorland. Scotland is much more compact and abrupt in its land use changes than England. Zigzagging through a maze of small roads, chased by my support car, I skirted Loch Ellrig and headed towards Avonbridge with the intention of continuing south through Armadale.

Armadale reminded me of my Edinburgh University friend Rob, with whom I once flat-shared alongside an OTC[1] member and law student called Neil. The village was his hometown and though he sometimes bemoaned its provincial nature, I'd once had an enjoyable run with him around its surrounding fields and footpaths. Rob was now a naturalised US citizen, having lived and worked as a teacher in Pasadena for many years but we still occasionally met up, usually in Edinburgh or London, whereupon we'd reminisce about youthful misadventures.

One such misadventure was running-related. When we finally parted ways from our shared student flat overlooking Bristo Square (so close you could probably run from our front door to the lecture halls in around ninety seconds, although we never tried), the occasion had to be marked. I'd managed to miss the others when they headed out to the pub that last afternoon, after we'd all scrubbed the flat from top to bottom to get back our deposits. I don't know where I'd been but I returned to the flat at about 11 pm on a winter's evening to find nobody home and no note telling me where they'd gone (we had no mobile phones in 1990). Annoyed at their lack of thoughtfulness, I began to vacuum my room, my last remaining cleaning task, in a moderate sulk.

I suppose I was still hoovering grumpily when my soon to be ex-flatmates bowled in, together with Neil's army buddy Justin. Several pints had been downed and the boys were in good spirits. I had little choice but to smother my churlish disappointment and join in with whatever they had planned.

It's interesting that I remember my peevish hoovering with more embarrassment than what happened next.

I can't remember exactly who had the idea – it certainly wasn't me, the only sober one in the group. But someone had a notion of going for a run together around The Meadows, on our usual three-quarter mile route, completely naked. Well, not completely naked – that would be ridiculous. We would of course be wearing our running shoes.

We set off, in near-zero temperatures, having first to cross a couple of roads and negotiate late-night revellers before we got to the relative quietude of the Meadows. Once there, peals of laughter coming from groups of girls making their way from Christmas parties, we hared away at a decent pace and very quickly something surprising happened – the run went from being a juvenile prank to something genuinely liberating. We overtook one pair of elderly ladies who leapt aside with a shocked gasp but everyone else that saw us definitely had their evening improved by the sheer surrealism of four men running naked in the middle of the night. Cars honked their horns as we began to feel oddly empowered. That Olympian athletes in ancient times would perform in the nude made a bit more sense.

That said, it was incredibly cold and it would have been sensible after one complete circuit of the Meadows to head back to the flat and leave our daft streak there. But as you've probably already figured out, sensible was not the mood we were in, so we set off on another circuit. Midway through lap two a police car mounted the pavement in front of us and, being stupid youths, we all shot off across the grass. Neil, being army trained, tried to duck for cover, perhaps forgetting that rather than wearing military camouflage, his pale British buttocks were reflecting police car headlights like a second moon.

Justin had the longest legs and was racing away in an entirely different direction when the second police car caught

the rest of us in a pincer movement. I ground to a sheepish
halt and covered my privates. Rob, a little way ahead, did
likewise and Neil joined us from the underbrush. Justin
could have eluded capture, except that he was going in
entirely the opposite direction from the flat and his clothing.
Wisely, he turned back.

 Rather unexpectedly, out of the first police car stepped
a rather attractive dark-haired policewoman and from the
second emerged a handsome young man and a pretty blonde
female officer. I'm not sure why this troubled me so much
but what I do clearly remember is the four of us standing in
a semicircle, hands covering our genitals, while Justin tried
to chat up one of the policewomen and the other officers
tried to stifle their laughter. Names and addresses were
taken, comically stern warnings were issued and we were
asked if we intended to head straight back to the flat. For
a moment I considered replying that we might do a spot
of late-night grocery shopping but thought better of it. We
dashed back to the safety of our accommodation and got on
with our lives.

Thinking about this youthful foolishness, I skirted around
Armadale. It wouldn't be the same heading through Rob's
home town without him. A mile or so further on I heard
a roaring sound that grew in volume and insistence as I
approached and resolved itself as the engines of some sort of
racing buggies – large wheeled 4 x 4 vehicles tearing around
a sloped farmer's field in the distance. Their aggressive roar
made a peculiar backdrop to my climb up and over a line of
hills towards the dramatically named town of Blackridge.
Surely this was a frontier town in the old west, rather than a
West Lothian commuter town?

 I passed a field of wind turbines under construction. To
me, wind farms symbolise, not a modernist blot on the
landscape nor an eyesore, but a serene and slightly surreal

reminder that we are a huge energy drain on the planetary ecosystem as a species and must find ways to produce the energy we consume without devastating our environment. It irks me when I hear people protesting about wind farms as if having their view 'spoilt' was a remotely sympathetic standpoint when stacked against the eradication of the ozone layer through the burning of fossil fuels and concomitant global warming. The good a wind farm does far outweighs, for me, any aesthetic considerations. I'm fairly sure when the first electricity pylons and telephone posts were threaded into the landscape, similar arguments were made. Few now would do away with electricity or telecommunications on aesthetic grounds. Besides, I don't find these silently rotating machines threatening or ugly at all. Far from it. As I ran beneath them, they resembled guardian giants keeping watch over the landscape (although such a fanciful imagery might in part be explained by my oxygen-starved brain becoming delirious at the end of a long day's running).

From Blackridge (no outlaws in sight) I made reasonable but exhausted progress to the road bridge over the M8, where I paused to film the endless stream of vehicles heading between Edinburgh and Glasgow. Then it was on to Harthill, where I finally ran out of steam. Somewhat sadistically, I thought, Carol was poised with camera ready near the top of a serious incline. I could hardly end the day with a grumpy walk, so I ran as hard as I could the last few hundred yards. If you haven't got a sprint finish left in the legs at the end of the day on a multi-day event, I think you've definitely overdone it.

We somehow located that exact spot the following day and I followed some more B-roads out of town and found myself running alongside a strip of preserved moorland, Longridge Moss, full of heather, wild grasses and flowers, framed by mixed deciduous and pine trees and maintained by the Forestry Commission. I noticed one such plot was up for sale and hoped that the houses built there would at least be tastefully integrated into the landscape.

Not too long later I reached the more substantial town of Fauldhouse and began to scout around for a route across the Pentland Hills. I felt I was almost on home turf now, since I'd been walking and running this range of hills (albeit about thirty miles further east) since I was a small child.

My parents moved to Edinburgh in the early seventies and to Colinton, at the foot of the Pentlands, in 1975. My primary school, Bonaly (a name which translates as 'the foot of the rocks' according to one theory), was positioned adjacent to the towering hill of Capelaw, at 454 metres. Towering, that is, to a five-year-old. Seven years later I would toboggan down that hill at speeds so terrifying that the only way to avoid the plastic sledge exploding into fragments in a ditch was to roll off into the deep snow near the end of each descent. I got more ambitious a few years later and tried to set up a sledge race with friends. The plan was to whizz from the treeline down through a couple of miles of forest track, hillside and black-ice-covered road to a car park 300 feet further down. A few of us tried it experimentally, and it proved genuinely terrifying. How we weren't killed, I'll never know.

Those memories belonged to the familiar and friendly Pentland Hills a five-minute drive from my parents' house. It was perhaps daft of me to imagine the whole range would be as well trodden and clearly signposted. My target of crossing the Pentlands by lunchtime was also unrealistic but I had a strong motivation. My old school friend Iain and his girlfriend Carol had taken over ownership of a restaurant in the quaint village of West Linton a year previously; when I mentioned I'd be running close by, Iain kindly offered to provide a free lunch. As I'd basically become a machine for processing calories and turning them into motion, there was no way I was going to pass up that offer.

To complicate things further that morning, my father and I had identified another likely place to fly the quadcopter, from the top of a shale bing at a place with the Douglas Adams-like name of Tarbrax. If I ran along what looked (on Google Earth at least) like a footpath alongside a working quarry, my dad should be able to get a great aerial shot of the hills with me standing out in my blue running top and white cap. This was assuming several variables fell in our favour, including the weather and my estimated timings.

As I found my way onto the hills alongside another quarry at Fauldhouse,[2] I quickly realised the terrain would not be kind. The footpath gave way to open fields, with footpath markers but few visible trails. When I eventually found a gravelled track that might be the remains of an old drove road, it wasn't leading me where I needed to go, namely south-east. Carol and my dad called me to inform me that if I headed for some wind turbines on a hillside beyond some forest, I'd be going the right way. Unfortunately, by the time I caught sight of these windmills, I seemed to be running away from them. Not having a map of the Pentlands, I had to rely on the 'blue dot' of Google Maps and recalibrate.

My new route took me down to the A706, whereupon I climbed a fence and tramped through a field of irritating grassy mounds that made running impossible, to reach a fringe of thick pinewood. Heading into the trees would be pointless – they were closely packed and there were no evident paths through them. Even my 'become a deer' method of forest lore wouldn't help me here. I tracked south alongside the forest, stumbling over tree stumps reclaimed by moss. The whole environment was vividly damp and my feet were soaked through in minutes. Eventually I reached a break in the trees where a logging road headed east and gratefully started running properly for the first time that day.

A couple of hours and several telephone updates later, I emerged at the back of a farm, climbed a couple of fences with one eye out for the farmer and found a tarmac road that seemed to be going the right way. What had happened to all the careful mapping I'd done before starting this challenge? Two casually scribbled words damned me – 'off-road section'. I'd been a bit cavalier where it seemed possible to head over open ground as there was often no way of knowing from satellite imagery whether a wiggly indentation was a footpath, a dried-up stream bed or a drainage ditch. I'd assumed it would all work itself out and it did – sort of. What I hadn't banked on was how much frustration would build up with delays piling upon delays. I probably lost around a week by not having Ordnance Survey maps of every off-road section of the run. Again, hindsight is a wonderful thing.

After letting my friend Iain know that I'd be having lunch in mid-afternoon, rather than at the conventional time, I reached the picturesque Cobbinshaws Reservoir just as thick drizzle began to descend. Unusually, this didn't deter my father, who seemed determined to fly the quadcopter anyway. I suppose having waited on top of an exposed shale hillock in the rain for over two hours, the last thing he wanted was for it to prove utterly futile. Whatever his reasoning, I'd like to say the end result was a glorious sweeping shot of me storming across the farmed moorland towards the town. Sadly, the shot somehow misses me entirely as the rain and the camera's altitude made it impossible to pick me out amidst the multi-coloured foliage (Scottish hills can be deceptively colourful in autumn – green grasses, browning bracken, purple heather and yellow wildflowers).

For my part, I was back to stumbling along. What had

seemed a path in the satellite photos might just have been the shadow of a fence? Or perhaps a path had been visible here when the mapping satellites last did their flyover. Now, seemingly, nature had reclaimed this route. I made agonisingly slow progress to Tarbrax, where I passed an aggrieved quarry worker who'd found it near impossible to get his massive monster-truck-wheeled vehicle past our parked support cars.

After more phone calls, with the rain turning torrential, we revised our plan. We'd still lunch at The Old Bakehouse but we'd have to drive there, then retrace our steps back to the A70 to run the last bit to West Linton after lunch. At around three pm I made it to the main road, located Carol and my father and we headed to the restaurant.

Iain and his partner Carol (amusingly, we now had two Carols and two Iains (although my dad's name is spelt differently) were incredibly patient and kind, considering they'd opened up the restaurant just for us and had waited for hours. It helped that they lived above The Bakehouse, but it was still an act of great generosity to provide a three-course meal for four hungry, weather-worn travellers. Iain and I shared a lot of reminiscences and he even produced an old photograph of us from over thirty years prior that I'd not seen before.

At the age of about nineteen, Iain and I once decided to take a cycling holiday around Skye and the West Coast of Scotland. We took our bikes on the train up to Fort William and cycled the 60-plus miles to the Kyle of Lochalsh. We did this having never cycled more than a dozen miles at one sitting before. By the time we sped through the last mile (thankfully downhill) to the youth hostel, the manager was about to give our beds away to a party of Germans. In my fanciful imagination, I see us skidding to a halt in the foyer as the manager's pen descends towards the guest book.

The following saddle-sore day we took the Caledonian MacBrayne ferry over to Skye (this is in the pre-bridge era) and proceeded to cycle round the island. We'd not bargained on two things – Skye is incredibly mountainous, possessing a dozen Munros; furthermore, the weather is frequently unspeakably bad. We battled both obstacles in our week-long excursion.

Our disaster-prone holiday, which spawned several incidents I've liberally adapted for screenplays since then, had its nadir on one epic journey between Portree and Broadford. The rain was coming down as if gushing from a battery of fire hoses. We both had on our rainwear but nothing stops Scottish rain when it's determined to inflict maximal suffering. I remember unwrapping toffees in my anorak pocket (I needed the consolation) and finding the paper covering them had dissolved into mush. We both clamped our frozen fingers over the handlebars and became cycling machines, our sole mission to get somewhere with a roof as soon as possible.

I was out in front and cycling as fast as my legs could manage. I'd assumed Iain was just behind me. Through the wind, rain and my anorak hood, I couldn't hear my own wheels and gears, let alone his. I guess I waited a little longer than reasonable to take a quick look back to make sure he was there. He wasn't.

I pulled over onto the grass verge, letting the cars and lorries spray me with fine mist as I waited for Iain to appear round the bend. Minutes passed with no sign of my friend. Reluctantly, I turned the bike round and headed about a mile back down the road. There I found Iain, sitting on a rock by the ditch he'd managed to skid and fall into while I, oblivious, cycled on. Iain was so angry that he swung a punch at me, which I ducked before apologising profusely. I think it was just the abject unpleasantness of the way the day was going that had riled him to the point of violence.

That I hadn't noticed he'd fallen off his bike was the last straw.

Iain and I could laugh about such misadventures three decades later. The fact that he'd once shared in my athletic pursuits perhaps gave him a bit more insight into why I'd attempt The Long Run, although he still professed amazement at my determination. I thanked him the best way I could – by wolfing down his tomato soup with home-made bread, venison burger with thick cut chips and lemon cheesecake like it was a condemned man's final meal. Before we left, I made sure we recorded a piece to camera in front of The Bakehouse. The restaurant trade is a brutally competitive one and I really hoped that he and Carol got the appreciative clientele they deserved.

Fuelled up at 4.30 pm, with about three hours of daylight left, I felt a renewed (although as it happens, misplaced) confidence as we drove back to the miserable A-road where I'd stopped before lunch. There were two signposts about a half mile apart, both suggesting footpaths over the hills. I chose the one closest to where I'd stopped before lunch. I remember feeling a little doubtful, since there didn't seem to be much of a visible trail through the coarse grass and heather. Still, the sign proudly proclaimed 'Public Path to Dolphinton and West Linton via Covenanter's Grave'[3] and directed me alongside a ragged fence between fields. The signpost seemed so absolutely specific – if it knew the way, so should I. I shrugged and set off, still in a thick soup of drifting rain. In retrospect, the signpost had been weathered and listing at an unusual angle. Sometimes it's not what the signs say that you need to pay attention to.

I realised fairly quickly that I was in some species of trouble. Not the sort of trouble that gets you drowned or dead from exposure, unlike the events of the 5th September. Rather, this was going to be a long, hard, mapless slog through awkward and irritating terrain in poor weather conditions.

There was no footpath . . . at all. There might have been once, perhaps in the mid-1970s when the finger sign had most likely been set in place. Nature had had other ideas, evidently. I followed the fence, unable to run more than a few steps before having to leap a ditch or zigzag through large tufts of reedy grass. Eventually, I found myself battling with proper marshland, tall fields of bracken, burnt and scratchy heather and yet more randomly arranged, ankle-twisting tussocks. It was impossible to run. I calculated I had about eight miles of this to get through in order to make it to the road to Baddingsgill reservoir that would lead me back down to West Linton again.

'Realised' might suggest a conscious moment of mental discovery but really it was an incremental process of hopeful-ness being ground down into grim determination. At some point in the early evening I got through to Carol with one bar of battery left on my phone and told her where I thought I was and what the terrain was doing to my progress, i.e. slowing me down to between twelve to fifteen minutes per mile. I wish I could say that we did sensible calculations and came to a realistic appraisal of how long it would take me to make it to the road for a pick-up. We did not. I probably suggested I'd be there in an hour and a half, or something similarly unrealistic.

At no point that afternoon did I worry about my own safety. However, my phone's battery died shortly after I gave that woefully inadequate ETA. There would be no more communication until I happened to bump into Carol. I hoped she'd park somewhere extremely visible. I think I already knew by then that she'd probably not be overjoyed by this turn of events. Nevertheless, irritated as I became by the landscape (and what is more futile than getting angry at bracken?), I knew I could get through it. Without maps or my blue dot to follow, I nevertheless knew I had to head between two reservoirs – Baddingsgill and Westwater. I tramped on, past rows of grouse hides and a water pumping station, scaring flocks of game birds and baffling sheep.

A glorious sunset brought the contradictory but simultaneous sensations of joy and trepidation, the latter because, although I could now see a reservoir, I didn't know exactly which one it was or if I could easily get down to it before night fell. I still didn't feel afraid, as such. And it has to be said, even though every footpath I found turned out to be the tracks of grouse hunters' 4 x 4s (where was the 'drove road' we'd googled at lunch?) I didn't lose hope. In an odd way, hitting that low point on the 5th had made me immune to common or garden frustrations.

Eventually one of the vehicle tracks crossed a proper footpath which led down to a service road and carried me down to West Water reservoir. My large-scale map didn't show a road leading to this reservoir but I knew there almost certainly had to be one. I negotiated a quandary of possible footpaths and got lucky. Gravel became tarmac and, bizarrely, I found myself running during glorious evening light through the middle of a well-manicured golf course. Confidence renewed, I belted down the last mile into town. There was no sign of Carol, but Iain told me she'd been driving up and down looking for me for some time. This didn't bode well. When Carol turned into the nearby car park a few minutes later, her expression said it all – I was in the doghouse.

For good reason, it has to be said. When Carol came on the project, my father and I had shown her edited 'highlights' of what happened on the 5th September in a spirit of honesty and, in part, to reassure her that this project now had real dramatic potential, despite the minimal budget. We did not foresee a repetition of the incidents of that traumatic day. After we'd lost contact, Carol couldn't have known that I was frustrated but absolutely safe throughout my misadventures in the Pentlands – without a working phone, I wasn't able to tell her that.

As a result, she'd be driving all around the roads of West Linton and up towards the hills for several hours anticipating my imminent arrival and watching the sun sink ever closer to the horizon. At what point would she be required to alert emergency services? Where exactly did her role as support driver and cameraperson begin and end? I confess I'd not done anything as formal as issue her a contract; it has to be said that production is not my strong suit in filmmaking. I much prefer to control the creative aspects than the pragmatic and administrative ones. However, on this pet project, I had no choice but to take on some production duties as well. In that capacity, I had failed.

Carol wasn't really talking to me as we drove to my parents' house and later, she absented herself to go for a drive and have a think. Unknown to me, she recorded a monologue to camera that features in the film. Meanwhile, I was also recording a video diary expressing my feelings of guilt and embarrassment and hoping she would not walk off the project. With my dad unavailable due to work commitments, if Carol left, it would be near impossible to replace her. The film and the challenge would be seriously compromised. I'm sure she knew this as she was considering her options. No one wants to walk away from a project but when it begins to feel foolhardy or actively dangerous, I'd not blame a crewmember for throwing in the towel.

As it was, Carol returned to the house and we came to an agreement, based on certain sensible safeguards we'd put in place. I hastily composed a contract which set out her exact duties and the limitations of her responsibility. I placed the requirement to safeguard my health squarely on my own shoulders, which seemed only fair as there were so many unforeseeable variables in this project. We also agreed the following measures:

1. We'd get proper maps of all off-road areas, or else I'd take roads.
2. I'd obtain some sort of portable phone charger and/or a second, calls-only phone.
3. We'd pre-arrange a 'last resort' plan, i.e. if I didn't make it to the expected pick-up by a certain time, support would return to a central location that I'd have to head for.

These all seemed eminently sensible. I obtained both a 'vanilla' phone which (the antithesis of a 'smartphone') was only able to make and receive calls and texts, and a portable charger which was capable of powering up my iPhone in about thirty minutes.

Disaster narrowly avoided, the following day we decided to ditch the original route via Eddlestone and another bit of Pentland off-roading and opt for B-roads through Romanno Bridge and the A72 to Peebles. The former town's name reveals its key attraction, a small humped, Roman-style bridge.[4] The A72 proved a bit of a return to the pleasures of dodging traffic I'd experienced on the first couple of days of The Long Run, albeit without all the rain. As I approached Peebles, which seemed to take an age, there was one particular set of serpentine curves on a narrow stretch of road with one lane of cars on each side and no verge to speak of. I had to creep along in sudden fits and spurts, including one near-sprint along the side of a high wall around an entirely blind corner, having to trust to chance that I wouldn't be killed by a speeding driver blasting round the corner into me. Certainly, bar the odd cyclist, drivers would not expect to see any non-drivers on this road.

It was well past the morning rush hour when I reached Peebles and hit pavement once more. With much gratitude and a rising hunger, I dashed into the town and found Carol. At this point in the experience, a morning without incident came as something of a blessing. In Peebles, a very quaint market town I've visited a few times in my youth, I found an old-fashioned sweet shop and bought some chilli-infused humbugs which I used as motivators in the days to come. Plus more fudge. There must always be fudge.

My mother had mentioned a relatively new railway path between Peebles and Innerleithen, which proved flat enough for Carol to do a bit of bicycle tracking as I ran past golf courses and alongside the sparkling River Tweed. I'd found following a bike always challenged me in terms of speed and so it proved this time. I'd been running at nearly 8-minute miles on legs that were beginning to protest loudly when I called a halt to this method of filming.

A little later, I cruised through a weird Stepford-wives modern-build village called Cardrona. Exactly the kind of place Prince Charles, with his famously conservative architectural tastes, would love, it even had its own village green and conspicuously archaic postbox. I couldn't decide whether it was pretty or just spooky, the quietude of all those semi-detached houses with their net curtains and manicured lawns rendered unfamiliar by the length of time I'd been away from anything suburban. I almost felt eyes upon me as I filmed a few comments on the green and dashed on. A little later, the skies opened and rain pelted down, turning everything into an obstacle course of puddles and slippery paving stones. I exchanged one of those 'We're both mad, aren't we?' moments with a passing cyclist and splashed down the verge of the next bit of B-road.

Next came Innerleithen, a small town where my father

had once helped renovate an old printworks for the National Trust for Scotland. I remember helping him, as a geeky teenager, lug cases of heavy lead 'sorts' up flights of steps and into the main room, where an old Eagle hand-press and typesetting benches were already in place. I didn't stop at Robert Smail's Printworks on my run through town because, despite a growing fatigue, I was determined to make it a little further before the end of the day.

Traquair was the next goal – a village famous for its grand twelfth-century house and gardens, once host to many royal visitors, including 'Bonnie' Prince Charlie and Mary, Queen of Scots. When I visited Traquair in my twenties, you were charged entry to the house but the gardens and woodland surrounding them were free for wandering. Commerce and the realities of keeping up a country house have since intervened and we were not able to detour through the grounds, unfortunately. Instead, I stopped that day at an unprepossessing bench by the side of the road, where I noticed something signposted as the Southern Upland Way. A little research later, Carol and I realised this off-road route could take me as far as the outskirts of Selkirk. I could turn off it where the River Tweed joined the Way and head, via a system of B-roads, south-east through the villages of Midlem, Ancrum, Nisbet and Morebattle, to hit Yetholm and the Pennine Way after approximately thirty-five miles.

All of which would have been a highly achievable plan and a great outcome were it not for my massively swollen left ankle. Over the course of the day, what had started as a dull ache had developed into a constant fiery pain. Each step followed the same pattern – a painful flash up the front of the ankle followed by a throbbing sensation which diminished until the next footfall. By the end of the day I was in perpetual discomfort. More worrying was the appearance of the ankle, which now consisted of a fleshy ring of soft fluid-filled tissue sitting on top of my shoe. Touching this swelling didn't hurt, as such, but it was evident that something was very wrong. It wasn't even as if this was the same injury as that which had forced a half-day in Fort William – that had been my right ankle.

Back home in Colinton that night, I discussed my options with Carol and decided that a trip to the Accident and Emergency was necessary. I had to find out what was going on in case it crippled me. My parents recommended the A&E department in Livingston, not far outside Edinburgh, since it would be under less pressure and I might manage to get seen more quickly. The following morning we headed down there as soon as the hospital opened and I presented my ID and sob story. Remarkably, I was seen just twenty minutes later, had an X-ray within half an hour and then a consultation with a specialist a little later. Fortunately, the consultant, Dr Stevenson, didn't mind us filming the discussion. What Dr Stevenson said next was surprising.

'You've got a small lump of bone on your tibia,' he remarked, drawing my attention to a faint bump on the X-ray image on his monitor, 'which is . . . odd.' The mysterious protuberance had a thin line down it, as if it was about to break away. Dr Stevenson surmised that the pain I was experiencing was the fascia of my shin rubbing against this unusual feature, something I'd not noticed before because I'd simply never tormented my ankles enough to cause the necessary irritation. In other words, it was a congenital oddity exacerbated by ultra-running. The prognosis was both encouraging and troubling. Encouraging in that Dr Stevenson told me it was unlikely that running on the ankle would cripple me; less encouraging in that he also made it clear it was unlikely to improve if I continued my extreme running. I could potentially be faced with weeks of fiery shin pain. Wonderful.

There was little I could really do, bar the usual recipe of

rest, ice, compression and elevation. Nothing short of my foot falling off was going to make me stop. That said, I decided not to run at all on the 16th September, which became a day for staring at maps, route-planning and accepting a bit of TLC from my mum once more, as if I was fourteen again and not a full-grown forty-four-year-old adult. You can't knock home comforts though and I willingly submitted to rest and relaxation. The following morning I was gratified to see that the swelling had gone down a little and, starting a little late, we decided to carry on.

From Traquair, the Southern Upland Way began with a climb of 292 metres, reaching a maximum elevation of 438 metres. In an odd way, this was good news – it meant there would be no temptation to run for the first half hour at least. Even uninjured, this was a slope I would be disinclined to run. The weather was kind too, starting off warm and dry. I rather enjoyed starting the day with a march uphill, rather than a pain-stricken hobble. After climbing, the route ran alongside forestry plantation and open moorland. There was even land art to admire, including Charles Pulson's Minch Moor circles (a grouping of thick rings shaved into the heather like unicellular organisms) and the Three Brethren cairns on top of Yair Hill.

Apart from being attacked by large black heather flies (also known as St Mark's Fly) amongst the peaty moors,[5] it was a pleasant and relatively speedy run over rolling hills to reach Yair Hill and a truly impressive view of the Borders' gently contoured landscape. On top of the hill, admiring those three impressive stone mounds, which resembled a cross between Scottish brochs[6] and partially buried eggs, I encountered an intrepid mountain biker, one of several I'd seen on the Way. He told me this was a regular route of his and we admired the view without much chatter. As we went our separate ways, I saw that he was escaping a dark mass of cloud swelling in the river valley below. It looked like the idyllic weather was soon to break. As I had done several times already that day, I called in to support and gave a progress report, a precondition of going off-road again. For once, phone coverage was reliable.

The greying sky began throwing down sheets of cooling rain before too long. Fortunately, the Way was all downhill to the Tweed River at Fairnilee and the rain was pleasantly cooling, rather than chilling. I crossed a stone bridge and rested in the support car as the rain cascaded down. Hoping to make up time to compensate for yesterday's day off, I ate a packed lunch with Carol and set off once more. The ankle started protesting more significantly when I swapped dirt and grassland for tarmac again. From that point until the end of the day, it would hurt whenever I ran. Nevertheless, as I alternated periods of walking with spurts of running, I knew I had to battle on towards the start of the Pennine Way. Nobody said this would be easy, after all – pain is an expected part of the ultra-running experience, just another tricky bit of mental terrain to overcome. I had to wheel out my usual tricks – inner promises of a slap-up dinner, a warm bath and a comfortable bed, the strategy of breaking down the task into manageable chunks. If I could just make it to Midlem, then four more miles to Ancrum, then Nisbet, then the intriguing-sounding (but as it happened never-seen) Teviot Water Gardens and on and on . . .

It would become one of the most challenging days on The Long Run and I had to marshal all my inner reserves, all that relentless determination which friends found variously laughable and remarkable, depending on how-directed.

My pain management strategies failed me after a half-day's running (and walking) a few miles outside the town of Ancrum. I just couldn't go on with the ever-present agony in my ankle, which was causing me to run-limp in a peculiar fashion. The limp was putting undue weight and pressure on other muscles and joints and I feared a knock-on effect. If anything else failed me now, it could prove disastrous. I'd managed about twenty-one miles and that seemed enough. The Pennine Way could wait one more day.

The additional rest helped. The following day I made it through the pretty village of Ancrum with its village green and war memorial. It occurred to me that the villages were looking a little more 'English' as I approached the border. Although it's hard to put into words, it's probably a combination of the layout of the towns around a central 'green'[7] and the type of building materials (more brick-built structures, more whitewash) that make these villages different from similar-sized settlements in Scotland.

I knew I wouldn't reach the border proper until I was on the Pennine Way itself, which spends almost a hundred miles flirting with the symbolic line separating Scotland and England. For now, my task was to negotiate a spidery network of B-roads to Yetholm. Measuring it carefully on the map, it appeared I still had thirty-five miles to run before hitting the start of the next national trail. Something had gone very wrong with yesterday's calculations.

I distracted myself from the growing pain in my ankle with musings on the different 'flavours' of bodily anguish I'd experienced on the run so far. I concluded there were three main varieties – a kind of round gnawing pain, a scratchy elastic one and a throbbing headache-like sensation. The middle of those three, with its concomitant flashes of fiery agony, was the hardest to suffer. Fortunately, on the 18th September, regular walking breaks and the relatively flat terrain allowed to cope as I approached the appropriately-named town of Morebattle, the biggest town before Yetholm.

I was also able to use the scenery to distract me from my agonies – the leaves by now were vividly turning and gusts of wind would scatter them prettily across my path. Watching

their trajectories became a way of redirecting my consciousness – a kind of meditation in motion. More prosaically,
a daily dose of paracetamol and ibuprofen at lunchtime
worked wonders. After lunch, I had only four more miles to
Yetholm and the sun was once again shining as I limped into
town and discovered it to be divided into Town Yetholm
and Kirk Yetholm, the latter a little way up a hill.

Someone had decided it was a good idea to build a hotel
and pub at what is usually the end of the Pennine Way and,
given my traumatised ankle, the sunshine and the triumph
of having made it to this landmark on the route, we decided
I would stop for the afternoon. Seldom has a pint of beer
tasted so satisfying.

MILES RUN: 411; MILES REMAINING: 689

---

1. Officers Training Corps.

2. Levenseat, suppliers of 'aggregate' i.e. gravel for construction.

3. Sadly, I never passed this legendarily remote headstone, a simple slab on
   the summit of Black Law dedicated to a fallen Presbyterian 'covenanter'
   who had fought and died for his faith during the Reformation at the
   nearby battle of Rullion Green in 1666.

4. It is also the name of the seventh novel by Scottish writer Andrew Greig,
   a Buchan-styled historical thriller.

5. Entomologists might know these as *bibio pomonae* – they sport some
   rather flashy red leg-markings and feed on nectar, hence their swarming
   around late-flowering heather in this mildest of autumns.

6. Brochs are distinctively cone-shaped iron-age dwellings peculiar to
   Scotland. www.scottishbrochs.com has some rather nice photos of most
   of the 500-plus broch sites in Scotland.

7. Not for nothing is The Kinks' *Village Green Preservation Society* a telling
   and satirical conceit.

KIRK YETHOLM to LADYHILL

'Don't Open Wasps'

An ancient white caravan, decorated with an inscrutable message. This was the unusual marker of the start of the Pennine Way, for me at least. Sure, there was a traditional map behind glass in a wooden casing and also a plaque set into a rock but I found more to wonder about in those three spray-painted, unpunctuated words. Was this a warning that the caravan was full of wasps? If so, why was it full of wasps? I've heard of beekeepers but not of anyone cultivating these serial-stinging picnic pests. Or was it just requesting passers-by not to open the caravan in case it filled with wasps? Or was this a threat – open the caravan and we'll set our wasps on you? Most surreally, perhaps it was just a message to the wasps themselves not to open the caravan's door.

It's funny how the mind wanders when you're trying to distract it from worrying about the task in hand. If I thought about the sheer scale of the Pennine Way – 267 miles long with dozens of peaks, fells, moors and farms to navigate – it panicked me a little. Given my recent history of poor navigation, it was wise not to dwell too fully on what lay ahead. Especially as the first section, from Yetholm to Byrness, was twenty-seven miles long without a single place of human habitation en route.

Things couldn't have been more auspicious on the 19th September, however – the sun was shining and the day was warm and pleasant as I set off on the climb up White Law to where Scotland met England. Being a 400-metre hilltop rather than a tarmac road, there was no visible marker of the border (at least none that I found), so I can't say precisely when I stepped into England for the first time. What I can say is that the Pennine Way meanders along the border for the next twenty miles, so I must have crossed that division many, many times.

The views were spectacular; I shared a few of them with hikers I passed on the route – some on their final day's walking the whole route, others day walkers from nearby villages and towns. The Way was not as popular as I'd imagined though. I must have passed ten times as many people on my first West Highland Way day as I did on the 19th September. That said, I was glad of the solitude. It allowed me to gather my thoughts as I alternated walking up the sometimes muddy hills and running along their tops. For the bulk of that first morning, things couldn't have gone better. Although I was a little fatigued, my legs were fine, the route was well marked and my map was serving me fairly well as I climbed to the impressive heights of Black Hag (549 metres) and The Schil (605 metres) with its rocky crags and stunning vistas.

Where exactly things went wrong remains a mystery. The plan was to meet Carol at Windy Gyle – she would walk up from the farm road at Cocklawfoot to intersect with the Way and wait for me there. We did have intermittent phone reception, so I was able to apprise her of my progress as I'd promised. Yet somehow, I took a wrong turning, following an erroneous footpath. I seem to remember climbing a fence at one point and knowing that the lack of a stile meant I'd gone astray.

Google Maps was fairly useless in this instance, having very few place names allocated to wilderness areas. My hikers' map was thorough but the problem was that, to this city-dweller, all the hills looked the same and there were many similar footpaths I could be on and many patches of forestry plantation I could be looking at, as well as dozens of streams. Each potential landmark had many clones. Without an utterly unique marker such as a radio mast or a reservoir of a particular size and shape, I wasn't a skilled enough map-reader to orientate myself. Signposts and way-markers were few and far between. Apparently there are 458 waymarks along the route but given its length, that works out at less than two per mile.

I'm making excuses. Of course, the fault was largely mine. I was too busy enjoying the views and filming impressive scenery to stop and recheck the map. In the days to come I'd develop a system of folding the map around the section I was on, slipping it back into its protective cover and running with it permanently in my hand. Before I thought of this simple system, I had to keep stopping to spread it out on the ground, using rocks to hold it down.

Sod's Law dictated that, although I'd passed a few walkers earlier in the day, now that I needed another person's input there was nobody in sight, bar cows, sheep and endless grouse, pheasant and partridges. Even though Carol had her own copy of the map, since I couldn't give her any clear indication of where I was, or where I'd stepped off the route, our broken phone calls served only to reassure her that I was basically okay, albeit in terra incognita.

I traipsed through many rough grazing fields, half hoping to see a farmer on a tractor or in a Range Rover. Used to going completely off-trail as I now was, I found my way by means of a sheep path down to a small stream then up another hill to attempt to locate a waymarker or signpost. No such luck. Instead, I followed a gravelled path up another slope and round the top of a second hill. I'm fairly certain that next I walked along a section of 'The Street', a long slash of shale and rock dug industriously from the hillside. At some point I turned west again, thinking I was still to the east of the Pennine Way. There's an exponential effect in getting lost – each additional blind turn makes you statistically less likely to be heading to where you want to be. I tried to keep my spirits up but by now, this was all becoming a painfully familiar experience.

Eventually, I simply gave up trying to find the Pennine Way. My new plan was to locate a fellow human and ask for directions to the nearest driveable road, then get Carol to pick me up. I'd return to do battle the following day.

Once the decision not to continue was made, things felt a little clearer. I descended a steep, scree-scattered hillside to where I could see a couple of buildings and a tiny dam, behind which lay a miniscule reservoir. I'd reached a place called Heatherhope, a couple of miles northwest of the Way. I was just about to approach a farmhouse, situated by a section of gravelled road when I heard the sound of motor vehicles, several of them, coming from the direction of the dam.

Suddenly, a whole convoy of Jeeps and Land Rovers bounced around a bend in the track, a selection of tweed and Barbour-clad gentlemen cradling rifles proudly within. I stopped the first vehicle and the gents amiably informed me where I was. They added that if I followed the path they were driving it would eventually become tarmacked and take me down to a village called Greenhill and then on to a junction with another road near the village of Hownam, eight miles east of Jedburgh. I thanked them and sent the happy hunters off on their way. I have to admit I mentally revised my opinion of people who shoot birds for sport just a little in the light of their painstaking helpfulness.

I could at last run again, even if it was a little pointless, given that I was heading north-west rather than south. I'd not had phone reception for a couple of hours but thought if I could just make it down to Greenhill, I'd be able to pick up a signal.

Around ten minutes later I saw a handful of houses

with gardens, fences and other signifiers of civilisation and stopped to make my call. Nothing doing, on both phones. I began to regret not making sure the 'vanilla' Nokia was on a different network, but suspected it wouldn't have made much difference. I was in a valley surrounded by hills, ten miles from the nearest town and it seemed that was enough of an obstacle to network providers. Not for the first or last time in The Long Run I threw some colourful curses their way.

I stopped the first car that passed me to ask if I'd get phone reception somewhere along the road and, as most locals do, its driver knew exactly where to go to make a phone call. After a bit of momentary reluctance I accepted a lift to the road junction near Hownam and managed to send a text, giving directions to Carol. Although it took the best part of an hour for her to find me in the network of little B-roads around Jedburgh, it was with much gratitude that I watched her distinctive purple Kangoo pull in.

I was doubly glad that Carol seemed in a fairly good mood. It seemed she had not taken today's misadventure as further indication of the futility of the entire challenge. We both managed to set aside our frustrations, vowing to return to the fray the following day. It hadn't been a life or death situation, after all and we'd been in limited contact whenever it was physically possible. Plus I'd used a map and local knowledge to get myself out of trouble. I think Carol had realised that, somehow, I'd always survive. Either that or she'd managed a Zen-like transcendence, perhaps aided by the unseasonably beautiful weather and location. However she'd managed to retain her sunny disposition, I chose not to question it.

The 20th September would prove a different kind of day. That's not to say I didn't get lost. Far from it. But at least I had someone to share some of the bewilderment with. Carol had arranged for her friend Stan, also an ultra-runner, to join me for the next section of the Pennine Way. Given my shifting schedule, this was not an easy thing to co-ordinate but Stan drove all the way from Ambleside in the Lake District to share his thoughts on ultra-running, so hopefully it would be a more successful day than yesterday.

We started well – we were gifted a warm, bright morning and had no difficulties locating the tiny farm road to Cocklawfoot, where we got ready to the sound of crowing cockerels (water, multiple layers of clothing, glucose gels, Vaseline applied to intimate places).[1] Our plan was to head up to Windy Gyle, where I was supposed to meet Carol the day before.

We headed in the wrong direction almost immediately and lost about ten minutes climbing to a signposted ridge about a mile further north than planned. Stan proved to have an acerbic, iconoclastic wit and was a fun companion to charge along hilltops with. Still a smoker, this arts venue manager had completed numerous fell races and had recently moved into ultras. His nemesis was the 53-mile-long Highland Fling, which he'd attempted twice but never completed. His second aborted attempt was due to a twisted ankle and his first due to sheer, ineluctable fatigue. Both times he'd reluctantly had to drop out after forty-one miles. Having run the route myself on the way to the Pennines, I can testify that the notion of completing it within the allowed cut-off of fifteen hours is a tall order. During The Long Run that route took me two days, albeit having run hundreds of miles beforehand and with half a day off due to stolen equipment.

Hailing from the Lake District and a member of the Borrowdale Fell Runners, Stan had no shortage of running routes and mountain scenery to enjoy back home. He said his main reason for running was to experience 'that solitary time when you can solve problems, reflect, de-stress', although a more prosaic bonus was being able to eat whatever the hell

he wanted. 'Fell running is what I really love,' he admitted.
'You run past all these hikers and the looks of disdain they
give you.' Possessing that true fell runner's attitude, he
talked about running a 9-mile fell run in a February bliz-
zard, saying he had 'never enjoyed a run so much . . . beating
against driving snow'. I don't think my Outer London cross-
country anecdotes quite cut it after that.

After about fifty minutes of running we stopped to talk
to two sturdy women hiking the Way in shorts and T-shirts,
which allowed us to definitively ensure that we were on the
right route. As we set off once more, we talked a little bit
about off-road technique and Stan recommended 'confidence and a lightness of touch . . . you kind of bounce'.

Minutes later I kind of bounced into a bog. Running
at speed over a flagstoned path through a peaty moor,
I put my foot firmly down on a stone that wasn't there
and abruptly vanished to my knee in sloppy brown mud,
smashing my shin against the rock on the way down. The
kind of agony that can only be dispelled with laughter shot
up my leg to my brain. Fortunately, adrenalin also kicked
in and my reactions fired quickly enough for me to get my
hands to solid ground and haul myself out. Shaken, with
bloody, grazed shin, I ran on, while Stan made jokes at my
expense in that teasing variety of camaraderie familiar to
the adventurous. It helped.

This got us talking about what we each did when things
got tough in a race. 'I shout,' said Stan. 'You effin' this and
effin' that . . . feel sorry for myself and then I just say "Get
yourself off".' I talked about the 'counting blessings' method
of dealing with obstacles. Stan's indomitability was unques-
tionable: 'It's like when I've been out and done an eight or
nine mile run or hike in the middle of nowhere and someone
says "What happens if you break a leg?"' Stan shrugged.
'Well, you crawl . . . you know . . . or you die.' I think he was
only partly exaggerating. I recounted my own horror story,

the saga of the 5th September. Ultra-runners bond with such tales, like old soldiers comparing war wounds.

Talking about his fellow fell runners, Stan said, 'I've got nothing but awe for these guys ... but you're not going to let them know that.' This, in essence is the nature of fell running camaraderie – admiration tempered with good-natured abuse.[2]

Pausing our conversation, we stepped off the flagstones for a troop of around two dozen heavily armed and backpack-toting soldiers who were marching at speed through the high moors. Those at the front looked considerably happier with the exercise than the pale youngsters at the back. Some of the squaddies appeared middle-aged, others teenage, all of them looked like people you wouldn't mess with. We remembered we were running through ground commonly used for military training, complete with block-lettered signs warning of misplaced munitions and warning flags for shooting ranges. When we got to an area called Green Chew, near the site of an old Roman settlement, the map sported the fearfully non-specific warning: 'Danger Area'.

At Green Chew we were hoping to meet Carol but, oddly, there were no cars in the small parking area at the end of the single-track road that wound through the valley. After waiting for ten minutes (need I mention we had no phone signal?) we decided to press on. Although we were running at conversational speed, we were probably managing 10-minute miles when we saw a couple of other runners coming up behind us. Stan's competitiveness spurred us on and, although we were mostly joking about not letting the approaching runners catch us, we were a little serious about it too. Unfortunately, my urge to film things and my cameras' irritating need for fresh batteries and memory cards slowed us down and our rivals caught us at a rocky bluff somewhere near Houx Hill.

Steven Fry (no, not that one) and David Stephenson

resisted the urge to just charge past us as we picked our way between tumbled boulders and we all stopped for a chat. When you're in the middle of the remote countryside and you meet others doing the odd thing you're also doing, it's only polite to share war stories. The newcomers told us they were on day one of a six-day attempt at the whole Pennine Way, raising money for the Marie Curie charity. Quick mental calculations made that an average of fifty-four miles per day. Stan and I were impressed; these were in fact the only other ultra-runners I encountered, apart from those I'd arranged to meet, during The Long Run.

They were both members of Bingley Harriers, whose famous alumni include fell legend Rob Jebb and Olympic triathletes the Brownlee brothers.[3] Stan knew more of the fell running names they mentioned than I did but we both stood in awe of these fifty-somethings' six-day epic. They suggested a meet-up and a pint in the town of Bellingham in the evening and I'd politely agreed that I might join them (knowing it was unlikely to happen). Bellingham was seventeen miles further down the trail and I already suspected I might not make it that far and that, if I did, I might not feel altogether sociable. As an interim measure, I felt certain we'd catch them up at Byrness, only a couple of miles further down the Way.

We were happy to discover the trail was almost entirely downhill from where David and Steven passed us, although it wound its way through some tricky and foot-trippingly narrow forest paths before emerging into a side road and car park on the A68. For once, we'd timed it quite well and my dad and an apologetic Carol were there to meet us. My father was planning to do a bit of quadcopter filming later in the day and Carol explained how she'd become a bit lost trying to locate Chew Green and had arrived after we'd passed. I felt a little vindicated that it wasn't only me with navigational issues.

At Byrness we found David and Steven standing by their own support car, parked beside ours, finishing their lunch and putting on bizarre daffodil-shaped hats for promotional photos, which my father gladly took. We all wished each other well as they set off, looking impossibly fresh. I had to remind myself that I had nineteen days of running behind me while they had half of one. Ultra-runners are nothing if not needlessly competitive!

A rather random packed lunch later (Byrness seemed little more than a row of houses along one side of the road) I waved goodbye to my support crew and followed the way I thought David and Steven had gone. I say 'thought' advisedly, because that's when the afternoon took a by now familiar turn into the unknown.

Stan wasn't with me – our fourteen miles together over hilly terrain had been all that he required that day. After half a day in such a loquacious and funny fellow runner's company, and with that impromptu meeting with Team Marie Curie adding to the sociable feeling of the morning, the afternoon felt very different. Quiet, uncertain, even a bit lonely.

After a moment of mild confusion where I thought I'd have to ford a stream, I located and followed the trail along the side of the River Rede, past a caravan park that sparked odd childhood memories I couldn't quite place. My unusually light lunch hadn't slowed me down as much as usual and I found I was making good speed amongst tall pines and on well-maintained forestry tracks. Their lack of waymarkings worried me a little but I shrugged it off – the trail's course seemed self-evident.

Something evidently made me turn west at Blakehope-burnhaugh (surely an unnecessary collision of syllables in that name) along what was certainly a trail, just not the right one. I was enjoying the ease with which these gravel-bedded forest trails could be run and I suppose I had grown complacent. As I rose into the hills, I could see the main road down below me to the left and that seemed evidence enough that I was heading the right way.

About an hour later, I had to admit that I clearly wasn't. Apart from a few trail markers for something called the 'Alternative Pennine Way' (which didn't bode too well) there were no Pennine Way signposts and the familiar white acorn logo of the National Trails network was noticeably missing. And yet this was a trail of some sort. Where the hell was I going?

I'll admit to being a bit bloody-minded when it comes to getting lost. I hate the notion of shamefacedly retracing my footsteps to the last correct junction, even though that might be the safest and most sensible thing to do.

I realised I was still, broadly speaking, heading south, albeit with a generous helping of west. I told myself that the greater goal was to run to Land's End from John O'Groats, not to painstakingly stick to the entire Pennine Way. Once I let go of the need to get back to the intended trail, my mission could be revised. I would press on until I could get a phone signal and direct the support car to wherever the day's running took me. I gave myself to the adventure of it out of necessity.

It started raining intermittently as I broke out of the forest for a while at Blakehope Nick and tried to get my bearings (impossible as I later discovered I'd run entirely off my map). A strange viewpoint presented itself at the side of the trail, with an information board detailing all the wonderful animals and birds that could be seen in the surrounding moors and forest. I was not in the mood for a nature tour, however.

After another half hour of running, a car drove by. I hadn't realised this was even a 'road' as such – I'd assumed the hard-packed gravel was there to allow access for logging vehicles. Perhaps twenty minutes later, another car passed me. No one seemed that surprised to see a runner out and about and I wasn't yet ready to ask for directions so I let them pass with a friendly wave.

A little later, signs saying 'Kielder Head Conservation Area' became apparent. I'd been running for about three hours with forest on both sides, bar a few denuded areas where logging had taken place. Clearly, this was no quaint little wood. It had a kind of beauty, it has to be said, all those rippling ranks of conifers. Britain doesn't have many large forests and this route was beginning to feel more like a trail in Canada than one in the heart of England. When I eventually made it back to civilisation, I did a bit of research on where exactly I'd been.

The largest man-made woodland in England, Kielder covers 250 square miles. 450,000 cubic metres of timber are felled there annually. It was initiated in the 1920s, expanded through to the 1960s with logging as the primary focus of operations. In recent decades, inroads have been made into conservation (for instance, more varied plantings, managed herds of roe deer and breeding pairs of rare ospreys) and active leisure (kayaking, cycling, even a Kielder Forest Marathon). More than half the UK's population of red squirrels are thought to dwell amongst its trees.

I got the oddest feeling of displacement running through this landscape – it was unlike anywhere else I'd ever been. I could see nothing but trees and open moorland in all directions. It was like an enormous Centre Parcs[4] after a virus has wiped out humanity. Still, the presence of the very occasional vehicle meant that I never quite let frustration get the better of me as the hours rolled by and I failed to reach a place of human habitation. Cars need roads and roads are interconnected, I thought, trying to keep my spirits up. If I kept running I'd hit tarmac . . . eventually.

As the afternoon eased into the evening, I began to wonder if I'd ever escape the forest. The road had wound its way up and over high moors, through cleared sections of woodlands and back into dense forest again, passing only one farm just before I hit the treeline. I was tempted to knock on the door of this remote farmhouse but something stopped me. I had just enough pride left to decide that, no, I wasn't really lost enough to call upon the kindness of strangers. It didn't feel right to give in just yet. I was becoming weary but there was enough strength in my legs and sheer bloody-mindedness in my spirit to give it another hour or so.

I began to see signs for Kielder Castle and Kielder Village, both of which seemed to be perpetually five miles further on down the road. When the gravel gave way, for no apparent reason, to tarmac, I rejoiced – surely there would be signs of human habitation soon. The signage increased, much of it directed at cyclists, with small but marked trails leading off the main road amidst the trees. I think I had arrived at a section of the forest managed for active leisure, rather than logging. This also gave me hope – surely soon there would be chalets or a hotel; anywhere with a postcode Carol could type into her car's GPS in order to find me. Of course, for that to work, I'd have to have some sort of phone reception – as usual, my phones were about as useful as two half bricks.

Eventually the road started to dip down once more and I began to see glints of dark water between the trees to my left. It had been raining intermittently and the sky was leaden but there was still enough light to make out a large lake opening out below me. The road curved down towards what I later found out was Kielder Water, the largest artificial lake in the UK.[5]

Built in the 1960s, the reservoir quickly became controversial as improvements in water conservation and changes in industrial processes quickly rendered it something of a white elephant. Nevertheless, it is a beautiful addition to the landscape, with up to a quarter of a million visitors per year. Futility can be surprisingly utilitarian.

I could just make out a distant glimmer of light that might be a hotel or houses on the curve of shoreline several miles below me but, I have to admit, I had exhausted my reserves of energy when a very helpful local called Thomas drew alongside me in a small van and enquired if I needed his help. I told him my tale of woe and he revealed, as was now customary, that there was a place nearby you could get phone reception – a lay-by about a quarter of a mile down the road. Apparently local people would drive to this viewpoint to make calls. I admit I felt sceptical but as he dropped me off at the rest stop in question, which offered an impressive view of the lake, there was already one car parked there, a man in his forties making what seemed like an impassioned phone call. As we pulled in, as if by magic, the reception bars on my iPhone reappeared, together with the 3G logo.

I called Carol, saying I'd head down to Leaplish Waterside Park (the glinting lights I'd seen on the lakeside). Neither me nor my rescuer had an actual address for Leaplish so I said I'd head down there and ask for a postcode in the bar / restaurant Thomas mentioned. I then accepted a lift a mile down to road to the car park, where I waved goodbye to my saviour.

It was 7.30 pm and we were in the realms of twilight by the time I availed myself of Leaplish's toilet facilities and tried to make myself presentable enough to hide out in the bar. Fortunately, as this was an outdoor activity centre, nobody batted an eyelid when a sportswear clad, mud-splattered forty-four-year-old staggered in and ordered a beer. I managed to down two pints in the forty minutes before the bar shut, then spent ten minutes shivering outside before Carol arrived, eyebrows by now permanently raised at my exploits.

Retrospectively examining my large-scale maps, I'd prob-ably followed a red dotted line that cuts almost in a straight line between the Pennine Way south of Byrness and Kielder, adding an unnecessary 12-mile detour almost due west. It also turns out I was still only three miles from the Scottish border; perhaps subconsciously I was reluctant to leave my home country? Because I'd gone so far off course, I now had two choices. The first option was to head back to Byrness and try again, with no certainty that I'd not get lost once more finding my way through the immense forest. Secondly, I could head back to that lay-by and keep going south, eventually linking back up with the Pennine Way. In terms of hours lost and miles added, both courses of action would be equally wasteful. My rules by now were fairly strict – no shortcuts and as little backtracking as possible – so it didn't seem much of a choice to me. The following morning, in heavy rain, I headed back to Kielder.

My only concession to compromise was to start from the car park at Kielder Castle, north of Leaplish but still about half a mile from the infamous lay-by. It turned out the road up and across the moors is a toll road with a coin-operated barrier and we didn't have the necessary change to use it. Given that I'd have to run nineteen miles to Bellingham, heading south-east, losing this additional half mile didn't feel like a cheat. I was, after all, running around twenty miles in total more than the route I should have taken. Kielder Castle turned out to be a moderately impressive eighteenth-century hunting lodge and Kielder Village a small settlement enhanced with ranks of utilitarian housing built for forestry commission workers prior to the expansion of the logging operations in the 1950s. Sightseeing wasn't high on the agenda on the morning of the 21st September though, given the foul weather and the gravity of the task ahead.

The road from Kielder was technically a dual carriageway but extremely quiet, so it seemed safe enough to run along the edge of it for about ten miles to Stannerburn. Eventually,

I decided it would be better to turn off onto a smaller road just before Stannerburn and head for Falstone, Greenhaugh, Lanehead and Charlton, making it to Bellingham (apparently properly pronounced 'Bell-in-jum') in time for lunch. A tall order? Perhaps, but I had something to prove.

Given how astray I'd gone the previous day, I felt today's running would almost be an act of penance. I had to show myself how serious I was about this country-long run. This wasn't a holiday and I couldn't waste any more afternoons touring regions of England that weren't even in the plan.

The day hadn't started especially well. We'd spent the night in a pleasant hotel in Bellingham, one of the top places to stay locally as evidenced by its perpetually full car park. One section of this car park dipped down on a steep rake towards ornate gardens with rose bushes, rockeries and topiary. After my wayward afternoon and evening we'd got back to the car park after dark and found the only space free was this precipitous section, requiring a sharp turn. Somehow, Carol had parked with finger's-breadth accuracy. A desperate desire for dinner, a hot meal and a shower can do that to a driver.

Getting back out the following morning, in gloomy wet conditions, with damp gravel spinning out under the wheels, reversing uphill to avoid a stone wall and several other vehicles, proved another matter entirely. Carol's car's turning circle in reverse was just not up to it, necessitating a three-point turn, except that every time she let the hand-brake off, the car slumped towards a two-foot drop into the ornate garden before the clutch caught reverse gear. The wheels span, gears ground and all that stood between us and a vehicle sitting on its nose in a hedge was a couple of inches of stone edging.

I got out to push, to little avail, before two gentlemen in their late fifties or sixties joined me to add manpower. We managed to prevent the car rolling with rocks under the front wheels until the clutch caught and Carol could reverse onto level ground. Unfortunately a smell of burning rubber and a cloud of foul smoke made it clear the engine was traumatised and overheated. We let the car rest for half an hour before driving off. Now both Carol and my dad had experienced vehicular trauma in the service of The Long Run. I found myself apologising profusely.

Later than planned then and under a grim, grey sky, I set off past Kielder village, around the picturesque shores of the lake where small yachts sat moored on the perfectly still water. Occasionally a logging truck would rumble by, shattering the quietude. Soon I was soaked through but warm enough. On the easily navigated route I found myself running around 9-minute miles for the 10 miles to the dam that revealed Kielder Water's artificiality. Thereafter, I slowed down a little but not significantly and was still managing 9:50 a mile by the time I recognised Bellingham up ahead and ended my morning's run in the very car park where we'd struggled with gravity earlier that day.

I felt vindicated and relieved. I was back on the Pennine Way and I'd had a pleasantly uneventful morning's run. Apart from hitting the 'marathon wall' at about eighteen miles and downing some gels and yoghurt-covered cranberries, it had been pretty pain-free. Was this epic adventure becoming oddly routine? I wouldn't allow myself to become complacent. After all, I was entering the 'anything can happen' world of the Pennine Way again.

The next part of the trail started off the B6320 south of the River North Tyne and I located it with ease, pausing briefly to chat with a hiker doing the Pennine Way south to north who seemed to have heard of my adventure – evidently my social media skills were improving. Unfortunately, I couldn't share much intelligence about the route north of Bellingham as I hadn't run it!

After a brief pause to call support and request the correct

shoes (trying to run in gloopy mud across a sloping field in road shoes is not advised), I began to enjoy the afternoon's running. The sun had come out and although I was starting post-lunch rather late (3 pm) I felt confident the next few hours would set me back on track. I knew I wouldn't make it south as far as Hadrian's Wall today but Ladyhill, nine miles away, ought to be possible. At first it was tricky negotiating the farms by hunting out stiles, signposts and the subtle white acorns of the Pennine Way but I soon developed a knack for reading the fields. I discovered that, with the sun low in the sky, if it was difficult to see a trail across an overgrown field, turning around by 180 degrees would sometimes reveal it through the knap of tramped-down grass.

I had a large mobile mast to navigate by on Ealingham Common and then a descent to an easy drove road connecting with a farm lane towards Hetherington. There, I took my first wrong turn, running around in a circle for about a mile before finding the correct route at Low Stead farm. I became used to negotiating my way around farms with names like Leadgate, Horneystead and Willowbog and (perhaps due to the proximity of the giant mast at Ealingham) got enough moments of phone reception to use the blue dot to keep me right when the map featured the worrying description 'no visible path'.

The varied and soft terrain underfoot meant my ankles and calves didn't suffer as much from the repetitive pounding, leaving me to focus on hydration and navigation. I'd got the hang of timing my sips and using electrolytes towards the second half of the day (untainted water felt purer in the mornings; after lunch I'd usually drop a couple of soluble tablets into my Camelbak). I was by now used to running with the map in one hand and my iPhone in the other — their presence reassured me and, to be honest, it saved time getting them out at every questionable confluence of pathways. In one field I counted nine possible tracks leading away from the gate. I took the most pronounced and, for once, got lucky.

After the confusion around Hetherington, I managed to get a text to Carol to tell her to head for Ladyhill and reached the forested section north of there by about seven o'clock. The Pennine Way had one of its habitual surprises in store for me though – an incredibly boggy stretch through the trees where I slipped and slid and sloshed my way through a painfully slow mile and a half to the last slope before the road where my car was waiting. Not knowing what I'd been struggling through, Carol was beginning to fret when I appeared from the treeline and did my best to attempt a sprint finish up to the last stile of the day, which I all but fell over in exhaustion.

As I stopped to catch my breath, the sun was busy setting in a fiery cauldron of light to the west. I recorded a relatively happy (but drained) piece to camera with the sunset's finery as backdrop. Sometimes timing is everything.

MILES RUN: 497; MILES REMAINING: 603

---

1. Stan was using the Vaseline. Although I used it to begin with (nipples, between the legs) to prevent the inevitable chafing that comes with hours and hours of running in often damp conditions, I found that wearing a pair of cycling shorts under my running shorts obviated the need down below. I used plasters on my nipples for a while but after a few days simply forgot to do so and never needed to again. I think the multiple straps of my backpack and gimbal pouch kept everything from moving around, reducing friction. Sorry to dwell on this, but the 'double shorts' tip, at least, is an important one, to anyone who's suffered from 'runners' rash'.

2. Stan even wrote a few blog articles for his club and they are fabulously offensive: http://www.borrowdalefellrunners.co.uk/

3. For an in-depth history and celebration of the frankly lunatic sport of fell running, I can't recommend Richard Askwith's *Feet in the Clouds* highly enough. It made me want to run up Ben Nevis and back down as fast as humanly possible, an ambition I've yet to fulfil. I'm also ashamed to say I've never visited one of the sport's spiritual homes, the Lake District, something I will rectify when I attend a friend's stag night in April.

4. For those non-European readers, Centre Parcs is a network of holiday villages, usually situated amongst forest, sometimes with water-parks under domes, and whose mission is to provide 'an exceptional short break experience in a natural forest location' (according to their website). I can't decide whether this is a good thing or a sinister commodification of nature. Perhaps I should try one?

5. That's largest by capacity, holding around 44 billion gallons of water. The largest artificial lake by surface area is Rutland Water.

LADYHILL TO THWAITE

Day four on the Pennine Way began slowly and somewhat lethargically but in a bright sunshine I was almost beginning to become suspicious of. This was the twenty-second day of my adventures on the paths and highways of Britain and it had only rained six times. Still, I was thankful for my good fortune as I fought exhaustion and headed off across fields strewn with the tiny jewelled nets of spider webs. My aim was to reach Hadrian's Wall by lunchtime.

Possibly more embarrassing than never having been to the Lake District was my complete ignorance of the huge Roman engineering project begin in AD122 that had resulted in the 'waist' of Britain being cinched by a limestone and turf fortification over seventy miles long and, at its tallest, up to twenty feet high. That is to say, I knew it existed and roughly what it was for but had never been there or learned much of its history. A lesser-known construction, the Antonine Wall, begun twenty years after Hadrian's edifice, provided a similar function (keeping out unruly northern tribes) between the Firths of Forth and Clyde. I'd seen remnants of that as a child but Hadrian's Wall remained an enigma.

The Pennine Way meets the Wall at Housesteads Crags and runs west along it for about eight miles to Greenhead, before ducking south again towards Alston. I was looking forward to this bit of the run and had a feeling I'd be able to capture some great sequences for my film. The eight miles to the wall begun with a slop through another boggy forest before I emerged onto Haughton Common to be faced with a chilling wind battling with the sunshine for supremacy. I found my way over the moorland to the next section of extremely wet and muddy forest and then down through the trees, which opened out to reveal an impressive view of the valley containing Greenlee and Broomlee Lough and behind them a suspiciously epic rocky ridge – could this be Hadrian's Wall? It seemed unlikely; the ridge was truly immense.

My progress that morning was a little hampered by the fact that I'd put my left contact lens in back to front. This impaired my depth perception, blurred my vision and irritated me no end as I ran across fields of hummocky grass and hardy moorland reeds. My map informed me that the Way ran between the loughs, so navigating was easy as I came to the slow realisation that I was both right and wrong about the geography ahead. This was indeed Hadrian's Wall but built, for this section at least, along a natural escarpment of dolerite, called the Whin Sill. Once a layer of extruded magma trapped between layers of limestone, the Sill was revealed after millions of years of erosion of the softer rock above and around it. The Sill added up to twenty-five metres to the height of the Roman defences at this point and no doubt improved the view of lookouts in its various forts and milecastles.

My amazement at a wall that seemed to tower fifty feet above the surrounding landscape was only tempered a little when I found the built part was of more modest scale. I climbed a stile over a fence at one of the 'missing' sections and, after filming a shot or two with my waiting support crew, clambered to the top of the wall and took in the view. The Sill and sections of well-preserved wall stretched off across the sunlit plain in both directions and to the west Crag Lough sparkled, sheltered by the Carboniferous escarpment towering above it. Sections of the wall were remarkably well preserved, with perfectly cubical bricks and impressively straight lines heading over the brow of the undulating landscape.

Walking into one of the milecastles I could almost imagine the layout – sleeping quarters over there, hearth against this wall, armoury here. But this was no time to channel Dan Cruikshank[1] – my explorations would have to be a little more fleeting.

There were many walkers and hikers traversing the wall but I was the only runner. Reactions seemed to range from amusement to perplexity to barely concealed hostility at the notion of somebody actually running the wall. I didn't stop to tell them I was only travelling a fragment of its length. The sun continued to shine down and my lethargy was soon forgotten as I enjoyed my snaking progress along the fortification. My only difficulty was the build-up of lactic acid in my calves and thighs whenever I tried to dash up a flight of steps to the top of a section of wall. I found this pain grew sharply and dissipated just as quickly and guessed that my body might have sacrificed something in the muscles required for climbing to divert power to those used in keeping me jogging along for eight to ten hours per day. At one point I descended a steep spiral of rocky ledges to the surreal sight of a kids' party in progress by one of the milecastles. Evidently, in the world of 'normal' people it was picnic weather.

I stopped at a place with the excellent name of Once Brewed, grabbing a lift with Carol and her friend Sorrell, also a musician and film-maker, who would be taking over from her for the next six days. Carol was off on an impromptu tour with her band Steve Ignorant's Slice of Life, supporting the zeitgeisty northern band Sleaford Mods. Sorrell was a trusted school friend Carol had not seen for a number of years who had expressed interest when Carol advertised the vacancy amongst her circle. I trusted Carol's faith in her friend implicitly and, fortunately, that trust was not misplaced.

The rest of the day's run, fuelled by a fortifying pub lunch was scenic and uneventful (in terms of navigation problems, injuries and other mishaps). You can't really get lost when you're running alongside a massive Roman fortification. I was forced after a while to relieve myself against the wall but, given part of its purpose was to keep out unruly northerners and Picts, it seemed poetically just. A little rain started falling when I reached the crags east of Walltown Quarry but it didn't trouble me unduly as I passed the ruins of twelfth-century Thirlwall Castle, gingerly dashed over a level crossing after a high-speed train rattled by and found my way round to the B3618 just outside of Greenhead. Exhausted and without enough daylight to sensibly embark on the next section of the Pennine Way, I decided to call it a day. I'd reached the end of the first of three Pennine Way maps – it seemed fitting to crack open the next one at sunrise on the following day.

I had Garrigill in my sights on Wednesday 23rd, mainly as it was the last village before what would prove the Pennine Way's toughest section – the rocky, barren summits of Cross Fell and Great Dunn Fell. Between Greenhill and Garrigill lay twenty-two miles of fields, commons and intricate navigation along only half-visible pathways. There was no way I'd be able to do another sixteen miles over mountains on top of that. Today would necessarily have to be another 'light' day's running. Or so I thought.

I got confused within the first mile, heading the wrong way past a mobile phone mast and bewildering a white-maned pony sheltering from the persistent wind under some gnarly trees. I then had a mildly disconcerting encounter with some cows protecting their calves. Cows have an unnerving habit of taking a few steps towards you as you approach, then stopping, as if to say 'I'm not afraid and am standing my ground.' I wasn't going to argue, skirting them while mouthing my usual meaningless platitudes, hopefully in a mollifying tone of voice. Invisible sections of footpath led me astray several times and I climbed more than one fence over the next seven miles to Burnstones, where the route hit a small village and where I stopped for lunch.

In the afternoon I orienteered as far as Slaggyford, where I confess I got frustrated of navigating in the rain through bafflingly identical fields in search of near-invisible flights of stone steps set into the drystone walls. I found a footpath running along a now-abandoned stretch of the South Tyne Railway and sheltered from the rain for a while under a road-bridge to consider my options. I was losing time and, if I didn't make it to Garrigill by sunset, I'd be loading an unreasonable burden on the already challenging route tomorrow. I decided to short cut a loop of the Pennine Way as far as Alston, following this footpath through the towns of Lintley and Kirkhaugh.

Having been reduced to stumbling around cowpat-strewn fields for the morning, I relished the chance to really speed up and run and I found myself managing 9-minute miles once more. Passing road bridges over the South Tyne Trail before Sorrell could get there and set up the camera almost became a cruel game. I waited for her for about five minutes at the first road south of Slaggyford and then decided that speed was more important than coverage and belted my way to Lintley, where the trail surprised me by becoming a still-operating narrow-gauge railway. No trains were running that afternoon but it was fun to imagine the steam-driven little trains linking villages together as I pounded the gravel.[2] It proved a pleasant distraction to observe the small stations, with their ornate nameplates, signals and points perfectly preserved.

I reached Alston and found myself sadly back in the world

of poorly signposted trails and non-existent phone reception. I managed to get a message to Sorrell that I'd be heading to Garrigill and swapped railway sidings for narrow forest paths. The next section of the route seemed to involve an unending tangle of fields and a sinuously curving river (the South Tyne) which I was perpetually on the wrong side of. A local farmer on a quad bike, whom I opened a gate for, pointed me in the right direction and I found myself following the river towards another glorious sunset. My usual early-evening delirium descended and I found myself composing fictional 'real' names for the explorer, mountaineer and TV presenter Bear Grylls[3] and making up a daft ditty about following the river as it went 'on and on and on and on and on ... '

Unable to contact Sorrell (not a great experience for her first day on the job) I made my way towards Garrigill, stopping to admire the lurid canopy of red, gold and blue unfolding above me as the sun sunk relentlessly towards the horizon. I got to the tiny, near-silent village at dusk, certain that Sorrell would be waiting for me in the chilly gloom. Sadly, mobile reception let us both down again. I waited patiently for about half an hour and greeted her arrival with gratitude, starting the process of thawing out as we drove through the pitch-black lanes towards our hotel.

Disaster almost befell me the following morning. After delivering what I hoped was a suitably perky and hopeful piece to camera at Garrigill, I set off up a rocky track towards the wild fells that constituted the next bit of the Way. After about five minutes I went to consult my map and realised it wasn't where I usually kept it, in my hand.

I dashed back down the trail at maniac speed to find the car still there and Sorrell filming a close-up of a Pennine Way signpost. I'd imagined me chasing her down the road bellowing about maps but my own insistence that she 'get plenty of cutaways' had saved me. Map in panic-sweating palm, I headed off once more.

Greying clouds soon began to hurl down icy rain as the path levelled off into a rough grouse-moor. The area was also evidently used for military training – I passed a personnel carrier parked in the middle of the stony pathway, a line of camouflaged and waterproofed men standing sentry amongst the heather, looking miserable and immovable at the same time. Perhaps it was some kind of endurance training. Certainly the brutal wind and slanting Arctic rain seemed designed to break the spirit. For the first time in The Long Run I began to feel underdressed.

I was wearing my running gloves and, as ever, a cap but was still clad in technical T-shirt, thin 'windproof' jacket and shorts. This outfit offered no protection against the driving, near horizontal precipitation. As moorland gave way to barren rocky wilderness, the right side of my face began to go numb. I had to hold the plastic-sheathed map against my cheek to protect it from what felt like stabbing needles of rain. Fortunately I didn't need the map much for navigation as the path looked like it had been carved out of the landscape with jackhammers and giant chisels as it arced up the side of Cross Fell, the highest point in all the Pennines at 893 metres (just 70 feet short of being a Munro). My feet were soaked after one too many encounters with puddles I was just too tired to run around and I began to search through the mist and rain for sight of a bothy I'd identified on the map that morning.

Bothies are communal hikers' huts distributed amongst the mountains and available to all travellers who obey the common-sense rules of well-behaved wayfarers. Usually furnished with little more than basic rooms, coal or wood-fired stoves and sleeping platforms, these huts are nevertheless a welcome respite for tired or soaked hikers. Many travellers on multi-day journeys choose to spend the night there rather than fight with tents in gale conditions. My frozen 8-minute mile dash to the Cross Fell Hut felt like a race for survival. I knew I couldn't spend much time there and would be unlikely to find the means to make a fire to get dry (nor did I have a change of running gear with me) but stepping out of the brutal weather for a few minutes would prove very welcome.

Situated about a hundred feet shy of the summit of Cross Fell, the hut had a little entrance hall, one room containing a few chairs, a noticeboard, visitors' book and a second room with a coal or wood-burning stove and sleeping platform. Without matches or fuel, I couldn't light a fire but I did find a smelly old blanket which I wasn't too proud to wrap around myself as I explored. The noticeboard contained evidence of fellow ultra-runners Dave and Steven's passing in the form of their laminated fundraising card. I was glad that they too had felt the need to seek shelter despite their heroism. I signed the visitors' book and filmed close-ups of discarded and ancient paperbacks, stubs of candles and squeezed-out toothpaste tubes. The hut was a pleasing reminder that I wasn't the only nutcase to wander this barren, rocky mountainside.

However, I couldn't stay there too long. As I squinted through the tiny windows I could see that the rain had abated a little although the hardy fir trees someone had planted near the hut in a futile attempt at additional shelter were waving around like the arms of drowning men. The thick stone walls were almost completely soundproof – only a thin wail across the chimney betrayed the presence of the Helm Wind, a weather phenomenon remarkable enough to possess its own Wikipedia entry. Apparently it is the only named wind in the British Isles, forming under the cap of cloud that almost permanently wreathes the top of the fell. Still sodden, after eating some energy bars and folding the blanket back where I'd found it, I headed back out to face down the full force of the Helm.

It's such a vivid memory I can still recall it with

remarkable clarity. I seemed to have to lean in to the wind to maintain my balance as I marched up the last one hundred feet towards the top of the fell. Running here was out of the question – wet slabs and shattered fragments of rock dominated the landscape, across which damp billows of cloud drifted. Remarkably, just as I was beginning to think I was probably walking to my doom, a figure swathed in a blue anorak and waterproof trousers marched cheerfully past me, alone but unperturbed. I exchanged a wave with this solitary walker, as our voices couldn't carry past the end of our noses. The wind was finding notches and holes in the rocks and singing with a peculiar rising and falling howl. All pretence at a marked-out path fell apart in the rounded dome of shale, gritstone and limestone pieces that littered the thin grass.

Despite the lack of a path, someone had engineered a huge four-armed slate shelter (laid out in a cross), giving me a chance to crouch down and consult the map and search for a blue dot on my phone. The attempt was futile – as thick blankets of cloud made their way across the hilltop thinning very occasionally to afford a rare glimpse of terrain, I couldn't reconcile the landscape with either of my maps. I had to navigate by intuition. I dragged my way through the mist over a rocky plain like the surface of an alien world and jumped into a trench of rock like a soldier under heavy fire. The rain had all but stopped at least, although the clouds provided plenty of moisture and the wind wouldn't let up its banshee wail.

After a few minutes sheltering and poking my camera, periscope-like up to film the chaos around me, a gap in the clouds formed for long enough for me to glimpse a route towards the next fell. I identified a steep descent to a grassy plain that gradually rose to a hilltop upon which stood a radar station like something from a 1960s sci-fi movie, complete with golf ball-like geodesic dome and mushroom-shaped antennae. On the way there I passed a few more heroic hikers, including one American woman who seemed intent on photographing two bearded strangers who were sheltering and smoking amongst the piled stone. Although their photographer waved cheerily, her subjects, who themselves looked chiselled from rock, wore expressions too stern and steadfast to challenge with more than a terse 'hi'. I turned and started picking my way down out of the tumult of cloud.

Down in the saddle of moorland between Cross Fell and Great Dun Fell, it felt like an entirely different climate – considerably warmer, still windy but not violently so. A line of flagstones led me across the heather and up towards the strange white structures comprising the radar station, which in their retro-futuristic stylings resembled a Space 1999 set.

This station, which actually dates from the 1980s, is part of Britain's air traffic control system, the geodesic dome (or 'radome') containing a revolving microwave antenna. Leading up to it is the UK's highest road, a service route leading from the nearby village of Knock. After descending from the fell, I ran down this strip of near-pristine tarmac for about a mile then followed signage across peaty, boggy moorland. The sun broke through patchy clouds and glinted on large pools of standing water like fragments of discarded mirror as I made good time down towards the village of Dufton. The trail grew steeper and rockier but I relished the chance to stretch out and run, fast but as controlled (I flattered myself) as a proper fell runner. Sheep scattered from my footfalls as I navigated by stone markers inscribed with gold-painted arrows. I think I'd pushed the potential dangers of Cross Fell to the compartment of my mind where the horrors of the 5th September still lurked. Now I relished the sheer contrast between being frozen, disorientated and wet and this feeling of gravity-assisted flight. I bounded over rocks and squeezed my feet into thin sheep trails, descending the 600 metres to the town with a serious lunch craving driving me on.

Sorrell had mentioned she'd found a pub serving half-decent food in Dufton but she wasn't sure if it would still be open after two o'clock. I made it into town, exhausted but reasonably pleased with myself and with about ten minutes to spare. Once again, in what was already becoming a bad habit, I had somehow wandered off the main Pennine Way about a mile outside of the village. A local farmer had pointed me via a local footpath into the town but I think Sorrell had been waiting by the Pennine Way proper, camera at the ready. Once I'd found her, we managed to persuade the local pub to cook two more covers – I think my ravenous appearance made it seem an act of charity.

Sorrell and I had agreed that I'd take small roads as far as Thwaite, thereby cutting off the thirty-three-mile loop via Middleton-in-Teesdale. Dufton to Thwaite by road should work out at around twenty miles, a considerable saving. I regretted not being able to see High Force Waterfall, which sounded exciting, but maybe it was good to save something for a future, completist assault on the Pennine Way. As it was, I was now eleven days behind on my (admittedly woefully unrealistic) schedule and if I didn't want to be running on into winter, I had to be more time efficient from now on.

So it was that I returned to small farm roads and looked up at the peaks towering to my left as I progressed through the villages of Keisley, Murton and Hilton. Having a generous three-course lunch might have proved a little unwise as the going was sluggish to begin with, although things improved, as they always did, as the hours rolled by. I would appear to have a cast-iron gut, not enduring so much as a hint of nausea throughout The Long Run, no matter what or when I ate. Still, I can't recommend downing tomato soup with crusty bread, sausages and mash and then apple pie with custard immediately before running twenty miles.

The rain came on towards four o'clock and the usual symphony of wind in the trees and birdsong was joined by the percussive drill of what was unmistakably a machine gun issuing from somewhere a mile or so away. The retort of rifles had by now become just part of the soundtrack of the country; machine guns were something else entirely. I could only hope a third world war or zombie apocalypse had not broken out, given that I'd not watched any news coverage for several days. The truth made itself known about fifteen minutes later when Sorrell drove down a country lane towards me, telling me to turn back. We'd reached the entrance to a restricted military zone, the Warcop Training Area. Scary signs warned of the dangers ahead and made it clear that no unauthorised vehicles should take the road I was on. I thought I'd probably be okay on foot but decided not to chance being separated from my support car for who knows how long. For once, a sensible decision was taken. Apparently the Area is still used for tank gunnery training. An encounter with a Challenger tank might have made for some great film footage but discretion won out.

Between Hilton and Sandford the sky decided to put on an incredible display of luminance and colour. The low sun sent Jacob's ladders through gaps in the clouds and the rain-washed road threw back bright reflections. I ran along a road across flat moorland, past large stables and on down to the A66.

On my large-scale map, the strip of A-road between Sandford and the turn-off to Warcop was less than a centimetre long. Unfortunately this translated to about a mile of stumbling along the grass verge past a thunderously busy road filled with trucks tossing up waves of spray into my tired eyes. Halfway along this route my dad chose to call me

1. With Dad at John O'Groats

2. Davey Henderson to the rescue, near Helmsdale

3. Left: On the Great Glen Way

4. Bottom left: Lost, somewhere off the Great Glen Way

5. Bottom right: Carol Hodge enjoys a rare moment of respite near Gairlochy

6. With the Three Brethren on the Southern Upland Way

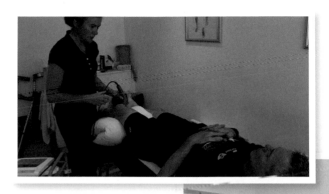

7. ABOVE: Receiving ultrasound therapy for my errant knee

8. RIGHT: My odd shin bulge examined in Livingstone A&E

9. On the Pennine Way with David 'Stan' Stanning

10. Helm Wind at Cross Fell

11. On the Pennine Way with Richard Durance

12. Alone on a wild, windy moor

13. The sun breaks through the mist

14. A spider's web by the roadside near Cowling

15. Blackstone Edge

16. A muddy trail in Somerset

17. Nearing Hebden Bridge

18. Kinder Scout

19. Planning at Edale

20. Sorrell Kerrison lines up a shot on the Yorkshire Dales

21. Dad cycling a towpath near Birmingham

22. A Cotswolds idyll

23. More car trouble and another rescue, this time near South Cerney

24. Georgian splendour in Bath

25. With author and runner Chris Thrall on the Devon-Cornwall border

26. Near Bosigran in Cornwall, on the South West Coast Path

27. At Land's End

to discuss his next visit (to film some quadcopter footage). I was rather grateful to step off the road at a lay-by and wander into a cornfield to take the call. However, I was only putting off the inevitable and given that it was growing increasingly dark and rainy and the traffic had its headlights on, I had to get off what was fast becoming a lethal route.

Gratefully, I waved goodbye to the A66 and Eddie Stobart[4] near Warcop and spent the next ten or so miles keeping up a running inner monologue as Sorrell helped me navigate the small roads towards the market town of Kirkby Stephen. The monologue went something like this:

You're exhausted, it's getting really dark and you've run over thirty miles today, including two huge fells. Why don't you just stop here? *No – I need to get to Kirkby Stephen*. Why do you need to get to Kirkby Stephen? *Because it's a biggish place and I like its name*. You do realise that's no sort of reason at all, don't you? It's totally arbitrary and you're beyond tired now – it's so dark cars can hardly see you. You're soaked through. Just stop, won't you? *But I promised I'd get to Kirkby*. You promised? Who did you promise? *Myself. I promised myself*. Well, you'd better break that promise or I'm going to fold up your knees and leave you in a puddle.

Eventually the body won out over the mind. It pretty much always does. Still, I can proudly say that when I stopped around three miles shy of Kirkby, at some nondescript farmers field we'd be lucky to locate the following day, I had nothing left. A near-full moon shone brightly the sky above me. The support car's tail lights glowed warmly, tempting me. It was time to call it a day.

As a sensible person might have predicted, the next day I was reduced to a zombielike shuffle as I headed for Kirkby and the B6270 towards Keld. Utterly drained, in a way I'd not yet felt during The Long Run, I knew I'd not make it very far. Every dragging step felt like a lead weight being hoist and hurled down upon unforgiving hard tarmac. A small blessing presented itself – the sun emerged early in the morning and it stayed warm and clear for hours. After the icy blasts of the previous day, it felt good to feel that tingling warmth on the skin.

Kirkby Stephen was advertising a 'Beer and Bangers' festival as I non-hurtled into town. I didn't stop for sausages though and tried to look heroic passing service stations, graveyards and suburban housing schemes. The front of my ankle no longer seemed to be an issue but now the tendon at the back of the left heel began throbbing. A tendon acting up was something to be very watchful of – should it become significantly inflamed or even snap, that would end The Long Run. I monitored the pain as I ran, trying to touch down with my forefoot to spread out each impact, a tall order given my exhaustion.

The B6270 was supposed to be an 'easy' alternative to the Pennine Way but nobody had informed it of this plan. The road quickly climbed over 300 metres from the small village of Nateby, most of which I walked in a state of ever-increasing fatigue, to the heights of Birk Dale. Fortunately, the views from the high dale were spectacular and, as I paused to say hello to my parents, parked in a lay-by offering the best views, I was glad of the scenic distraction.

The transition from Cumbria to Yorkshire was marked by the appearance of meticulous, almost fanatical lines of dry-stone walls creating an irregular tessellation of fields as far as the eye could see. Yorkshiremen, it seems, will build walls anywhere – steep hills and high summits are no obstacle and the skill with which these walls and their attendant stone barns are constructed is awe-inspiring. I remembered our encounter with drystone dyker Davey Henderson on day two and was sure he'd see much to admire in this stonework.

The geology seemed to change too – bluffs of hard,

overhanging rock appeared on the high hills and fells to the
north. At one point I passed the remains of an old-fashioned
covered trailer, its decrepitude nicely framed by the cliffs
overhead – this would be an excellent place to film a rural
horror film, I thought as I ran (location spotting is a habitual
obsession). Somewhere in the green valley to my right a small
river must still be carving out this ancient landscape. I could
hear it but catch only glimpses of it. I passed a couple of
hikers, backs laden with heavy packs and then, remarkably,
descending the steep road to Keld, a cyclist pumped his way
uphill, managing a grimace in greeting. More understand-
ably, I saw a lot of motorbikes, in pairs and touring groups
– the views, dramatic sweeps and curves of the road would
make this a favourite route. The traffic wasn't busy and the
road was wide enough that I didn't have to worry unduly
about speeding motorists.

Keld was pretty and marked a return to level running
through valleys reminiscent of James Herriot's novels and
the TV shows based on his Yorkshire veterinary practice
through the thirties, forties and fifties. A favourite of my
mother, James Herriot's books, including *All Creatures
Great and Small* and *It Shouldn't Happen to a Vet*, managed
at once to be comically parochial and yet universal in their
themes. Along with that other legendary Yorkshire-set TV
show *The Last of the Summer Wine*, Herriot's works had
made the county a semi-legendary place in my childhood,
full of dourly humorous farmers and delinquent pensioners.
One of Yorkshire's biggest towns, Sheffield, where I studied
film, felt very different from the tiny villages I found myself
running through now. Everything was vividly green and
the pace of life seemed to slow down by degrees as I ran on
through Angram and headed towards Thwaite.

Despite my fatigue, which was now reaching epic propor-
tions, I remember the road to Thwaite as one of the most
vividly beautiful stretches of my journey. There seemed to be

a gentility and kindness in the behaviour of locals who gave way for me, nodded hellos and generally seemed to accept this odd character jogging past their workplaces. Farms were everywhere, quad bikes ambling over hillsides, sheepdogs herding errant ewes. The roads were almost ridiculously twisty, which slowed the traffic to a comparative amble. I think this suited the locals just fine – this was a land without the modern sense of panic-stricken urgency. Everyone had his or her own job to do and took the time to do it. I'm aware that there's a growing problem of depression amongst young farmers, who often feel lonely, underappreciated and economically pressured. I'd watch a local TV news report on this very subject a few days later. Yet, as I ran through Yorkshire's busy farming communities, what I noticed was dignity and a respect for the landscape. It's a place to which I'd gladly return.

Although I was utterly drained of energy, my spirit felt enriched as I progressed through the dales and into Thwaite. The square where I stopped contained a perfectly positioned bench, onto which I dropped gratefully to await my support car. A few yards away stood the guest house in which we'd be staying that night, hikers peering curiously at me over pints as they sat by picnic tables outside. As I ran into the village, I composed a motto for the town: 'Thwaite – it's worth the wait', which made me smile. A woman smiled at me in passing as she hung out her laundry. The comfortable hospitality the town seemed to offer felt entirely in keeping with the way I'd been feeling all day – weary but welcome.

MILES RUN: 598; MILES REMAINING: 502

1. For non-Brits, Mr Cruikshank is the endearingly enthusiastic and quintessentially English presenter of such television documentaries as *Around the World in 80 Treasures* and *Adventures in Architecture* (both BBC).

2. South Tynedale Railway was instituted in 1852 between Haltwhistle (perfect name for the end of a railway line) and Alston and now runs as a tourist attraction, still steam-powered, with services running through the spring and summer months. Plans are afoot to extend the line back to Slaggyford.

3. Disappointingly the ex-SAS paratrooper and adventurer's real name is Edward Michael and not Hieronymous Spoonfodder as I'd supposed.

4. Omnipresent UK and European Logistics company whose vehicles are all heavily branded with Mr Stobart's moniker.

THWAITE TO BLACKSHAW HEAD

I'd hoped my fatigue would lift a little after an afternoon off and a good night's sleep in Thwaite. As I dragged myself out of bed on the morning of the 26th September it was evident that this had been wishful thinking. Although I felt a little better, I was still having issues with momentum – it took a lot of brute willpower to keep me moving. Anything more than a shallow incline reduced me to walking and this being the Yorkshire Dales, I was always either heading uphill or downhill. The 25 per cent incline road sign I stopped to film at one point was far from unique. Eschewing Great Shunner Fell (713 metres) felt like a necessity and I decided to take the roads between it and the euphemistically named Lovely Seat (675 metres) instead. There would be plenty of time for fells in the days to come. As ever, I reminded myself of the greater goal as my muscles warmed up and battled inertia.

The town of Hawes would be my next immediate goal, beyond it a 14-mile stretch of fields and fells to Horton-in-Ribblesdale. That would amount to around a marathon in total mileage. Without my current level of fatigue, I would have easily coped with that and more. As things stood, it would prove challenging. As ever, I began the day optimistically though, enjoying the sunshine, the dales views, and the fact that, no matter how awful my legs felt when I began running each day, I could be confident they would 'thaw out' and allow me to keep going, albeit not indefinitely.

As ever, the road quickly climbed, reached a plateau, wound around a few contours and descended towards

Hawes. On the final, steepest part of the descent, my legs protesting each impact, I ran by a local runner heading up the slope. Hill training works on a grander scale in Yorkshire than back in London. He asked me, 'How far are you going?' A mischievous impulse made me reply 'Land's End'. His reply: 'Fucking hell! Well done!'

It was oddly encouraging to have that reminder that what I was doing was out of the ordinary. Somehow it's easy to forget after almost four weeks of doing something like The Long Run that it is in any way exceptional. The body and mind quickly adapt to new routines, however unusual. It's probably this quality of adaptability that has allowed *homo sapiens* to thrive, surviving ice ages, global wars, technological revolutions and economic collapses. As a species, we just get on with it.

I had a light lunch at Hawes with Sorrell and my parents (forgoing the local Wensleydale cheese), having by now realised that large amounts of stodgy food would just slow me down. Calories were more effectively taken on in the early morning or in the evening, after I'd stopped. The engine could run on empty if it had to – all that would happen is that, running out of carbohydrates, my body would switch to the less efficient but longer-lasting fat-burning phase. In Christopher McDougall's book *Natural Born Heroes* he quotes Phil Maffetone, fitness coach and fat-burning guru: 'Even an athlete with 6 per cent body fat will have enough fat to fuel exercise lasting for many hours.'[1] My experience on The Long Run would seem to bear testimony to the truth of this – there's simply no way I was taking on enough carbs each day to run on sugar alone. Fat had become my secret weapon.

After almost two days on roads it was good to return to the trail out of Hawes, which began a little way beyond the suburb of Gayle. A local boy pointed me down the tiny passageway between houses where I picked up the marker posts. After navigating a few tricky fields, farmland gave way to rough fell country once more and I started climbing the contour lines to 587 metres, where the path met an old packhorse route. Wensleydale's prettiness gave way to a starker, flatter landscape as West Cam Road met Cam High Road, now a tarmacked access route but once known as 'The Devil's Causeway' and before that, a Roman Road running between Lancaster and the fort at Bainbridge. The satanic nomenclature might, in part, be explained by its barren aspect and exposure to whatever vicious winds are cutting across Dodd Fell. As I ran it, however, the weather was amiably breezy, cool and overcast. The wind was light enough for my father to capture perhaps the most successful aerial footage in the film of The Long Run, a swooping shot following me for around a mile towards Cam End. At this junction between footpaths, I had one of my moments of map-reading doubt but eventually did the right thing (for once) heading due south on a much rougher and steeper trail. From the top of Cam High Road to Horton-in-Ribblesdale was a steady descent of 300 metres over six miles (less than half the distance Sorrell had mistakenly estimated). Apart from my ankle pain flaring up and having to be silenced once more with painkillers, I was making almost alarmingly good progress.

The sky began to put on an impressive display once more as I wound down the valley, throwing shafts of light down to illuminate Horton-in-Ribblesdale, where I decided to end that day's running. It would be another 'easy' day – just seventeen miles – but I could sense that the ankle's tolerance was being tested, even on this relatively soft terrain. Given that the route out of Horton included two epic fells, it seemed wise not to push my luck. On a practical note, there probably wouldn't be the time to essay the 14.5 miles to Malham (the next potential collection point) before night fell. The landscape would dictate its own pace. I was also about to finish the second Pennine Way map and there was something satisfyingly neat about starting the final one the next day.

After a tricky plunge down a rubble-strewn pathway into Horton, I noticed an unusual number of bicycles – whole groups of lycra-clad cyclists lounged outside pubs or raced one another down the high street. A pre-race vibe had over-taken the little town. It transpired that I'd be running two of the fells that form the Three Peaks Cyclo-cross race, the toughest of its kind in the UK with a total distance of 38 miles, 20 of which are on trails, and a total climb of over 5,000 feet. As I'd discover the following day, much of that climbing would be challenging in the extreme.

The following morning, as I recorded a piece to camera, I was able to announce a milestone – I'd done 550 miles, making Horton the halfway point in my journey. This and the weather, which was warm and sunny, set me off in a good mood towards the towering triangular peak of Pen-y-Ghent. Hot-air balloons rose in the valley below and, as I slapped on sunscreen and donned my running sunglasses, it felt almost like a summer's day. The hill ahead was named in Cumbric, an ancient language related closely to Welsh. Pen-y-Ghent probably means 'head of the winds', although other readings include 'hill on the border' (of Cumbria).[2] Certainly, the driving wind at its summit would support the first reading, although once you've felt the full force of the Helm Wind, other winds pale in comparison!

There wasn't much running to be had over the first hour as I made my way up 400 metres to the sheer rocky face of Pen-y-ghent. Midway, I found a folded sheet of paper tucked into a stile – a map and instructions for one of the cyclo-cross marshals. The bikes didn't pass me, though, since they weren't due to hit this part of their route for another three hours. However, a keen local fell runner dashed past with a long-legged stride as I neared the base of the hill proper. He smiled happily and I almost felt like explaining why I was marching, rather than running. Runners' competitiveness doesn't really switch off.

Perhaps that was why I decided to run the last few hundred yard to the top – I had something to prove. I made it to level ground with heart pounding in my chest and lungs bursting. The view from the dome-like top was my reward. A rocky trail vanished over the summit's edge and the land fell sharply away, revealing an epic plain of fields and hills, cradling a bright band of low-lying cloud. A few wispy contrails stood in for clouds in the vividly blue dome overhead. The sun was a painful ball of fire, even behind sunglasses.

I didn't tarry long as I could already see my next target – Fountains Fell to the south-east. First, though, I had to pick my way down a sheer, rocky stepped trail without injury, not an easy task on aching quads with almost a month's running in them. Again I was inspired by the sight of a couple of fell runners leaping up past me like mountain goats. The glorious weather was bringing out the intrepid. Fountains Fell proved greener and rounder than Pen-y-Ghent – as well as wetter and muddier. It seemed to be named for the many little rivulets and streams running down off it, some of them feeding or emerging from a small tarn set into its north face. I wish I had known the tarn was there (I only spotted it on the map later) as I might have been tempted to swim. One of my lasting memories of a brief visit to Tasmania was walking the Cradle Mountain trail and chancing upon a high pool where, under shimmering late summer heat and secure in the mountain's solitude, I stripped naked and swam for half an hour. It's probably a good thing Fountains Fell's tarn escaped me – I had a long way to go before lunch.

One more thing about Fountains Fell impressed me –

even here, at 668 metres, ambitious Yorkshiremen had built a wall defining the boundary of the National Trust owned Malham Estate to the south. I began to see the woods and blue square of Malham Tarn below me, driving me on. Although I began to experience a lot of ankle pain, accompanied by a fiery flare up the left calf, the beauty of the forested trail alongside the lake kept me nicely distracted. I took a tiny detour down to the water's edge and was almost hypnotised by the glimmering clarity of the water as I snacked and drank. Shaking off sudden lethargy, I rose and hobbled on, having developed the fastest limp in England. Rounding two sides of the tarn and passing many walkers and day-tripping families with obstreperous children, I emerged from the trees into a flatter, bleaker plane and headed down into Ing Scar, a rocky gully strewn with awkward boulders that slowed me down and made each footfall a heightened risk.

The pain in my ankle began to overcome me. I found something to take my mind off it in the shape of Malham Cove, a curving cliff of limestone forming a natural amphitheatre 260 feet high, below which runs Malham Beck. In the distant past, a waterfall once plunged over its dramatic heights. In December 2015 Storm Desmond re-enacted this spectacular sight and, for a few days only, water flowed over the cliff edge once more. Generally though, rainwater from the top of Malham moor finds a more secretive path to the bottom via channels scoured deep into the limestone.

The Pennine Way next took me around the west side of the Cove and over a section of grooved limestone pavement unlike anything else in Britain. The porous structure of this particular limestone, combined with aeons of meltwater flow, has made a giant jigsaw out of the rock. I had to leap from one piece of this giant's puzzle to another to make it across to the grassy slopes to the west. Dozens of families

were delighting in the other-worldly geology of the place.
I stayed as long as I could but my stomach was already
complaining and the pubs and cafes of Malham were
calling.

Malham was a dangerous draw that Sunday lunchtime
– hundreds of people enjoying leisurely lunches and pints
in the sun. Perhaps that's why we opted for tea and scones
in a small gift shop café. I was back on the trail within an
hour, running alongside the sparkling beck, following the
contours of the land through Hanlith and Airton. At one
point I stopped to film horses in a field, accompanied by the
sound of church bells. From rugged prehistoric scenery to
comfortable and cosy English rural charm – the Way was
providing a lot of variety to stave off the worrying trauma
in my left leg.

The afternoon's terrain was gentle and unchallenging,
exactly what I wanted after my mountaineering morning.
Only after the Way left the river's side past Airton did I have
to pay much attention to my map. The trail began crossing
green fields north of Gargrave; at one stage I thought a cow
had taken to stalking me up a hillside path until I realised
that animals too might follow the route most-trodden. I
began to realise that I was spending more time these days
in the company of livestock than humans. This is not necessarily a bad thing.

Without any incident more noteworthy than occasional
wayfinding confusion, I reached the town of Gargrave at
around five o'clock and, discovering juice left in the tank,
decided to keep on for Thornton-in-Craven. After two light
days, I felt a need to rack up some mileage and, I realised
with surprise, the day had been nothing but enjoyable. Why
stop now? Thornton would be 'only' 25 miles from Horton
but with about 460 metres of off-road climbing on a questionable ankle, it would feel like a good day's running.

At East Marton the Way took to a pretty section of the Leeds

and Liverpool canal towpath before veering off again across
one final field, whereupon the trail turned into a surfaced road
leading DOWN to Thornton. In yet another glorious magic
hour, I reached Sorrell, waiting for me in a suburban cul-de-
sac with camera poised, and concluded a near-perfect day's
running.

That night I had a good look at the ankle, which was still
ringed with a doughnut of now hard flesh but which didn't
seem to hurt unduly. Could I keep running on it indefinitely?
Common sense would suggest that I probably couldn't but
then common sense and ultra-running are rarely compatible.

The following day had an unpleasant significance about
it – it was the day that, it my pre-planning naiveté, I had
believed I would be finishing The Long Run. In reality
I wouldn't even be leaving the Pennines. Still, that kind
of negativity wouldn't get me very far. I was still running
more than double the mileage per week than I had ever run
before – and I was surviving – just. I decided to let bloody-
mindedness propel me on; it is the ultra-runner's constant
companion and best ally.

And so on the 28th, I tried to banish the demons of
self-doubt and disappointment and set off from the pretty
village street at which I'd stopped the previous day.
Tracking down the next part of the Way by a coop of oddly
free-range cockerels (they were wandering up and down the
pavement making friends with Sorrell when I got there) I
headed up a flight of overgrown stone steps into the first of
many fields.

I immediately got lost ... again. That is to say that,
having had a bit of assistance from a local farmer in locating
a very well-hidden stile, I followed a muddy trail of boot-
prints into the middle of a field where they seemed to stop
abruptly. The field was shaped like a dome so I couldn't see
a wall at the other end where there might be a stile, gate or

finger sign. I could see a farmhouse which didn't seem to be on my map. Through some country sleight of hand I'd managed to end up in the wrong field.

An important fact you have to bear in mind in following an English Trail is that certain routes over private land are what is known as 'permissive paths'. Not to be confused with BOATs, RUPPS, restricted byways or green lanes, permissive paths[3] are controlled by the landowner who may divert the course of said path or close it, without legal recourse, at any time. Generally, as such routes are negotiated with National Trails, local councils and other conservation organisations, goodwill generally prevails. However, sometimes for good ecological or safety reasons, paths are altered and occasionally disputes may arise, resulting in a trail diversion. Though these are usually well signposted or marked with temporary laminated notices, they won't of course appear on maps, unless they become permanent changes and the maps are revised. All of which is to explain that it is not always bad map-reading to blame for walkers becoming momentarily lost.

On this occasion, I never found out why I went so far astray that I had to climb two barbed wire fences and vault a small stream before getting back on track. By now I had a bit of a laissez-faire attitude to getting lost. That said, the delay put a bit of a dent in my confidence. Things improved significantly once muddy fields gave way to bridleway at Thornton Moor. As I ascended to the road crossing, I was amazed to see a small herd of wild roe deer racing across the crest of the hill. Perhaps youngsters, one of the deer suddenly leapt many feet into the air – the jump was so unexpected and dramatic that it seemed a product of nothing more than spontaneous joy. The sight made me feel a little embarrassed about my increasing grumpiness at the lack of proper signage. As I crested the hill, crossed the road and began a gradual descent to the village of Lothersdale, I vowed to try to enjoy myself more.

After Lothersdale came Cowling and the sun broke out from a gauzy haze of low-lying mist. I resisted sunglasses though, having discovered fellow walkers and runners just aren't as welcoming to a person who has hidden their eyes. I was even briefly harassed by a bumble bee as I put on sunscreen; it must have mistaken my brilliantly white T-shirt (for once washed in an actual machine) for a giant flower. What mist remained sunk to the valley floors and low hillsides, although it sometimes seemed to be threatening to follow me as I made for the moors proper. Picturesque Ponden Reservoir came and went, punctuating the conspicuously wilder landscape that had taken over from the irregularly shaped fields and graceful hillsides. Lunch in my belly, I left the reservoir's side with my legs in seemingly good shape and in a better frame of mind, noticing as I clambered over one stone sile that I was finally leaving the farms behind. Between Cowling and Hebden Bridge lay eleven miles of moorland now branded as 'Brontë Country' as it was here that the famous literary sisters wrote such novels as *Jane Eyre*, *The Tenant of Wildfell Hall* and, of course, *Wuthering Heights*. The latter has always been one of my favourite novels. I find it deeply modern in its cruel pessimism, layering of variously unreliable narrators and an air of barely restrained lustful longing. *Wuthering Heights* quite possibly says more about Emily Brontë's psychology than the society in which she lived, but I still wanted to see those famous moors. Quoth Emily:

'"Wuthering" being a significant provincial adjective, descriptive of the atmospheric tumult to which its station is exposed, in stormy weather. Pure, bracing ventilation they must have up there, at all times, indeed: one may guess the power of the north wind, blowing over the edge, by the excessive slant of a few, stunted firs at the end of the house; and by a range of gaunt thorns all stretching their limbs one way, as if craving alms of the sun.'[4]

I was not disappointed. Expecting only to see a landscape typical of the bleak, wild places described in Emily's novel, I didn't anticipate that, in the midst of a hilly plain called 'Withins Height', I'd encounter the remains of a small farmhouse whose aspect, if not architecture, may have inspired its creator. A plaque laid there by the Brontë Society, in somewhat equivocal language, pays homage to this remnant of literary archaeology. Apart from an odd row of shacks that I'd passed on the way to the Height, each equipped with water butts and small chimneys, (refuges for shepherds or peat-cutters?) this was one of the only signs of human habitation for miles.

The weather seemed determined to add to the melancholy atmosphere of the extraordinarily flat, bleak moorland all around. Low mist began to roll in all around me as I followed a sinuous path of flagstones between the reeds and heather. Bird calls and the perpetual thrum of the wind in my ears provided an accompaniment to the percussion of my footsteps. Aside from a picnicking couple at the Withins Height house, I passed nobody bar groupings of stalwart sheep. Quite suddenly I stopped, realising that, if someone had blindfolded me and spun me round I would have had no idea which direction I'd come from and which way I was going. The views were identical. As the mist thickened to fog, I could see no further than twenty or thirty yards ahead of me. Oddly, the effect was soothing, rather than worrying – meditative, even.

I was beginning to lose track of time when I felt the trail begin to descend towards the three Walshaw Reservoirs. I ran out of the fog and back into sunshine and sustained myself with a home-made flapjack that one of the Three Peaks race marshals had given Sorrell a couple of days ago at Pen-y-Ghent. It was one of the most delicious things I've ever tasted. That said, I was extremely calorie-deficient and anything sugary tasted like manna from heaven. The small act of kindness in giving me this restorative treat made me more certain than ever that people are generally helpful and appreciative. This is one of the most encouraging theories I was able to confirm on my trip. Mean-spirited people remain in a distinct minority, even though I suspect a fair few of them congregate in London, where I live.

Hours of climbing and descending exhausted me by the time I reached the wooded valley at Heptonstall and got momentarily lost amongst the tangle of forest trails surrounding the tributary stream that flows down to Hebden Bridge. A local and his dog provided a guide to the right way across the river and I trudged up another steep trail and through a field to a road along which was strung a row of houses known as Blackshaw Head. It was there that I finally ran out of both daylight and energy. It would have been nice to reach that day's target, Hebden Bridge, a couple of miles to the south, but the sun was performing a colourful display as it sank below the horizon and I'd simply run out of steam.

Of course, because I'd told Sorrell I'd make it to Hebden Bridge, that's where she was waiting and, when I finally got a message to her, I knew I'd have another shivery wait for a pick-up. Still, I'd raised my spirits, persevered, enjoyed most of the running and passed through some unforgettable land-scapes. One more stretch of Pennine Way stood between me and the B-roads of the Midlands – it would have to pull out all the stops to impress me more than the 200-plus Pennine miles I'd already covered.

MILES RUN: 685; MILES REMAINING: 415

1. Christopher McDougall *Natural Born Heroes* Profile Books, London 2015 p265.

2. https://en.wikipedia.org/wiki/Pen-y-ghent

3. BOAT – Byway Open to All Traffic; RUPP – Road Used as a Public Path. For further elucidation of the many confusing definition of public rights of way and access see http://www.iprow.co.uk/ (website of the Institute of Public Rights of Way and Access Management – things are so much easier in Scotland!)

4. Emily Brontë *Wuthering Heights*, Everyman edition 1991, p2.

Section Three

ROUTE: CANALS

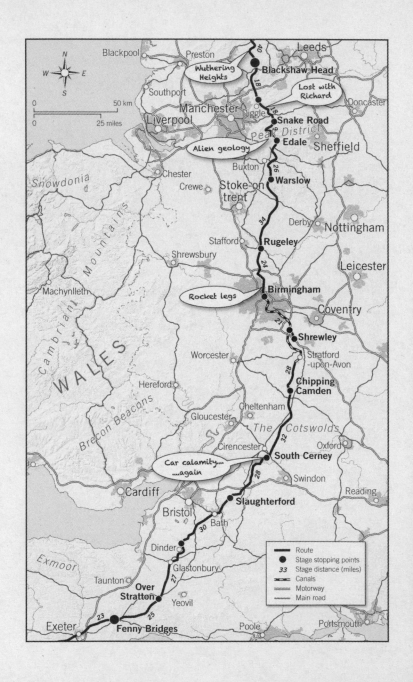

BLACKSHAW HEAD TO EDALE

I thought I'd experienced fog and plenty of it but this was something else entirely. An icy, static, ominous white wall of moisture, filling the lungs with a thick and strangely chemical sensation, like dry ice. This was definitely the kind of fog that giant black dogs emerge from, fangs dripping with blood.

It was just as well we'd made the decision that morning to skip a little more of the tougher trail in favour of a stretch of the canal between Hebden Bridge and Todmorden. My legs were leaden, stiff, sore and unyielding. I felt like a mummy, swathed in unravelling ribbons of fog, staggering down the hillside towards the valley. I rationalised my decision by telling myself that there was little point in running through beautiful countryside if you can't see it.

The Pennine Way intersects with the Hebden valley about a mile west of the town proper, which felt advantageous for another reason – there would be less people to see how pathetic my gait had become. A vicious zigzag of pathway cut steeply down to the valley where a road, a river, a railway and a canal all followed the contour lines. Braking on this descent was especially painful. Once on the level ground of the main road I found the Rochdale Canal with relative ease and felt immediate relief as my legs settled into a predictable and economical stride.

The canal was walled-in by old converted mills and factories in places and ran in tandem with the river Hebden Water for a while. I could hear but not see the whoosh of trains on the wooded track uphill and to my right. There were a few walkers and cyclists but, once the working populace were in their offices, shops and factories after 9 am, it quietened down for the morning. Around seven miles of canal lay between me and Walsden, where I'd decided would be the best place to rejoin the Pennine Way, via an intersecting footpath.

Oddly, the fog that I'd passed through in the high fields wasn't present in the depths of the valley and I got some good footage of the well-maintained and historic strip of canal. Built in the 1790s, it is unusually broad and boasts 91 locks over the 32-mile extent between Manchester and Sowerby Bridge (narrowboat users had better not be in a hurry). At one such lock, over which passed a small road bridge, I encountered a gaggle of white geese who did not take kindly to my appearance. As they honked and hissed their way towards me, I lured them under the bridge, then ran across the top to rejoin the canal behind them. The subterfuge gave me a disproportionate sense of achievement.

Finding the footpath to take me back up to the Pennine Way proved something of a challenge as I first stomped up a steep suburban street, located a bridleway, abandoned it as unhelpful and was eventually forced to follow a drystone wall up through the fog which was still drifting across the high moors. I reached Warland Reservoir some thirty minutes of bewilderment later and was able to run again along its long straight edge, following the 375-metre contour line towards White Holme Reservoir. The fog had thinned a little to drifts of mist blown on a strong westerly wind as I made my way round to yet another reservoir near Greenhalgh, in time for lunch as a serendipitously situated pub, the White House. The level stretches had done wonders for my legs which now pumped out steady miles. That it would all go a little bit wrong in the afternoon was perhaps inevitable. There seems to be a natural equilibrium of good and bad fortune in multi-day ultra-running.

Somewhere between Greenhalgh and Blackstone Edge I lost my way. There were two huge landmarks with which to orientate myself – Green Withins Reservoir, which I could see down in the valley far below me, and the M62, which I could just make out some way ahead. The problem was that I couldn't understand why the trail, which at this point was unmarked, seemed to be heading me down towards the reservoir, rather than towards the motorway. I knew I had to cross the motorway via a footbridge and didn't want to hit the road several miles too soon then have to run along the hard shoulder or potentially unnavigable, verge or, worse, play Frogger again with rush hour commuter traffic.

I'd somehow missed the sudden right-angle turn that the Pennine Way makes along a bridleway between Lydgate and the amusingly named Dick Slack. I think I may have been heading down something called Broad Head Drain but I'm not entirely sure. All I know is that once I decided to give up on bridleways and trails that all appeared to lead me in the wrong direction, I ignored all marked routes and headed for high ground. For once, I used my compass and the landscape to navigate, heading as the crow flies over boulders and springy heather to locate the shattered ridge of dark rock called Blackstone Edge. I probably lost about 45 minutes making the wrong guesses so it was a relief to get back on track.

From the Edge I could see the M62's constant stream of huge trucks, coaches and cars and was glad I'd not risked hurling myself across it. It felt peculiar to be picking my way alongside a black gritstone escarpment looking down at this conduit of modernity.

The trail fitted the map's criteria of 'no visible path' down to the motorway so I ended up following the fence, although it seemed that many other walkers had done the same thing, as evidenced by sections of muddy boot-prints and discarded litter. Eventually, I met a stretch of visible trail arriving from the left with two hikers strolling along it – probably locals. The bridge over the motorway forded a roaring river of vehicles streaming east and west. Then appeared a radio mast, another road and more wind and mist as the moors reasserted themselves once again. There would be no towns or villages of any sort for thirty miles. Instead, I'd have to end each day at a suitable road crossing, choosing between five A-roads or the village of Edale. Running beyond a road crossing near the end of a day would commit me to reaching the next one before the sun went down (or turning back which, as you'll have gathered by now, I don't like to do).

About ten minutes after crossing the motorway and A672, I reached a fence with a marker denoting the most easterly point in Lancashire, which was odd as I'd assumed I was still in West Yorkshire. Doubly odd as Google Maps shows Lancashire as stopping significantly north of the M62. There was also a sign telling me I was entering the Marston Moor Estate, administered by the National Trust. The Battle of Marston Moor, fought during the English Civil War in 1644 between the Royalists and Parliamentarians, was the largest ever held on British soil and helped cement Oliver Cromwell's leadership credentials. I didn't know this at the time, my knowledge of English History being shaky at best and so ran with grumpy ignorance over the graves of countless Englishmen as I headed south.

I say grumpily as, unaccountably, this was one of those days where I'd just woken up in a bad mood. There was nothing concrete to point to as the source of this angst, perhaps just cumulative fatigue coupled with how far I was from finishing compared to my initial goals. The spate of getting lost before lunch hadn't helped my belligerent attitude and I do remember apologising to Sorrell for being a little more brusque than usual. I also remember telling my handheld camera that if the Pennine Way annoyed me again today, I'd find a way to punch it!

Fortunately, this didn't happen. The moor was suitably bleak, flat and desolate, befitting its status as an epic battle-field. The heather and peat was dotted with marshy ponds, whose surfaces were perpetually rippled by the relentless winds that scoured the plain. A rocky trail quickly rose to a high limestone escarpment at Close Moor, which offered a spectacular view of the Castleshaw Reservoirs to the south-west. The irregular chunks of rock near the cliff edge provided another chance to practise my rock-hopping skills as I ran. I turned to see a mountain biker speedily merrily along the trail and shouted a question: 'I'm on the Pennine Way, yeah?' I think he nodded in the affirmative.

My mood improved slightly as blue skies dominated the afternoon and the endless wind proved more cooling than chilling. Wind-rounded tors of limestone punctuated the cliff edge as I paused to look down over the valley between Diggle and Denshaw. It was a glorious sight and I was reminded how fortunate I was to have the time, good health and ability to run there. I was then further rewarded by a continual descent along a mostly visible and grassy path with occasional finger posts to reassure me that I was indeed still on the Pennine Way. In fact, below Diggle, I was also entering the Peak District, so-named for its comparatively high aspect. A little further south I'd pass into Derbyshire, though I'd never have known it – county borders meaning little to the Pennine Way.

My ankle was aching by 5 pm, nagging me insistently but without severe pain. As I headed back down to the road, I vowed to try to complete the Way the following day. It would be a tough day of twenty to twenty-five hard miles but it seemed possible, injuries notwithstanding. When the blue rectangle of Brunclough Reservoir and the equally blue glint of Sorrell's Renault Clio made themselves known below me, I gratefully decided to stop. Hopefully I'd awake with a more positive attitude on the 30th September.

Sorrell had arranged for me to meet one of the ultra-runners I'd contacted some time before the run, Richard Durance, a highly experienced veteran of races including the Marathon des Sables and Caballo Blanco Ultramarathon. I was a little nervous about meeting such an experienced long-distance veteran (he had knocked off over 100 marathons) and hoped I'd be on top form.

Richard and I weren't due to meet until around lunch-time, which was just as well as the 30th September started off in thick, freezing fog, the densest I had yet encountered. The path through the section of Pennine Way between the A62 and Wessenden Moor was well defined but I could only see around twenty feet in front of me. I had about ten miles running to do before lunchtime and a giant white expanse surrounded me as I ran along a thin gravel path, and then a peaty trail which quickly gave way to well-placed flagstones. The fog was so dense that I nearly ran straight into the water of the first small reservoir on the accurately titled Black Moss. Its rippling waters vanished into white nothingness. The temperature, appropriate to the season for once, kept my pace up as grouse scattered and clucked out of my way and I focused intently on not slipping on the wet stones. My legs could do without further trauma, although my ankle, for once, was mute.

The footpath seemed to lead me along the wrong side of this reservoir and away from the correct Pennine Way, leaving me with a three-way choice – continue on which-ever way this new footpath was taking me, double back or attempt to draw a perpendicular route and meet up with the path I'd meant to take. You can probably guess that I did the most dangerous thing and took the third option, using my compass to point me due north-east and heading off into a cloud. For once, my gambit paid off and I found the flagstones again after about five minutes. As it happened, had I continued on that other trail, it would have led me to a different crossing with the A635 and then back to the Pennine Way around four miles later. Fate seemed intent on being a little kinder to me that morning than yesterday. The flagstones began to descend and I found myself easily managing 8-minute miles down to Wessenden Reservoir. An impressively steep valley contained this and Wessenden Head Reservoirs and it should prove easy to find my way around them and up to the next A-road.

I say easy as nothing in ultra-running is ever as easy as you might hope. I followed narrow gravel trails alongside the southern side of the valley, then muddy paths through knee-high bracken, my feet squelching now, wet with accumulated moisture from the fog and foliage. My lower legs were whipped by fronds and sharp grasses as I crossed and re-crossed a small feeder stream, complete with impressively stepped miniature waterfalls. I crossed it one time too many, apparently, because I ended up making a short detour up and back down a tributary valley. This required a weir crossing and a careful dash along quite badly eroded paths back down to the intended route. The path rose above the first Wessenden reservoir then crossed a few fields where piles of new flagstones had been airdropped, ready for laying by some hardy landscapers.

Despite the fog and the cold, I was enjoying myself. I'd slept well in the Diggle Travelodge the night before and sleep is definitely the best 'secret weapon' in a multi-day runner's armoury. The latter part of my morning route coincided with something called the Kirklees Way, a 73-mile circuit of West Yorkshire and occasionally part of the unusual 'wineathlon' schedule of booze-fuelled ultra races, inspired perhaps by France's famous Marathon du Medoc[1] where runners can sample local vintages and cheeses at every checkpoint. There was not so much as a half a Tetley

Bitter waiting for me though as I made my way to the road
and a quick consultation with my support car. Given the
fog, it seemed sensible to plan each little stage of the day.
My father would be meeting Richard, Sorrell and I at the
car park by Torside Reservoir in about an hour's time, if
all went well. He hoped to get a couple of good quadcopter
shots if the fog let up in the afternoon.

So it proved, fortunately. The blue sky was decorated
with huge white cumulus clouds as I charged down the steep-
walled valley north of Crowden. The trail rose along narrow
peaty pathways, climbing to 375 metres at the incredibly
precipitous Black Tor, where the contour lines met at a
dangerous edge, protruding blocks of limestone standing
like watchtowers along the cliff. I was high enough to see the
fells south of Torside, rendered a misty blue by atmospheric
perspective, the last peaks of the Pennine Way heading
south. In a vicious wind, it was all I could do to remain
rooted securely on the Tor to take photos. Remarkably, as
the wind fortuitously blew me away from the edge, a pair
of hands appeared grasping the limestone and a young man,
unassisted by ropes, pulled himself over the lip of the tor and
then, dressed in nothing more than jeans and a thin anorak,
walked calmly past me. I was too stunned to ask what he was
doing and, in any case, my ears had become wind tunnels of
roaring noise. I suppose statistically, there's always someone
out there crazier than you (unless maybe you're that French
bloke who scales skyscrapers without ropes).[2]

After enjoying the view from the heights, I picked my
way carefully down to Torside, where I discovered a
lakeside forest trail. The compacted pine needles made a
fast and springy surface for running as I sped down to the
A-road, dam and car park. My support crew were waiting
and Richard (and lunch) were scheduled. My foul mood of
yesterday had vanished.

Mr Durance turned out to be a friendly, lithe fellow in his

early sixties, bald as a turtle but keen, agile and energetic. He had many somewhat rambling anecdotes about ultra-running, having got into the sport through the unusual route of, as he puts it 'being the world's worst footballer' and injuring his eye. Perfect vision being less essential to long-distance runners than footballers, Richard (at the insistence of a friend) took part in the very first London Marathon in 1981, when there were only 6,255 finishers, around a fifth of the today's field. From that moment, he'd caught the bug and proceeded to enter race after race, going ultra when the marathon novelty wore off and eventually competing in the aforementioned MDS and other arduous events. Sadly, many of his stories didn't quite make it onto film as the radio microphone I'd prepared for him didn't seem to work (I'm not the most technically able of film-makers) but enough remains 'in the can' to attest to his positive attitude and energy. He certainly kept me going during that difficult period immediately after lunch.

We climbed a steep trail to the top of Bleaklow Head, running when we were able, 'bimbling along' (as Richard puts it) when the ascent became too demanding. At one point a small bird seemed keen to act as a mascot, hopping along the path ahead of us as if leading us on. I was engrossed by Richard's tales of endurance (I avoided the obvious pun involving his name) and determination and impressed by how, he told me, he had recently taken a bit of a competitive back seat to support his wife Penny in her own charity-driven race running (she recently completed a marathon a month for a year, aged 60). I got the impression that nothing would stop Richard running completely, however, bar drastic ill-health or life's ultimate 'cut-off time' being called. I hope that I will remain as keen and vigorous as Richard is over the next few decades.

I was so entertained by his company, and found myself opening up with my own tales of misadventure and recent struggle, that I clearly wasn't paying enough attention to my map. Signposts were rather rare 633 metres up on the hillside and somehow we ended up running a near-circle through black peaty or sandy stretches of moor, stopping to try to get our bearings by the remains of some sort of shack-like structure. Alfred Wainwright, who wrote early definitive walking guides to the Lade District and Pennines, wrote of this area that 'lives have been lost on Bleaklow', a simple but stark statement of how dangerous these high hill landscapes can be in inclement weather.

Fortunately, for Richard and I the sun shone brightly and warmly and the wind, although persistent, was not appalling. That said, we did get lost. I can't even begin to tell you where we went wrong but, after about an hour of meandering we located the trail again and headed down Hern Clough, the local sandstone blown to actual sand in places, which made me feel a little like I was running between dunes down towards a distant beach.

My father had prepared an impressive shot of the Devil's Dyke, a straight watercourse along sandy soil down to the nicely named Snake Road (more prosaically, the A57). Richard and I paused briefly to let him set the buzzing drone camera off and then raced one another (not seriously, yet with a noticeable increase in speed) down to where Sorrell had set up an end-of-day shot of her own.

It was past 5 pm and I had to make one of those difficult decisions about whether to go on or stop for the day. Richard would probably have joined me if I'd decided to continue but with around seven miles still to go to Edale and tricky terrain ahead, it seemed wise to stop. We shook hands and parted. It was most definitely the right decision.

Alone once more, I set off from Snake Road the following morning, not as early as I'd have liked, given the vagaries of hotel breakfast times, but still before 9 am. I was excited by the prospect of completing the Pennine Way. It had proven so much more challenging than in my naivety I had imagined. In Scotland it's all too easy to think we have a monopoly on spectacular scenery with epic lochs and hundreds of mountains. However, the West Highland Way, beautiful though it is, winds along the valleys between the Munros. In England, the trails more frequently go over the top of the highest available peaks. So I didn't expect an easy morning on the 1st October but I did still hope to get to Edale in plenty of time for lunch.

The day began with thick fog, if anything more dense and impenetrable than the previous morning. The route from Snake Road began easily enough with a fairly straight set of flagstones extending across level moorland. My left knee for some reason had begun to send fiery shots of pain up my lower thigh, an injury I'd not detected at all the previous day. I hadn't slept much either but all in all, despite these ailments, I was quite enjoying the run, finding myself becoming a little introspective. Perhaps when all you can see in front of you is a white wall of nothingness, it forms an excellent screen upon which to project things.

I was thinking in particular about my parents, especially my mother, who hadn't been very well of late, with gastric pains and nausea, and who was waiting for the results of various tests. Both her and my dad had always been very supportive of my unlikely activities whether it was distance-running, writing stories or making strange short films. They seemed to realise why these things were important to me and why I would never be happy in a nine-to-five office job that didn't engage the creative or exploratory parts of my nature. I feel sorry for would-be explorers, artists or sportspeople who don't have that bedrock of familial support – it is a vital component as the fragile sense of self is developing. The outrageous levels of self-belief you need to succeed in sport or the arts (or really in any ambitious endeavour) are built in childhood and adolescence. I've always had that support. It felt important to record my gratitude to camera now, as I trotted through a misty and mysterious landscape. Especially so as Sorrell had left us the previous night and my father was taking over support and camera duties once more.

Occasional quizzical sheep and the forlorn calls of wetland birds were my only companions as I ran on, pausing to get my bearings at a ramshackle cairn on the top of Mill Hill (545 metres). There a stone route-marker with the familiar acorn logo and a gold arrow, headed me in the right direction. Broadly speaking, my route that morning should describe a large 'W', following the lay of the land and the precipitous cliff edges of Kinder Scout, the last significant peak I would climb before Edale.

The sun's sphere could just be seen trying to push through veils of cloud as I began to climb the broken, rocky trails to Kinder. The effect of the shattered rock and protruding edges of the Sandy Heys cliffs emerging out of banks of mist was spooky but picturesque. The wind, howling at near gale force, was driving me towards the cliff edge this time so I erred on the side of caution and kept at least a dozen feet away. What awaited me at the top would exceed my wildest expectations.

Kinder Scout is the name given to a high plateau (over 600 metres) surrounded on all sides by steep cliffs and grassy slopes descending around 100 to 150 metres to the moors and valleys below. Once privately owned, it was the site of a famous 'mass trespass' of around 400 ramblers in protest against the lack of access rights to open spaces, the culmination of a lengthy and frustrating campaign. This act of civil disobedience, which included scuffles with the Duke of Devonshire's gamekeepers and resulted in several arrests and jail sentences for participants, contributed significantly to the Right to Roam becoming enshrined in law.[3]

It did seem a fitting backdrop to revolutionary protest as I rose through what now seemed more like clouds than fog, clumps and veils of it drifting across the plateau and revealing or concealing what lay ahead. Once at the top of Sandy Heys, I was able to run, carefully, on hard-packed dirt and blown grit pebbles that resembled the industrial salt used to prevent roads from freezing over. The gritstone that formed the top of the plateau had been sculpted into dramatic, sometimes biomorphic shapes by the perpetual winds – literally sandblasted by eroded particles carried by the wind, as well as by driving rain and centuries of freezing and thawing conditions.

That morning was relatively warm for Kinder, I suspect. Although the wind, intermittent visibility and my acting-up knee troubled me a little, what I chiefly felt as I ran on was wonder and awe. From heavily striated stacks of rock to overhanging precipices to rounded Henry Moore-like natural artworks, there was plenty of unusual geology to admire as I wound my way around the western and southern edge of the plateau. I forded Kinder Downfall, a sometimes dramatic waterfall plunging a hundred metres down to a river flowing towards the reservoir a mile to the west. It clearly hadn't rained much over the past few weeks on Kinder, so the falls were more of a trickle today.

Far more impressive was the sight of the reservoir and green valley below with fast-flowing rivers of cloud passing over them, as viewed from as close to the edge as I dared get. I took a lot of photographs and shot many scenic video clips. This undoubtedly slowed me down but it wouldn't do to pass through this stunning region without recording it for the film. In the end, my enthusiasm got the better of my (admittedly non-expert) route-finding skills and I missed the path down something known as the Swine's Back and then on to the Jacob's Ladder path. Instead, I continued east as far as Crowden Clough and in so doing passed through the strangest region yet.

Ahead of me was a landscape of flat sandy earth punctuated with large, rounded boulders and towers of gritstone, almost like a field of creatures standing as sentinels, guarding the way forward. Whereas I'd encountered forms reminiscent of Henry Moore earlier, this was a landscape as envisioned by Salvador Dali, Yves Tanguy or perhaps a piece of landscape art by Anthony Gormley, whose 'field' of tiny terracotta figures it somewhat resembled. On my map these formations were designated the 'wool packs' because they also look a little like agricultural bales. I ran over one formation without paying much attention only to look down and realise I was racing over the tops of towers a dozen feet high with gaps of one to three feet between them. A last-second instinctive leap averted disaster – my childhood-learned rock-hopping skills saved me once more.

The urge to use my gimbal to get swooping Steadicam-like sequences was making me run some sections faster than was perhaps wise but at least my knee had quietened down a little. I stopped to get my bearings and saw a hillwalker making her way up a steep trail from the valley below. She smiled as she passed and this reassured me that, although fearsomely steep, the way she had taken was a reasonable route.

I scrambled down and found it slow-going but not dangerous. Unfortunately, it also required me to make a steep yet controlled descent on fragile legs. Suddenly, presumably on one of my jumps from rock to rock, I pulled something in my left thigh. This hurt like hell whenever I had to use the muscle as a brake, something I had to do constantly between the top of Kinder Scout and the Vale of Edale below. The pain got worse and worse and quickly rose beyond the level of inconvenience to something potentially disastrous. I didn't want to admit it, heading down to Edale, but it was probably going to end that day's running, unless it improved significantly over lunch.

Some pain reaches its own level and stays there, allowing you to manage it. My thigh sprain did not seem to find its plateau and kept getting worse, even as I hobbled through a grassy and very pretty valley towards the village, trying to turn my grimaces of pain into smiles for passing hikers.

I'd managed to message my father, although we'd had no phone reception for most of the morning. I knew he'd be waiting on the trail somewhere with a shot prepared. Down in the valley, the glorious sunlight and verdant greenery belied the season. A local train service rattled through the valley and there were many walkers and hikers out.

I was a little surprised, therefore, when I made it all the way into the village without seeing my father. Perhaps he had become bored waiting for me and found somewhere to eat. There sat the car, parked with a few others outside the local school and The Old Nag's Head public house. I'd made it, but the welcoming committee was AWOL. I tried my phones – no reception on either – then went into the pub, borrowed a pen and left a note on the car windscreen. This was becoming worrying – had he slipped and fallen on some unwise attempt to find a high vantage point?

Fortunately, after leaving word at the pub, café and a local shop that I was waiting for him, Dad wandered back into the town square, exasperated. He had waited for several hours at a beauty spot on the wrong trail. The pub's signage seemed to suggest the Way started from the back of its car park. An official fingerpost dad hadn't noticed (to be fair it was in shadow and relatively low-key) told otherwise.

I was perfectly sanguine about the mix-up, however. I'd had a nice rest, some food and plenty of time to think. My thigh wasn't going to magically heal itself – it needed a few hours off. Dad and I agreed that the rest of the afternoon would be better spent poring over his large-scale AA map-book and plotting a route through the tiny B-roads south of Edale towards Birmingham.

We sat in the beer garden of The Old Nag's Head and got our maps out. I made a list of all the villages I'd pass through, so Dad would know which of the unnamed and unnumbered roads I'd be on at any given time. In honour of the final county I'd traverse on my adventure, I drank a pint of the Cornish ale Doom Bar. We sat in the sun. It was restful, a rare respite from the hardships of ultra-running. One might even think we were on holiday.

MILES RUN: 730; MILES REMAINING: 370

---

1. http://www.wineathlon.co.uk/ or http://www.marathondumedoc.com/ but don't say you weren't warned!

2. Alain Robert: https://en.wikipedia.org/wiki/Alain_Robert

3. http://kindertrespass.com provides a useful summary of the events of 1932.

EDALE TO BIRMINGHAM

Edale was a significant milestone – the end of the Pennine Way, which had felt at times like it was trapping me in a complex tangle around the spine of England. I had sometimes felt like I might never escape its patchwork of fields, moors and fells. I'd been lost more often than I'd ever expected, had compromised and taken short cuts. Everything had taken twice the time I'd estimated in my pre-planning ignorance. In its last few miles, the Way had brought me extraordinary beauty but also inexplicable pain. The thigh really worried me – this was not an injury I'd ever experienced before. Knee pain was so omnipresent, even before The Long Run, that I paid it as little heed as the common cold. But a deep pain within my thigh was new and perplexing. Perhaps I was just wearing myself away by degrees. What would be the consequence if I had to pull out of this endeavour now?

I would feel like an abject and utter failure. My master plan to use this run to reinvigorate my sense of self would collapse.

On a practical note, giving up halfway would leave me with half a film (i.e. no film at all) and writing a book about the experience would be pointless. Nobody wants to read about a man running from John O'Groats to the middle of England and then giving up. I had invested almost everything I had into this film, both metaphorically and literally. The additional days added to the project were rapidly eating up what remained of my redundancy pot but stopping now, with nothing to sell at the end of it, could ruin me.

The consequences of failing hardly bore thinking about but consider them I did as I took that first tentative step away from Dad's camera on the morning of the 2nd October.

A shamble became a shuffle. Which developed into a slow jog. After about a mile I could finally admit that I was running. Not without some discomfort, but running nonetheless. I could postpone those gloomy thoughts for now and watch the villages crawl by. The relief was palpable.

Sparrowpit, Peak Forest, Old Dam, Smalldale, Hargate Wall, Millers Dale. I'd already realised our maps contained only a fraction of the roads that existed in reality, so we'd constructed this list of places from online sources, expanded to the maximum size on our phones to reveal the hidden detail. Little white roads like veins criss-crossed the countryside, linking farms to villages. Few of these roads had names or numbers, most of them were single-track and some of them lacked evident passing places.

Nevertheless, we'd left The Old Nag's Head confident that this new method would work – as long as my dad leapfrogged me relatively closely and stopped on any road junctions where he wasn't sure which way I'd go. At least, that was the theory and it seemed a sound one.

As we drove back into Edale the following morning, the atmosphere was again performing a dramatic display. Large white banks of cloud had coalesced in the lower valleys, leaving vacant blue sky above. Brilliant sunlight illuminated these clouds, making them glow vividly. We were witnessing a temperature inversion, so-called when layers of warm air trap colder air beneath them, holding in the moisture, which forms thick mist. I remember witnessing one of these when several friends and I climbed Ben Nevis in 1990. Eschewing the tourist path, we took the rocky arête linking Carn Mor Dearg (1,220 metres) with its more famous neighbour. As we rose above the arête, waterfalls of cloud poured over it. All around us, mountain tops emerged from a thick eiderdown of cloud.

Edale was surrounded by mist, deep in the middle of one of these troughs of cloud. As I ran south towards Sparrowpit, the road ahead of me had become a giant blaze of white light, like a 1990s special effect (perhaps an abduction scene in *The X-Files*). The clouds were acting like a reflector, bouncing and diffusing light in all directions. On the narrow, winding roads I had to exercise extreme caution as I knew cars coming towards me would not be able to see me in time to react. Eventually I rose out of the clouds and could admire their beauty from above.

That morning I was experiencing a cocktail of pain – aches in both calves, the now-muted throb in my thigh, a sore right foot and the occasional flash of fiery pain up my lower back. It's likely the latter two ailments were caused by me changing my gait to accommodate the pulled muscle in my thigh. The body is remarkably adaptive but not infallible. As ever though, I had no choice but to continue. I did allow myself to intersperse periods of walking, even on straights; perhaps 30 per cent walking to 70 per cent running. I doubt I managed better than 10-minute miles. I did some mental arithmetic and concluded that even if I walked all day, I could cover twenty to twenty-five miles. If I managed 10 to 12-minute minute miles on average, that worked out at 5–6 miles per hour. Over just six hours of running I could accomplish thirty-six miles at best. I told myself I wanted to finish within ten to twelve days, perhaps 14 as an absolute maximum. Such inner deals are easy to negotiate and difficult to realise.

Coming down a winding hillside road, I found footpaths short-cutting through the fields and eagerly limped down them. I played a game of 'catch me if you can' with two local cyclists, who took the long way round and passed me several times on the road. Distractions like this and the clouds lazily filling the valleys helped me ignore the pain. It helped too that our navigation plan seemed to be working – Dad set up camera positions and shots ahead of me which I variously walked or jogged through. Having the camera there made me loathe to walk more than necessary until I realised that this kind of adversity was part of the story and if I had to walk, my audience would understand why.

So I walked. Revising my estimates for walking, I realised I could do 12–15-minute miles and therefore cover 3 to 4 miles per hour. Eighteen to twenty-four in a six-hour day. The ultimate mile count would be somewhere between my walking and running calculations. I had no end point in mind for the day – there seemed no point given that it was touch-and-go whether I remained on my feet at all.

Still, faulty mechanism though I was, I made it to Miller's Dale, a distance of thirteen miles, by noon. Our plan then was for me to follow an off-road route, the Monsal Trail, through a picturesque river valley we had driven past the previous day. From a high viewpoint on the road above, we were able to look down on the Trail and I knew there was a potentially glorious and cinematic shot to be had of the trees, steep hillsides, river, ornate bridge and a row of old stone cottages. We decided that my dad would find his way there and wait for me as I ran the trail. I'd call him just as I was about to emerge from the trees below and he'd get me running over the bridge and past the houses.

Dad and I sat on a retired train station platform at Miller's Dale and had a quick packed lunch with real coffee from a food van while a family on bicycles prepared for an excursion nearby. The trail ran the course of a discontinued railway line to the west, then followed the river as far as Bakewell. I wasn't planning to run to its end point though. I'd spotted a quarry, at Topley Pike, where I guessed I might be able to head up towards the A5270. In this part of England, avoiding A-roads might prove impossible but I had a notion that the more digits there were after 'A', the less busy the road might be. I concede that as a theory, this is less than scientifically rigorous but at least my father and I had agreed on a course of action. Generally, any plan, however naïve, is better than no plan at all.

The Monsal Trail rang a vague bell in my memory. I had visited Monsal Head with a film school friend, Rob (not the California-dwelling one) in about 1997 and we'd had a lovely walk and a couple of pints in an ancient pub part-constructed from a stone cowshed (booths were hung with the names of the animals that had once dwelt there; somehow this avoided being corny). But Monsal Head wasn't on my route, unfortunately, being a few miles away to the east. Still, I expected the run to be pleasant and quiet. So it proved, occasional cyclists or walkers passing me but a peacefulness pervading the verdant channel, which occasionally passed through echoing railway tunnels and eventually cut between impressive cliffs, the A6 lurking somewhere above. I saw birds of prey wheeling in the thermals above the cliffs. Soon I was really enjoying the run, my leg pain having diminished considerably. Then it all came to a perplexing halt.

I was about to cross a bridge over the river when I saw a fence had been erected there with a 'Private Land' sign and a warning about trespassing. A fingerpost nearby was lacking a finger, which seemed to have been torn off. I followed a flight of steps down to another path which ran alongside the River Wye. I called my father and told him that I wouldn't be running over that picturesque bridge after all as some landowner had blocked the route. The downside of a 'permissive path' perhaps? Renovation work? I found out much later that the trail did indeed end at that bridge and the fingerpost was to be replaced but the effect at the time was more than a little worrying.

Dappled sunlight and the gentle trickling of the river made the diversion a pleasant one until the trail broadened to a gravel track and then a road and petered out in a car park. I followed the road round and eventually found the quarry. As I'd guessed, a footpath ran up its eastern edge. After telling my dad the new plan, I took this route. A few minutes later, I passed a couple of elderly walkers coming the other way. This boded well. The new trail became rocky and heavily vegetated, the quarry owners having fenced it off and paved it with fist-sized chunks of aggregate. They had also decorated this fence with signs warning of the dangers of 'Blasting' and, more worryingly 'Quicksand'. I waited for a sign warning of rattlesnakes. Fortunately, at no point did I encounter any of these dangers. What I did have to struggle through were lengthy regions of tall nettles. Stings were inevitable. My run was quickly reduced to a hopping jog as I found my way through the foliage and piles of scree. The gully deepened, its sides V-shaped and no more than thirty metres wide in places.

Strange birdcalls punctuated the afternoon as the path wound a little way up the side of the gully, around stunted trees and under dense canopies of leaves. I passed a plaque dedicated to Alan R. Reece,[1] an engineer renowned for inventing a landmine-detecting military vehicle, and then a cave, which seemed big enough for a family to reside within (perhaps a family of prehistoric bears).

The trail was leading me more west than I wanted but I had no choice but to follow it – climbing a 50-foot wall of scree did not seem sensible. Eventually, it widened out and reached a fence with a gate and a large public information sign. It turned out I'd been running through a SSSI (Site of Special Scientific Interest), designated such for its rare wildflowers and ferns. On the other side of the gate, sheep maintained the close-cropped grass and a copse of rowan trees provided colour, their red berries contrasting with the blue of the sky opening up ahead. The cliffs fell away and the gully reached a farm and then a main road. Serendipitously, although I'd hit the A5270 several miles west of where I'd intended, I was only half a mile from the turn-off to the B5053, which would take me due south to King Sterndale. I dashed along and across the main road, made the junction, and all but skidded to a surprised halt.

At the head of the B-road stood a large warehouse-like building with a car park and a sign proudly proclaiming Brierlow Bar Bookstore. It was so unexpected, I had to look inside. In truth, I can rarely pass a bookshop without investigating. It felt peculiar to wander round a civilised store while dressed in long-distance running gear so I didn't stay long – just long enough to spot a book of twentieth-century plays I wanted to get for my dad. He was thinking about writing one based on a collection of short stories he'd created about his time as a printer's apprentice in the 1960s. It's tricky to segue from ultra-running to shopping though, especially when you don't have your wallet with you. Fortunately, my dad drew up in the car park moments later, quite coincidentally. I bought him the book and we had a quick afternoon break. Our plan had modulated a little but hadn't failed. We revised the list of villages and I vowed to reach Warslow, a further ten miles south.

A mysterious jolt of energy took over, perhaps engendered by the fizzy apple juice I'd consumed. I even found myself running uphill, past the entrances to more quarries, looking into the low afternoon sun (eventually I resorted to sunglasses). The B-road was busier than I would have liked and not every driver gave me enough room in passing but I kept positive, amazed that I was able to run uphill at all this late in the day. Soon a sign announced 'Welcome to Staffordshire' and I immediately thought of the one thing I associated with the county – potteries (an Australian cousin and aunt are both talented potters). I hoped to reach Birmingham in a couple of days, where the eighteenth-century canal network had first been built, partly to help transport goods like Staffordshire pottery to the major cities.[2] For perhaps the first time I realised I was in the heartland of England – the Midlands – and heading ever south. Every so often you need a really straight road to convince you of your progress in a run like JOGLE.[3] The road to Warslow via Earl Sterndale and Lognor did not disappoint.

In a town called Wigginstall I saw a sign advertising 'Logs, Sticks and Hot Max'. I wondered who Hot Max was and whether he was popular.[4] The road inevitably rose and dipped – I was, after all, still in the Peak District National Park – and I realised I was doing a strange running limp to minimise the generic all-over ache emanating from my right leg. It reminded me of the old music hall performer Max Wall,[5] which makes me seem impossibly old. At times my gait almost resembled speed-walking, an Olympic sport I have always found intrinsically embarrassing. Now I just wanted to get the day over with but I was determined that Warslow, which I had originally meant to reach at the end of day *seventeen*, would not elude me.

As the sun sank low towards the horizon, throwing a golden light through the trees, I reached my destination, rejoicing in the sight of a Warslow sign and then a pavement. Somehow, despite my selection box of ailments, I'd managed over thirty-two miles that day.

The following day began in a now familiar morning mist and with something of a real chill in the air. I hoped this would encourage me to raise my speed towards my comfortable 9-minute mile pace. I do often run faster in cold weather and find the chill air on my exposed legs helps to numb whatever pain I'm feeling. I could actually see my breath as I headed out of Warslow and back onto the B5053.

Mid-morning, with the mist still clinging to the valleys, I began to pass a lot of bicycles, their riders wearing numbers revealing that they were in a race, possibly something called 'Change Gear – Moorlands', a 116-kilometre loop. Tired as I was, I tried to wave or shout a supportive 'Hi!' Ah, the fellowship of the cardiovascularly challenged! The race seemed quite spread out – no heads-down pelotons here but individuals struggling with the hills or pairs egging one another on. Our routes parted company after a few miles and I made my way towards the town of Froghall.

As it happened, Froghall felt more like a suburb than a village or isolated town. The map was beginning to reveal a thicker density of housing. Froghall lies on the A52 between Cheadle and Ipstones, which explains why I almost thought I'd hit Rugeley too soon. After Froghall came a town with the rather grandiose name of Kingsley Holt. Running up one street of semi-detached post-war villas, I saw my father talking with a local minister and spied a sign advertising a coffee morning. After three hours running, the notion of a sit-down and injection of caffeine seemed too good to pass up and as the minister waved me to a halt, I gratefully accepted an impromptu break. Several chocolates and a cup of instant coffee with a group of pensioners and housewives later, we thanked the Kingsley Holt Methodists and I headed on my way.

Remarkably, they'd also donated £25 to my charities, despite the fact that they were fundraising for their own causes. I'm not sure that leaving with more money than you'd brought is how coffee mornings are supposed to work but Dad and I were grateful. Not for the first time in recent history, I revised my assumptions about the godly. As a firm atheist, it's sometimes too easy to become cynical about the motives of the religious, but I can say with certainty that nothing but generosity of spirit motivated the kindness of those parishioners.

After Kingsley Holt and until lunch, things turned a little more rural. I began to feel deeply fatigued. I'd not had a good night's sleep and had dreamt a peculiar dream in which I shot myself in the head, then heard bystanders comment 'Well, he's made a right mess of that.' As I stopped by a field to change a memory card on one of my cameras, a herd of cows shuffled towards the gate, presumably expecting me to let them out somewhere. I found myself apologising aloud to them. It was going to be a long day.

The endless hills of the Peak District continued, rolling me over and down to villages nestling in the valleys. My fatigue deepened as the morning wore on and I began to have difficulty enunciating clearly and constructing proper sentences for the camera. I fantasised about the terrain levelling and some sort of flat fenland taking over but I was in the wrong part of England for that. At one such village, Hollington, I ground to a halt around 1 pm and had lunch (chilli con carne with rice and a Coke).

I managed only a pathetic shuffle immediately after lunch but, as ever, my gait improved as my digestion did the essential work of extracting all that food energy and moving it to the muscles. After an hour or so I crossed the A50 to Uttoxeter, with its two enormous JCB factories on both sides of the overpass. My plan was to make it another fifteen miles after lunch to Rugeley, not far from Birmingham, largely following the B5013.

This task was rendered a little tougher by the fact that pretty much everything below my waist and my upper back was now aching in a symphony of disapproval. I began to take some walking breaks to salve my feet and ankles. Usually when the pain gets particularly bad I can distract myself with the scenery but this part of the country offered little more than endless grassy fields, busy roads and hedgerows. A pretty tea shop appeared suddenly on one nondescript and straight stretch of B-road but turned out to be closed, which was probably just as well. Any temptation now could tip my weakness of will into a decision to call it a day. I stumbled on.

A field of impressive oak trees and the Blithfield Reservoir gave me the distraction I needed as Rugeley loomed ever closer. For some reason I began to see a lot of motorbikes whizzing past, including one vintage vehicle in whose sidecar sat a floppy-eared spaniel – a lot of Brummies appear to be bikers, even the canines. The western sky began to turn pink as I ran along a road that bisected the reservoir, as fishermen stood in waders or drifted by in rowing boats. Impressive light beams angled down from the clouds as I began to pick up a little end-of-day speed. I found a train station on the map to the north of Rugeley and fixed that in mind along with images of a hot bath and, as always, dinner.

Just outside the town I stopped to take a photo of a set of cooling towers on the horizon. In the foreground was a seemingly ordinary grass verge that someone had seeded with a variety of wildflowers – the contrast of industrial heritage and wild prettiness caught my eye and made me get my camera out. As it happened, the man who had planted those flowers saw me taking the photo and we chatted briefly about civic pride and about my mission. He said he'd actually met a long-distance walker doing a JOGLE a few months prior and let him camp in his garden. I found this quite reassuring. About a mile further on I found the station sign and took a call from my dad who was waiting in the car park. Amusingly, one of the next trains was leaving for London Euston and, as I staggered up to my dad, I joked that I was tempted to get on it. If this fatigue didn't let up, the remaining 400 miles or so could potentially finish me.

The 4th October brought sunshine and a pleasant surprise. In the station car park where I'd stopped the previous day was a sign advertising the 'Chase Heritage Trail', a walking route covering ten miles from Rugeley to Cannock Chase. This would allow me to avoid taking any of the big A-roads or B-roads out of town. I could cut from Chasetown over the A5 near Brownhills and take smaller roads via various hamlets to Kingstanding and the road to Birmingham.

It proved a little tricky to find the start of this trail. I was imagining something green and verdant, whereas the first part of it runs through the old centre of Rugeley, crosses a park with a small but noisy duckpond, heads across a major road, through another park and only then becomes trail-like. Consulting a local cyclist didn't help much; I found the trailhead by chance in the end. A plume from Rugeley's cooling towers produced virtually the only 'cloud' in the sky as I ran along a wide gravel path into a pine forest, suddenly passing a dozen mountain bikers tearing down a prepared cycle track alongside the main trail. The forest was remarkably pretty with a gently undulating terrain and tall trees through which the sun strobed as I ran. My fatigue lifted and the aches and pains temporarily dissipated. Ten-minute miles was about all I could manage but compared to the previous day's slog, that was near-Olympian.

The trail soon diverted into a number of different paths, some of which were marked with distances and difficulty warnings for cyclists. I consulted another local and took a high road that led me via a bit of open parkland to Brindley Heath where, remarkably, I found a heather-purpled moor, beds of bracken, small birch trees and variegated grasses. A little later I passed some fishing ponds where groups of men sat whiling away the afternoon, their rods balanced on metal supports like miniature cranes. The path took me through a muddy stretch of forest by the side of a busy road and then petered out into a suburban housing estate.

Urban orienteering is the phrase I'd use to best describe how I got to Birmingham from Cannock. This close to the city, the density of roads and housing was such that I resorted to following the blue dot on Google Maps on my phone. I reached Burntwood and was disappointed and frustrated to find I had no choice but to race along yet another busy B-road with no pavement. I picked my way along the verge and inter-mittently dashed along the tarmac, managing spurts of faster than 8-minute miles (easier to do when one's life is in danger).

I found respite on a small farm road leading to the village of Stonnall, where we'd arbitrarily decided to have lunch. This was perfectly timed, as I'd just hit the 'marathon wall' where

I'd burnt off all the glucose in my system and was moving into fat-burning mode – the transition is never pleasant. Kicking up autumn leaves along the pavement I dragged myself into the car park of the local pub, feeling a little disconsolate. I didn't think I'd reach Perry Park and the start of the Birmingham Canals in this state of mind and body.

A three-course pub lunch can work wonders. Although my dad and I waited an inexplicable time for our meals in the Old Swan, when they came, they were filling and well prepared. The landlady made a donation to my charities and all was forgiven. Despite the growing delay, I insisted on having dessert – chocolate cake warmed up with cream. I guess I was malingering, afraid of the pain that surely lay ahead. Plus I do really like chocolate cake.

Despite it being a sunny Sunday, I found the traffic tearing along the A452 unexpectedly heavy and fast-moving. A car roared past me every second. Fortunately there was pavement, or else my task would have been impossible. With food in my belly, I began to gain pace and energy and kept up a respectably 10-minute mile speed.

When I was ten miles outside of Birmingham, the sun a blazing ball of light overhead, the houses grew notably grander and more detached. I hit the leafy avenue of Kingstanding Road and something bizarre happened – a spate of 'rocket legs' took over and I began running faster and faster. It was only an hour since having lunch and I was flying along, entirely free from pain and managing sub-8-minute miles according to my Garmin. It would have been useful to take some blood and analyse the chemistry of what was going on within my body. I'm fairly certain it involved endorphins – a joyous feeling and a sensation of boundless energy contributed to the most purely enjoyable running I'd experienced since Kinder Scout. My father could scarcely keep up with me – he kept setting up his tripod only to find I was upon him before he was ready to hit 'record'.

Coming over the summit of a hilly section of Kingstanding Road, I could suddenly see Birmingham appearing in the haze beyond the distant trees. Towering office blocks and walls of shimmering glass felt as good to me then as the sight of the Emerald City to Dorothy. Those trees turned out to be the northern limit of Perry Park and, crossing a small bridge, I spotted a reflective strip of canal below me. I decided to run on the few hundred metres to Perry Park as I knew my support car was waiting there.

The park was bathed in the idyllic light of endorphins as I realised that I still had around three potential hours of daylight and I had all but reached my goal. We just had to start on the canals and find a road-crossing at which to stop. Dad was waiting in the car park of an adjacent Wickes DIY superstore. We sat in the car for a few minutes and planned how we would get some bicycle tracking shots on the canal. Unfortunately, as we made to drive off, to go and locate a better parking place closer to the canal, we saw that someone had put lockable steel posts across the entrance, trapping us in. Perhaps we should have noticed that we were the only vehicle in the car park and remembered that 'big box' shops are only allowed to open for six hours on a Sunday. This could prove disastrous.

Then I looked more closely at the metal poles and saw that all was not as it appeared. I got out the car and tried to lift one – it came up easily in my hands. As did the others. They weren't locked – this was a pantomime of security, fortunately. We drove out, replaced the bollards and fled the scene.

Ten minutes later, having parked somewhere readily escapable, my dad sat astride the second-hand fold-up bike he'd bought on Ebay and collected from a Birmingham resident the previous evening. It was a rather ramshackle contraption but it would fulfil its function admirably. We set off, my dad motivating me with a reasonable pace. The canal was leafy and colourful – autumnal shades, red-brick walls and lots of graffiti, some of it quite accomplished.

I don't really mind graffiti when it's vivid and well done; what I object to is endlessly repetitive 'tags', a moronic way of claiming ownership of the street by signing it as many times as possible. Spray-can artistry is fine by me though. Anything that adds variety is good for the ultra-runner keen to top thirty miles after a couple of bad days.

The canal became increasingly industrial – lots of red-brick factories, recycling plants, builders supply yards – and I didn't mind this either. After all, if we want to enjoy all that modern convenience and technology has to offer, it would be hypocritical to object to the industrial work that goes into making life that convivial. You can't have your loft conversions, fridge-freezers, fork-lift trucks and basic, functional sanitation without a lot of heavy lifting behind the scenes. Businesses once used to abut canals because they provided logistical routes to get products to market; now canal-side developments are about high-density housing, each home with its own balcony, giving people views of a liquid artery to remind them that life keeps flowing along – and so must we. We are drawn to watercourses because they seem to embody life, even when as comparatively still as a canal. Even the Birmingham waterways boast herons, swans, moorhen, carp gliding by amidst the pondweed and discarded cans of super strength lager.

As I ran that first section of canal from Perry Park towards the centre of Birmingham, I might have lost my 'rocket legs' of an hour previously, but there was still enough left in the tank to get me to Aston Locks, around three miles from where we'd started. My dad and I parted company after two miles and agreed that I'd call him when I'd had enough and would stop near a road and obtain a local postcode for his satnav. As ever, my 'having had enough' coincided pretty well with the sun sinking behind the office buildings and factories of Birmingham, not long after I'd negotiated one of the most hideous multiple-flyover junctions I'd ever seen.

Under several concrete loops and bridges, a dark and

sluggish stretch of canal forked into three possible directions. My brain was too addled and exhausted to make much sense of this using online maps on my phone so I took a stab in the dark (an appropriate metaphor given the environment) and headed down the Aston branch. Around half a mile later, something felt wrong and I'd all but run out of light, so I got back onto the roads and found a local corner shop for a snack (and a postcode). Serendipitously, I'd stopped near a poster advertising the Sleaford Mods and Steve Ignorant's Slice of Life,[6] Carol's band. She'd been in Birmingham three days earlier. A meaningless coincidence, admittedly, but oddly encouraging.

MILES RUN: 814; MILES REMAINING: 286

---

1. https://en.wikipedia.org/wiki/Alan_Reece – I'm glad I didn't know this during the run. What with the remote location, Reece's occupation and the danger signs, I could have started fretting about unexploded landmines.

2. For more on this I'd recommend Jenny Uglow's excellent book *The Lunar Men* (Faber & Faber, London, 2002).

3. The common acronym for John O'Groats to Land's End. Its converse, LEJOG, seems even more fey.

4. Google destroys the mystery – Hot Max is a brand of artificial log, made from made from compacted, recycled softwood dust and particles.

5. https://en.wikipedia.org/wiki/Max_Wall

6. Steve Ignorant was one of the original founders of the anarcho-punk band Crass. His new direction is a little gentler. But only a little. Try this for size: https://www.youtube.com/watch?v=S_a-C5YldMA

BIRMINGHAM TO
CHIPPING CAMPDEN

The following day I retraced my steps, needlessly as it turns out, to the horrible knot of overpasses at Salford Junction and took another route, heading onto the Grand Union Canal after Saltley. The small foot- and road bridges over the waterway provided shelter for more graffiti artists, whose colourful works adorned the red-brick and concrete. At times a sweet-sharp taint of chemical processes caught the back of my throat. I passed a few walkers and the occasional jogger but the stretch of canal closest to the city looked like it would benefit from a bit of investment to make it more inviting as a resource for locals. Given how central Birmingham is to the canal network, it's a shame there hasn't been the renovation many London and Scottish canals have enjoyed in recent decades.

The stretch of canal I was running, had I followed it for several days, would have joined up with the section I used to run while marathon training in my mid-thirties. I wouldn't be heading for London, however. Instead, my plan was to skip the capital by leaving the canal at a place called Little Shrewley, chosen primarily because it seemed that the canal was interrupted there, having been filled in. Later, I'd discover that the satellite image on Google Maps was misleading – at Shrewley the canal merely vanishes into a 396-metre-long tunnel then keeps going.

I had slightly leaden legs but no real pain as I plodded along the towpath, watching Birmingham's industrial arteries bleed out into a hinterland of suburbs and farmland. It took the best part of an hour to finally leave the city and its graffiti behind and I made 9 or 10-minute miles in an unremarkable light drizzle, with the intention of reaching a place with the evocative name of Catherine-de-Barnes[1] for lunch. Autumn was in full-flame by now and I ran over piles of reddening leaves, fallen damsons and crab apples. I met my dad mid-morning and, in a period of brief respite from the rain, he cycled ahead of me once more for a couple of miles. Patterns of rain and leaves on the canal drew my eye and I took more photos than I had expected to.

At Catherine-de-Barnes, we found a local pub, The Boat Inn, where I dried out and ate my usual hearty lunch. In the car park outside, Dad and I just caught a female runner heading off, her support vehicle pulling away. I wish I'd been able to ask her where she was running to but I think she must have been heading north. Either that or I was simply unable to catch up with her – not an unlikely scenario.

The rain having stopped and the countryside being quite pretty, we filmed another bit of bicycle tracking. The Kings Arms in Knowle kindly let us use their car park and my dad got back on his fold-up. I think he was enjoying the easy pace and flat terrain of the canal towpath along with the turning leaves and waterfowl that became more common as we progressed south. Stately herons, who always seemed to be posing for long lens photography, flapped away in seeming slow motion as we rattled by. From here, there would be many more narrowboats, an occasional pleasure boat or private dock. There was more of an air of the canal being an opportunity for leisure and for residence, rather than an industrial by-water or remnant of a forgotten age.

Canals are a little strange, however. Their endless contour-following curves are misleading. What looks like half a dozen miles on the map becomes ten when you factor in all the wiggles and turns. I'd imagined I might make it to

Snitterfield today, once I'd left the towpath for B-roads but the canal had other ideas. It twisted and turned and teased me on. Running on black mud, grass, gravel and leaves was easy enough on the legs and the terrain was hardly challenging but I began to have a feeling that this might never end – the canal became a watery ribbon stretching out indefinitely ahead of me.

I had a peculiar encounter a few miles on. A young female Friesian calf had strayed onto the towpath and was happily munching berries from the hedgerows. She had probably broken out of an adjoining field for this very purpose; such is the impetuousness of youth. I slowed to a walk and tried to sidestep the animal but she took fright and trotted off ahead of me. Each time I caught up with the calf and tried to slide past her, she would skittishly bolt further on down the trail. I felt like I was in danger of adopting her and worried that she might get too far from her own mother and herd and forget her way back. Fortunately, a few hundred yards later, the towpath widened enough for me to skirt around her. I looked back to see her gingerly stepping down into a ditch and back into her field.

A little later, at a place called Kingswood, I came upon an old metal signpost pointing down a fork in the canal. It read 'Stratford-upon-Avon'. Looking at my map-book, I realised that I'd planned to reach Stratford by road the following day. Taking the canal might prove both quicker and more pleasant. Unfortunately my phone reception had predictably vanished the moment I left the Birmingham city limits. I tried to call Dad to leave a message that I might head down the Stratford branch but couldn't get through to him. I decided to run on to Shrewley as planned, where he would be waiting. We'd drive back to somewhere near Kingswood the following day and start from there. More extra miles, in other words.

Given that these last miles were 'bonus' ones, I felt some

relief that I reached Shrewley at a little after five pm, as the rain began to lash down once more. I ended that day's running at the mouth of the village's epic tunnel, eschewing its black depths for a rainy dash to a warm and waiting Ford Mondeo.

The junction at Kingswood split once more, with another branch heading north-west to join the Worcester and Birmingham Canal at King's Heath. The junction was pretty enough to warrant a few set-up shots as I began my day on the 5th October. A local running club passed us as we were filming, making the most of the dry, bright weather (overcast but warm). I made good progress, passing more narrowboats and walkers as Stratford drew closer. At Edstone, a narrow but impressive viaduct carried the canal over the road and railway – the reflective strip of dead-straight canal pointing me like an arrow towards the distant spires and hills.

The pleasant weather did not last and the rain began to pour down like something biblical as Shakespeare's birthplace approached. The outskirts of Stratford were unexpectedly industrial and commercial – not that different to Birmingham really. Things became a little prettier as I made it into town and headed for a hotel car park where I'd told Dad to wait. I was utterly soaked, cold and craving lunch. A towel and a quick change of clothes later, we were dashing from car to café in a retail park stippled with puddles and gurgling drains. I was already thinking how unpleasant the afternoon's running might get if this didn't let up. I'd planned to find a trail along the Avon's banks as far as its junction with the Stour, then follow something called the 'Greenway', yet another repurposed railway line, to Long Marston. From there I'd be negotiating farm roads and villages into the heart of the Cotswolds.

The Avon's banks were graceful and decorous with willow trees, swans and partially glimpsed church spires contributing to a picture-postcard prettiness. I filmed a compulsory shot of Shakespeare-referencing statuary in a nearby park and proceeded along the Avon's banks. Fortunately the rain had temporarily abated so my dad was able to film from the park without constructing his usual umbrella-and-bungee-rope contraption. Swans waddled around the lush lawns as I followed the line of trees to a woodland trail that quickly climbed to fields south of the city.

After recent memories of the Pennine's wildness, everything was just getting a bit too domestic. Right on cue, filthy black rainclouds glided overhead and emptied their contents on me as I squelched through a grassy field. I've seldom felt such rain – it quickly soaked me to the point where there was no longer any reason to avoid puddles or indeed to care about being wet. I decided to enjoy the lunatic precipitation, pausing only briefly under a road-bridge tunnel to watch rivulets of brown water pouring off the fields.

Oddly, the trail I was following seemed to want to pass within twenty yards of the Greenway without actually meeting it. A patch of nettles, a partially broken-down fence and a small, muddy embankment separated me from my intended route. Feeling more than a little crazed, I shouted 'Banzai!!' and belted through the wet foliage, which exacted their revenge in the form of a dozen stings. Scrambling over the fence and up the embankment, I followed a muddy path clearly made by many other short-cutting walkers.

The Greenway was a surreally straight corridor between trees flanking flat, expansive fields. Enormous puddles had formed along its length and, as the rain gradually eased off for a while and the clouds broke open to reveal patches of blue, I chose to rampage through the puddles with childish glee. My shoes threw swathes of water over the path as I splashed up to my shins. It's my basic belief that to live in Britain and complain about the weather is an exercise in utter futility.[2]

The temperature and fun of acting so outlandishly made

me speed up and I was running eight and a half-minute miles for the next hour or so. My dad braved the squally showers to film me breaking from one wide section of the Greenway through a pair of gates to the narrower stretch which stopped at a road junction just south of Long Marston.

I definitely found myself 'in the zone' during the afternoon's running. I didn't quite have the turn of speed I'd enjoyed on Kingstanding Road but if you look at some of the footage I shot, I'm wearing the fixed stare of an athlete seeing the approach of the finish line. In ultramarathon terms, this can happen with an hour's running still to come – you feel a sharpening of focus and determination, a kind of monomania of running. Long Marston Road was a busy thoroughfare and I had to run through the puddles at the side of the road as cars tore by, throwing up spray. I didn't care, for once paying the cars and the puddles no heed in my determination to get to the Cotswold town of Chipping Campden.

We'd been staying in that town for the past two nights and had found it astonishingly picturesque but marred by a glut of perpetual traffic. It was as if the denizens of Gloucestershire (where it now appeared I was) all owned multiple Range Rovers and other 4 x 4s[3] and were determined to parade them around the small village all day. Trying to ignore passing cars was a perverse and, it has to be said, slightly aggressive strategy brought about by the undeniable feeling I had that many of the drivers just didn't give a damn about my safety. I kept a peripheral awareness at play, ready to jump out of the way if I had to and I always ran as close to the road's edge as possible. Sadly, the incidence of drivers giving me little clearance as they passed, not slowing down on narrow stretches or seeming actively hostile to my presence definitely increased as I entered the moneyed Cotswolds. Need there be an equation between income and propensity to behaving idiotically? Apparently so. I began to feel no guilt whatsoever in slowing down the traffic on tight corners or narrow stretches of wet road. This was running as a kind of minor rebellion – an act of defiance against the highways of Britain being entirely given up to the car and to the most selfish kind of motorist.

I'm probably exaggerating somewhat and, in my endorphin-fuelled mind, everything probably just felt that little bit more intense but I really did feel an air of antagonism descending as I tramped along the B4081 that afternoon. Mickleton passed with its Tudor cottages and provided a pavement and also a baffling moment when I paused by a pub whose menu board seemed to read 'The Long Run'. It turns out that my dad, whose tripod was set up across the street, had been mischievous with a piece of chalk. I ate a chocolate bar in the car and determined to reach Chipping Campden. It would make a change to stop for the day in the town where I would actually be sleeping.

When I got to the town, it was only 4 pm but there was just too much temptation to stop. I was wet, muddy and exhausted. A bath and my bed were only metres away. I met my dad on the medieval town's high street and recorded a piece to camera. I then sent my dad out on a quest for cutaways (everything in Chipping Campden is exquisite, bar the traffic) while I headed for the solace of hot water and soap.

MILES RUN: 863; MILES REMAINING: 237

---

1. Known to locals as 'Catney', the town's name is a bastardisation of Ketelberne, the name of the twelfth-century lord who owned the land.

2. As Billy Connolly famously said 'There's no such thing as bad weather. Just the wrong clothing!'

3. SUVs as they are known to Americans.

CHIPPING CAMPDEN TO BATH

I once won a race. Just once, so the memory remains vivid. It was in late summer in 2010. Ealing Primary Care Trust[1] and Ealing Council had jointly organised what I think they hoped would be an annual event for their staff – a 5K race around some playing fields and tracks in Northolt. For a reason which is not entirely clear, team colours were allocated – black, green and red. Participants were encouraged to 'walk, jog or run' and the event was evidently allied to both organisations' health promotion policies.

It was reasonably well attended. I seem to remember each team having about forty members. Most people turned up to the race early enough to participate in a group warm-up. Partly through being as late and lost as ever, I missed this, which means I also missed the team photos that were taken. Still, I remember the race having an astonishingly wide-ranging field, from fellow runners to those who chose to stroll round the route.

I started near the front. I had no idea if any of my fellow participants were 'proper' runners (with PBs and Garmins and training plans) or whether everyone was just there to improve their health, socialise or because their colleagues made them attend. I do know that two of the faster members of my then running club, Ealing, Southall and Middlesex, who both worked for the Trust, were not in attendance. Of this I was almost glad – both Tom and Alison would have given me serious competition and quite probably beaten me down to third. That said, none of this was really going through my mind as we received the countdown (more 'ready, steady, GO!' than a gunshot); these realisations came later.

I bolted, overcompensating for my lack of knowledge about the field, and quite quickly found myself out in front by about thirty yards. I'd been expecting a road 5K but the cross-country aspect of the course actually played to my strengths – unlike inexperienced runners, I didn't slow down much on grassy or muddy surfaces – my shoes gripped well enough to let me increase my lead on these sections. Halfway round, hearing the pounding of young footfalls behind me on the gravel path, I expected to be passed. But it didn't happen.

The marshals were inexperienced but then so was I, at winning. If you are the front-runner, the onus is on you to navigate. I passed one marshal who was too busy clapping to point me the right way. I shouted an enquiry and was misdirected. I think she thought I was on my first lap, rather than my second and final one. I'd realised by then that there was a chance I could win, which filled me, largely, with panic. Suddenly, from this being just an event I'd agreed to go to because I knew one of the organisers, it had become a milestone race.

Pounding down the home straight, well ahead of the second and third placed runners, I felt both triumphant and just a little bit ridiculous, as if I was almost putting too much effort in, like a kid turning up to school sports day with a personal trainer. Still, it's the only way I know how to run a race – all out, to the point of near-collapse. Crossing the line came as a merciful relief. Accepting my laminated certificate and a money-off voucher for Sweatshop that I never got around to using, I smiled for the cameras, mildly bemused that this had happened at all. It would not happen again.

The reason I bring this up is that there's a point in any race or run, when you suspect you're going to achieve your goal – either a win, a personal best, a sub-3-hour marathon or something more amorphous. Around the 7th October, with the toughest trails behind me, winding my way through the Cotswolds with no significantly debilitating injuries, I began to have the feeling I had when I turned that last corner in 2010 and saw the finish tape.

Except this time the finish line was still 300 miles away.

That Wednesday began in middling to heavy rain and under a canopy of fast-flowing grey cloud. The legs were in good shape as I set off as early as the Volunteer Inn's breakfast service would allow. The ultimate goal for the day was Cirencester (and perhaps a little beyond), around thirty miles to the south.

Despite the rain, I found plenty to enjoy that morning – in fact, the water made the colours of the Cotswolds in autumn all the more vivid. The whole area through which I'd run as far as Cirencester was composed of a notably yellowish rock. It's a colour very characteristic of the region – an ochre hue familiar from postcards and photos. That autumn, with leaves of similar shades tumbling all around, the effect was harmonious and painterly, even in the rain.

Prettiness is one of the greatest palliatives to the long-distance runner and, as the rainclouds glided eastwards towards lunchtime, I scarcely noticed the miles flying by. Upper and Lower Swell and Upper Slaughter passed, proving almost intolerably beautiful. Upper Slaughter even boasted its own flour mill, currently being renovated to full working order. My high-speed tourism prevailed – I was managing 9-minute miles with the intention of running close to twenty miles before lunchtime. As it happened, I didn't quite make it to the picturesque town square at Northleach before I hit the familiar wall of glucose deficiency and ground to a halt.

Northleach was recently featured in a British TV drama based on J. K. Rowling's *The Casual Vacancy* and proved as picturesque as you might imagine. The town square had space enough for Sorrell and my father's cars, enabling them to do another handover. Sorrell had returned to do another six days on the project, before my dad returned finally to see me to Land's End. Comically, when I reached the town running, it took me about half a dozen attempts to escape it again. Eventually I found the correct road, a lane right by the café where we'd had lunch. I must have said my good-byes to Dad several times as my support crew unpacked and repacked their vehicles.[2]

A new endurance strategy had formed without me really noticing – whereas back at the start of September (seemingly a lifetime ago) I'd attempted to divide the day into four chunks of roughly ten miles, now I was trying to notch up twenty before lunch and ten to fifteen after. The 'morning break' had been replaced by longer periods of walking, which were more efficient in terms of helping me recover my breath and resting the feet and ankles without everything seizing up. It felt like a more natural division of effort.

Just outside of Cirencester, however, both knees began to protest, sending the occasional shooting pain up the front of my thighs. Aside from self-medicating with ibuprofen and paracetamol, there didn't seem to be a lot I could do about this, so I perhaps rashly decided to ignore the pain. Sorrell and I agreed that, since the B-roads and farm tracks were easier for me than heading in and out of towns, we'd skip Cirencester, where I'd run the 24-hour event described in the foreword. A new route was plotted via Coln St Dennis, Coln Rogers, Preston and Siddington. Now that I wasn't planning to stop in Cirencester, I had no idea where I'd end up, but that felt okay. Despite the pain, I was still making good time and now I had the added pleasure of my route veering south-west, towards the leg of Cornwall (literally, the last leg of The Long Run).

My mood remained optimistic as I passed the marathon mark and headed towards thirty miles, by now a daily psychological boundary after which point stopping would not induce guilt and continuing would feel like a triumph. My optimism was slightly dented when a white car (my ignorance of cars won't allow me to be more specific) apparently decided that I was not worth moving the steering wheel for and roared past with about an inch to spare as I sidestepped at the last minute. I confess, I turned and bellowed the darkest of all Anglo-Saxon insults as the driver blithely failed to take my life.

Amusingly, the effect of screaming the C-word at a total stranger flooded my system with endorphins and I had a spate of sub-9-minute mile running though the high farmland between Clapton-on-the-Hill and the A417 east of Cirencester. It may in part have been the fear of this maniac turning round and catching up with me, carjack in hand to dash my brains out.

Uncharacteristically, Sorrell wrong-footed me a little, sending me west from Ampney St Peter to Cirencester Road, the main artery into the city from the A419. When I hit the main road and realised I had to run along it, at rush hour, I knew this would be all but impossible. Traffic sped by in unending convoy, commuters impatient for their dinners. I crossed to the side I needed to be on for the turn-off to South Cerney and stood on the grass verge, which was unkempt and bristly, not much fun to run or even walk along. My spirits fell – until I saw what lay on the other side of an adjoining ditch and barbed wire fence.

It looked at first like an abandoned airfield but I quickly realised the weathered tarmac roadway ran in a giant loop, perhaps three kilometres in circumference. Its surface was worn, grass and weeds growing from cracks in the tarmac in places, the buildings in the distance seemingly abandoned. A racetrack of some sort – perhaps a test track for new cars? Maybe it was used by go-karters? I didn't know and, I'll admit, I didn't use my smartphone to check. All I knew is that if I got over that ditch and fence, I could follow the circuit round and then climb another fence to reach the turn-off. A slightly desperate plan, involving trespassing, to be sure, but a solution to my immediate problem.

Leaping the ditch was touch-and-go, especially as I chose to film my crime. I scrambled across the fence, realising I'd be visible from the road, as quickly as possible. The sun was low in the sky, burnishing the clouds with bronze light. A beautiful backdrop for an illicit intrusion. At first I started jogging on the grass, half-expecting a vehicle full of angry officials to pull over beside me. When I realised this wouldn't happen, I grew emboldened and took to the tarmac. I suppose it took me around seven minutes to run the 1.5K to the far side of the track and I'll admit I felt the thrill of a naughty child doing something forbidden. Of course I was harming and inconveniencing absolutely no one.

Still, it was a relief to see a gap in the hedge, a tiny road behind it and two paltry strands of barbed wire between me and escape. I trotted down the road, having called Sorrell and ascertained that she was parked near the entrance to South Cerney golf course. A few hundred yards further on I saw a beaten and faded sign on the barbed wire barricade I'd just crossed:

MINISTRY OF DEFENCE: THIS IS A PROHIBITED PLACE, WITHIN THE MEANING OF THE OFFICIAL SECRETS ACT. UNAUTHORISED PERSONS ENTERING THE AREA MAY BE ARRESTED AND PROSECUTED.

Oops.

If I'd experienced the worst of arrogance in terms of a driver nearly killing me the previous day, Thursday the 8th October started with a vivid demonstration of what can happen if, as a motorist, you err on the side of generosity.

Sorrell and I were shuttling along the B-roads, heading from Chipping Campden to South Cerney when signage diverted us from some roadworks down the narrowest of farm tracks. Given that this was 8 am, a stack of locals were trailing us as we drove as fast as we could along the sinuous bends. Without the diversion, I imagine this road was usually quiet – its single-track and lack of passing places would not normally be a problem. We crossed our fingers for a clear road ahead but as we rounded a bend at speed, Sod's law provided another vehicle coming the opposite way. Sorrell saw her opportunity and pulled over into a dense grassy verge, only for the left side of our car to suddenly slew downwards, as if into a hidden ditch. Metal ground on dirt and the engine stalled. We jumped out, the car behind us stopping to see if we were okay.

We were fine but the little Renault was struggling. Its front right wheel had dropped into a giant hole, perhaps left by the removal of a dangerous boulder (oh, the irony). There was a small dent where the bonnet had dislodged a rock on the way down. There was no way we were going forward and little chance of reversing out. The men and women who emerged from their vehicles behind us offered opinions and ideas but we were all a little stumped.

Meanwhile cars were building up in both directions, creating an impasse. Astonishing fortune shone on us, however, in that one of the vehicles behind us was a low-loader carrying a miniature digger. Filming proceedings on my GoPro, I ventured a tentative opinion that we might get out in reverse. The workmen from the low-loader agreed and with amazing presence of mind, backed the digger off its carrier and onto the tarmac. A belt was procured and tied to our rear axle and moments later, the Renault was pulled out of its pit. The pocket-sized digger and its operator accomplished the rescue with ease. We thanked our saviour, Lol, profusely and got back in. Our problems weren't quite over though with over a dozen cars behind us and three or four ahead, on a road where nobody could pass one another. Common sense and the majority prevailed, the cars ahead of us reversing back to the nearest road junction and Sorrell and I shamefacedly following the low-loader. We had no time to be polite – there was running to do.

About half an hour later, somewhere near Oxey, I ran round a corner and was stopped in my tracks by that most iconic of English sights – a medieval church in a field of dappled sunlight. Philip Larkin would have approved of the effect, if not the purpose, of this sight.[3]

There was something idyllic about the flavour of The Long Run in those early October days – gone were arduous trails and navigational uncertainty. If I missed the wrong farm track, an alternative would present itself. Everything was clearly signposted with every village named and miles accurately listed. All I had to do now was run. Bath was my next destination – a stately and ancient English town named after its Roman remnants but also boasting impeccable Georgian terraces and circuses. I'd wanted to run through Bath since I'd first visited it – its hilly, cobbled streets and architecture reminded me a lot of my home town, Edinburgh. I knew it would make a picturesque addition to the film and its surrounding hills would offer vistas and variety. I couldn't keep stitching endless villages together all the way to Land's End – the (admittedly photogenic) monotony would finish me.

Midway through one piece to camera that morning, I gave up whatever inconsequential drivel I was spouting in sheer exhaustion.[4] Fatigue had crept up on me again and my left hip had taken over pain-giving duties from my knees. Throughout the morning I battled this injury and the urgings of the inner voices telling me to stop. In the credit side of the balance sheet was the weather which, although a little cloudy, was gloriously warm at around 19 degrees Celsius. I ran in my T-shirt, smeared in factor 30.

It also helped that I was continuing to run through some supremely attractive little towns and villages. At Oaksey the quietude of another medieval churchyard gave way to the excited battle of a school playground. The villages seemed to be getting closer together and the hills were less formidable than in the heart of the Cotswolds. This meant that there were more people walking between villages and therefore more careful drivers, making my experience a little less fraught. I noticed the Cotswold stone begin to give way to a greyer, less sandy rock.

The roll-call of English hamlets continued – Little Somerford, Great Somerford, Upper Seagry, Stanton St Quintin, Kingston St Michael (many of the villages in these parts named after their prominent churches). I began to imagine becoming a judge on a 'prettiest Cotswold village competition' and made an inner list of my preferences, revising it as I ran.[5] I took inspiration and diversion where I could. At one point I was stopped in my tracks by a field of newly cut hay, its perfection decorated with the curving tyre marks of tractors. Another time I heard a strange engine sound buzzing like a giant fly above me and looked up to see a red WWI biplane cruising beneath candyfloss clouds. The day passed without high drama and in a gentle, ambling manner that belied my discomfort. Reaching Bath, however, was now a hopeless and unrealistic dream.

I ran under the M4, which felt like another milestone and crawled on as far as Slaughterford, which seemed ramshackle and sinister, and oddly appropriate to my mood of mildly delirious fatigue. I was longing for a change, for something other than fields, farm roads and villages. But more than anything, what I needed was to sleep, renew my energy and *heal*.

Slaughterford was even scarier the next day, when I

started there a little after nine am. I stood swathed in freezing fog, a pronounced chill in the air. In what I felt was a nice touch, the sound of a buzzing chainsaw accompanied me out of the village and up the first narrow, steep farm road. There were even tiny, dew-dropped cobwebs strewn between the hawthorn hedges, adding to the Halloween vibe. I felt considerably more positive, nevertheless, as my breath clouded visibly around me. The road I was on was entirely empty and, apart from the rustling of leaves, my breathing and footsteps and a smattering of birdsong, it was extraordinarily peaceful.

After 38 days of running, my inner bargain now was to manage 30-plus miles per day and not worry about specific geographical targets. I added another motive to the stockpile of reasons why I was doing this – to better get to know the country in which I live. Not just the major cities and attractions, but the lesser-known towns, villages and hamlets, hidden beaches, pocket-sized woods and gurgling streams. What better way to celebrate a country than by passing a continuous strip of it under your feet, literally feeling the entire terrain of a top-to-bottom treadmill composed of tarmac, earth, sand and grass?

Crows cawed and flocked over fog-hidden fields and the sun, keen to break through all this moisture, lit up the fog ahead like a giant bank of Kleig lights. At times, the fog was so thick that the sun's disc looked more like a full moon. Approaching Colerne, I took to a B-road which had a little strip of footpath along one side, fortuitously so as the fog seemed to be getting thicker, rather than dispersing. Trying to run along a narrow road like this with, at best, thirty feet of good visibility, would be foolhardy indeed.

Leaving villages for open farmland, I took the Roman Road towards Bath as far as possible but, as ever, town planners disappointed me by removing the pavement about a mile south of Colerne. In thick freezing fog, it was impossible to continue on the main road. I found a 'foot-path' sign (no destination indicated) and headed down the grassy track in search of an alternative route. After a bit of uncertainty, I followed a tree-lined path, a strip of road and then a green channel between hedges, past gnarled oak trees and eventually to an unusually ornate black-painted wrought iron fence with another inviting fingerpost nearby. The fact that I could see absolutely nothing more than twelve feet in front of me as I headed into the field did not dissuade me. Rampant bulls aside, this was still safer than playing chicken with articulated lorries on the main road.

Looming out the mist appeared a herd of cows, eyeing me with much suspicion as I followed a clay and gravel bridleway which described a giant loop through the fields and down a valley towards the By Brook. Expensive-looking wrought iron fences contained everything on what appeared to be a fairly well-to-do estate and I began to worry that I'd strayed off the official footpath onto someone's private land. It was difficult to see anything at all with clarity, so I kept to the footpath and hoped an angry landowner wouldn't roar up in a Range Rover and send me back the way I'd come. Unfortunately, I was wearing my road shoes, so some of the thicker clay and mud presented a bit of a hazard as I ran parallel to the forested riverbank. After about ten minutes though, I emerged onto a farm road, turned and saw another 'footpath' sign, admittedly pointing into a neighbouring field. Most probably, nobody would have cared but the fog and uncertainty had increased my paranoia. Plus, nothing had gone seriously wrong on The Long Run for a few days – I was probably due a calamity.

Half an hour later, I reached Batheaston, a suburb of the city proper. In fact, Bath's suburbs sprawled for several miles to the east of the city centre and as I exchanged farm tracks for major traffic arteries, the run became less of an adventure and more of a slog. I'd already run around ten miles by the time I began to recognise Bath's Georgian grandeur and, as ever, immediately thought of Edinburgh. I decided to stick to my original plan to run right into the heart of it and stop on the lawn at Royal Crescent.

Rather wonderfully, the sun decided to peer out just as I climbed a hilly path around the side of Hedgemead Park and then ran along a series of pristine cobbled streets, sunlight colouring the Georgian townhouses' sandstone a pale blonde colour. Like Edinburgh, Bath is quite easy to find your way around and, having been there only twice before, I nevertheless managed to navigate up to The Circus, an impressive circular terrace, and then on to the great lawn in front of Royal Crescent, the sensational sweeping arc of thirty terraced houses which sits high on a hillside, commanding an unbeatable view of the city. Designed by John Wood the Younger and built over seven years, it was completed in 1774 and is, of course, Grade I listed.[6] I decided to allow myself a bit of a rest in the sunshine on the lawn in front of the Crescent. Groups of tourists were snapping photos as I sat down on the grass, ate a flapjack and drank some water.

It was tempting, given the lovely weather and peaceful surroundings, to forget my mission but it was only mid-morning and Somerset lay stretched out before me like a very green patchwork quilt. Ten minutes later, I set off once more.

MILES RUN: 923; MILES REMAINING: 177

1. An NHS administration centre where I worked for some years.

2. For kit fetishists and adventure completists, there is a list of what we had in our support vehicle in Appendix II and a list of what I habitually had on my person as I ran in Appendix III.

3. The poet's best-known work 'Church-going' eulogises an atheist's appreciation of the English village church. Hear Larkin himself read it here: https://www.youtube.com/watch?v=w5aKknj-q3o

4. Something about the ubiquity of Cotswold stone giving way to other building materials but, even watching the footage back, it's unclear where I was going with that thought. The body's states feed the brain.

5. The definitive top three: In third place Kingston St Michael, in second place Lower Slaughter but, traffic aside, Chipping Campden still holds the number one place. I'm sorry I have not run through your village.

6. For those that don't know, Grade I is the category reserved for buildings 'of exceptional interest'. Only 2.5 per cent of listings lie within this grade. Source: https://historicengland.org.uk/

BATH TO FENNY BRIDGES

Getting out of Bath proved as easy as, well, getting out of a bath. I used the famous blue dot of my iPhone's mapping system and followed it south, down to the river then up a suburban row of early twentieth-century houses impressive in their own regimented way. The hills I'd seen in the distance were the Mendips, about which I knew absolutely nothing. By now, I'd become rather blasé about hills – they exist (unless you live in the Low Countries) and you'd just better deal with them, was my motto.

Bath gave way rather abruptly as I headed for the nearest village, Englishcombe. The terrain sank and rose as I tried to run as much of it as I could. Disaster almost struck when I left my phone on a roadside verge and ran on for a mile before noticing its absence. I must have managed close to a 7-minute mile as I raced back. The streets were deserted and the iPhone lay in the shadow of a hedgerow. I kept it close at all times for the remainder of the challenge. Lose my phone, with its detailed map and (occasional) internet access and I'd lose one of my most useful tools. I think that although the fatigue of the previous days had lifted a little, the brain cells remained slow to recover.

The weather continued to be absurdly warm. I was perspiring about as much as I would on an average summer's day – except this was the 9th October. Thin bands of fluffy cumulous floated low across the fields but the skies overhead were mostly azure and clear. The unseasonal warmth was filling the air with swarms of what looked like mayflies as I headed through high fields for the village of Tunley. I'd have covered eighteen miles by then and could stop for lunch. Sorrell was keeping close tabs on me and heading me off from wrong turnings, as she had in the Cotswolds. By now we'd managed to get a rhythm going and I suppose she now knew my average speed over different terrains. Confusingly, Tunley was also signposted as Priston, having once been home to Priston Colliery, according to a hand-drawn sign 'the last deep mine sunk in Somerset'. I had no reason to doubt this assertion and no headspace for it either, since my brain was filling with visions of sausages and mashed potato.

Pleasantly fuelled, I set off from Tunley at a stiff jog. The landscape stretched out rather flat below me as I headed downhill to Camerton at unimpressive 12-minute miles. My thirty miles per day rule meant I had to complete a minimum of another dozen miles, but I hoped for fifteen or sixteen.

One hour after lunch I was back up to 9-minute miles, the legs having loosened off. Running had become easier and less painful, were it not for an impossible network of tiny roads, some of them not on my support car's satnav. Like the veins on the back of my hand, I might look at the map a dozen times an hour but memorising its chaotic jumble of routes proved impossible with a tired brain. I reassured myself that, so long as I headed south and west, I'd not be in too much trouble if I took the wrong road.

I also found myself rambling a little incoherently to the camera – needing its admittedly one-sided companionship. Tall hedges and flat, straight roads once more predominated but I tried to focus on the little details of the landscape, including a peculiar conical hill which appeared in the distance, almost volcanic in appearance. This, it transpires, was not a hill at all but the Old Mills 'batch' or spoil heap from the town's once thriving colliery. As the sun sank ever nearer the horizon it flashed spasmodically through the trees, throwing dappled sunlight at my feet and bright splashes into my eyes. Once again, I resisted sunglasses, perhaps unwisely. There was plenty of evidence that this sunshine was not especially unusual for the region – I passed an enormous bank of solar panels filling a small field south-west of Midsomer Norton.

Anvil-shaped clouds were forming in the landscape to the northwest, flat-topped cumulonimbus, suggesting that the heat of the day had drawn plenty of moisture up into the stratosphere. Did this bode ill for the future? I hoped not. A mile or two later I began to see the first apple orchards – fields of dwarf trees heavy with red and yellow fruit. 2015 was a bit of a boom year for English apples, it seems – an estimated 160,000 tonnes were produced, making it possibly the best harvest for twenty years. Nobody can have failed to note the boom in the popularity of cider in recent years. A vice of mine as a teenage drinker, cider was once again fashionable in the trendy city bars and country pubs up and down the UK, in both hellraising and connoisseur variants. A nation of keen, if not obsessive drinkers, we were even importing Scandinavian and Irish ciders and that just wouldn't do. It was good to know that English producers were fighting back with a bumper crop.[1] This most British of fruit would prove a constant decoration to the landscape over the couple of days I took to cross the county.

Towards the end of the 9th October, I got a little lost in the labyrinth of English villages. I'd made it as far as Binegar (which to my addled mind seemed a highly amusing name) then attempted to find the right small road towards Dinder and Shepton Mallet. This proved all but impossible. I came upon Gurney Slade by mistake and asked some locals, including a woman who called her husband outdoors to help; a few minutes later, one of the largest men I've ever seen emerged from the house; I felt guilty for making him get up, especially as between the three of us we still couldn't plot a sensible route. When the locals don't even know where you are, you are in trouble.

A little later, another local man walking his dog tried to be helpful, looking at my laminated maps and scratching his head. It didn't help that there was a sliver of map missing between the two pages I was carrying. My iPhone's battery had died and, daftly, I'd not charged the emergency battery. The dog-walker used his own phone and tried to match what he saw with my maps, with much difficulty. Five minutes later, we were still conferring and phrases like 'you should have gone down here' were being bandied about. Backtracking being anathema to me, I asked him if he was sure I couldn't keep running the way I was heading. As it happened, there was an (admittedly not ideal) route I could take by just keeping on going. Music to my ears.

The 9th October ended strangely – I had seen the same purple-blue hatchback several times during the day (or thought I did) when I eventually hit the insanely busy B3135 and decided to stop. There was no safe way to run along the B-road in the fading late afternoon light. At the junction of the B3135 and the road to Binegar sat the hatchback, parked opposite an isolated house. A woman waved at me from the garden and I nodded back and decided to assume she was just very friendly and not some crazed stalker. On second thoughts, she probably thought I was following her – after all, I was the one loitering opposite her house.

The following day, with the B-road still too dangerous to run, Sorrell and I decided to give the now semi-mythical 'Road from Binegar' another try. Dinder and Crosscombe were the immediate targets as I set off in a thin morning mist. My support car stayed close and between us, we managed to find the right junctions to take me along the back roads, skirting Wells towards Glastonbury. The home of Britain's most famous music festival seemed achievable by lunchtime, so long as I didn't get lost.

A decision would have to be taken about the A-roads. There was really no way to avoid running along a stretch of either the A39 or A361. Hopefully, as this would occur only about two to three miles from Glastonbury, there was a chance there might be a pavement. When I was about five miles out, I could see the uniquely nipple-shaped tower on top of the rounded hill of Glastonbury Tor. Keep that in sight and I couldn't really go wrong.

There was nothing ailing me that day but a slight clicking coming from my left knee – nothing that I ought really to worry about, I decided. All that was really troubling me was the lack of eventfulness. As a film-maker, I began to worry that this section would simply become too repetitive. As a runner, I was beginning to long for a change of scenery – a major town, some hills, anything to break up the monotony of what was an extremely flat part of England. Born and raised in Edinburgh, I'm just not used to large flat expanses of landscape. I feel like it's harder to judge distances and speeds with so few visual indicators of progress.

I found myself looking for details to appreciate – the sinister buzzing of overhead power cables, patterns of irrigation ditches between the square fields, the sun's pale disc glimmering through thick clouds, a roadside thistle. All of these helped stave off boredom – one of the ultra-runner's worst enemies. Oddly, boredom is something I hadn't encountered much in my trip so far. There is a surprising amount to think about when you're engaging on a task like The Long Run. There's route-finding, dealing with injuries, thinking about food (fuel), keeping hydrated, taking care of equipment, filming and photographing things of interest, monitoring pace, keeping an eye on traffic, thinking about things to say to camera, watching the different landscapes give way to one another. To put it another way – although

I'd brought an iPod shuffle with me, I used it about five times for perhaps a total of two hours out of more than 384 hours of running. The intensity of the experience alone rendered any sort of lasting boredom impossible.

That morning I had intended to head west to the A39 but somehow arrived at the A361, which did indeed boast a strip of pavement. It was still fairly early in the morning so I thought I'd try and make it to Glastonbury, climb the Tor for a view of the terrain ahead and then keep going as far as possible before hunger overcame me. Small fields of apple trees and ramshackle farms appeared along the side of the perpetually busy A-road leading into the town. Even a couple of miles out, I could sense I was entering a different sort of place than anywhere else I'd visited on the trip. I'd always meant to go to the Glastonbury Festival but had never quite managed it. Of course I'd heard reports of the horrors of unending rain, thick slurries of mud and life-threatening sanitation but something had always appealed about the spirit of shared fandom. Music has been a very big part of my life as the son of a jazz musician, avid purchaser of vinyl and occasional guitarist. I was looking forward to seeing what all the fuss was about in terms of Glastonbury the town. A place swathed in mysticism and legend would surely not disappoint.

Well, it did and it didn't. Once I'd located the turn-off to the right which wound up to the Tor (and it was a fairly well-hidden one) I began to climb steadily, relaxing into a quick stride and wondering how far I'd have to spiral around this hill before it let me in – of course, this all added to the suspense. A little way up that narrow roadway, a brightly coloured mural on the side of a house reminded me that I was in the hippies' Mecca. Further on a small fountain trickled from the overspill of a hidden reservoir – a mystical fountain? I didn't stop to take the waters.

Around ten minutes later, a tiny car park, National Trust

signage and a gate denoted the entrance to the Tor. Even though it was midweek, overcast and very windy, there were perhaps fifty couples, groups of friends and families exploring the conical hill and its fourteenth-century tower, all that remains of St Michael's Church, the bulk of which was demolished in 1539. There is evidence of buildings on the site dating back to Saxon times and the terraced mound of sandstone that rises from the surrounding clay soil does have a very ritualistic feel. It can be seen for many miles in all directions and, on bright days when there is a lot of low-lying mist, a *fata morgana*[2] effect can cause the Tor to look like it is floating.

The Tor was possibly not at its most majestic in late morning but I was impressed by the commanding view it gave of the surrounding landscape and something impelled me to dash up the last few hundred stepped yards to the top and film a 360-sweep of the terrain below. Using the compass built into my Garmin, I was able to look at the direction I'd be running from Glastonbury. To my relief, it looked fairly flat but I was also aware that looks can be deceptive when perspective and a high viewpoint come into play. I spent a few minutes there enjoying the view then remembered my mission.

Heading back into Glastonbury, things went rapidly from quasi-mystical to rather tawdry. Garishly painted vans proclaimed 'You are Love' and various shops offered healing crystals, reiki, tie-dyed clothing and other 'spiritual' paraphernalia, although I was a little disappointed by the lack of druids. A more surprising sight was a field of very relaxed-looking Highland cattle. Haight-Asbury this was not.[3] Glastonbury was ultimately a fairly nondescript, perfectly decent rural town that has sprouted a huge music festival; it is not really the town's fault that it doesn't really imbue the hippy vibe very convincingly.

That afternoon, I pretty much relied on my support

for route-finding. Beyond the prosaically named Street, at the village of Compton Dundon Sorrell had found me an off-road section to skirt a swathe of the B-road and bring me round to Bramwell. The trail she located on her satnav comprised thick mud, deep puddles and absolutely no tarmac or gravel for about a mile. Even a 4 x 4 would have trouble negotiating this; in my road shoes I skidded through the mud and over the puddles but I enjoyed the variety, having run on tarmac for several days. Emerging at the end of the trail, I discovered a signpost describing it as 'Slippery Batch' which, although accurate, seemed a bit rude.

The next chunk took me through a series of farm roads which were not visible on paper maps or the satnav. The sun glimmered weakly in a grey wall of cloud as I wriggled my way further south and west. Somewhere near Somerton we had lunch (my memory is hazy but it was not, sadly, in the nearby villages of Beer or Stout). Throughout the day I began to notice more and more thatched cottages, built in stout grey stone, their impressive roofs crafted with a blend of traditional materials and modern detailing. I reached the town of Martock around mid-afternoon. I'd managed around twenty-eight miles by that point and was beginning to hear the inner voices urging me to stop and rest. Without any major town or village as a specific goal, it was proving difficult to fight their insistence.

I distracted myself with the poetry and history embedded in the names of the places I passed through. One signpost boasted Coat, Long Load, Kingsbury Episcopi and Shepton Beauchamp, names encoding landowning families, Catholic dominions, ancient watercourses and archaic trades. In the age of Google, it is easy to demystify the origins of place names. I preferred not to, allowing me to make up my own fanciful stories as I passed through. Towards the end of the day I jogged past a pile of pumpkins and a sign suggesting a £1 payment, cash to be deposited in a pipe protruding from the hedge. This reminder of impending Halloween spurred me on – I could not still be running on All Hallows' Eve.

As we started filming the following morning, the publican at The Royal Oak, Over Stratton poked his head out of an upstairs window inquisitively. As with most curious spectators, once we explained what we were about, he seemed unperturbed by the sudden appearance of a tripod, camera and yawning runner outside his place of work and residence. He wished me a bleary-eyed good luck.

A jungle-like channel of road between tall banks studded with ferns and ivy lead me to the Roman road between Lopen and Dinnington. Its straightness took me speedily between the endless hedgerows on another grey but dry morning. Tall trees and a profusion of ferns and water-loving plants flanked the narrow lanes – everything a riotous green even under the overcast sky. Of all the counties through which I passed, I'd have to say that Somerset was the greenest. Long gradual inclines took the place of more obvious hills that morning and roads devoid of cars allowed me to hear the birdcalls and rustlings of small mammals and wildfowl amongst the undergrowth.

I didn't entirely succeed in avoiding major roads, however, hitting the A30 and having to run a quarter mile along it before the next turn-off. By now I'd learned to either trot along the grass verge or just pick my way at walking pace, so as not to alarm motorists coming round the corner at sixty miles per hour. I knew there would be another tiny lane to carry me on to Chaffcombe and beyond. In fact, the lane was so miniscule and obscure that it wore a moss mohican along its centre – always a good sign for a runner. Blissfully peaceful forest opened up on both sides of the road and I drank in oxygenated air. Although this helped me manage a steady 9-minute mile pace, I had to contend with the day's special ailment – a solid all-over ache in my left calf.

My pleasure at running through forest was mildly impaired when I passed an opening to the left, barricaded with a tree limb. A beautifully varnished plaque nailed into a nearby tree proclaimed 'Private Forest – Keep Out'. A path evidently ran parallel to the road and, had I been in Scotland I would gladly have louped[4] that barricade and taken to the forest trail. It seemed more than a little mean-spirited for the landowner to claim exclusive ownership of the trees, since it would do nobody any harm whatsoever for me to run there. Still, having trespassed a couple of times in England so far, I didn't push my luck.

Chaffcombe proved a village in touch with its own history to the extent that it preserves a village 'pound'. Used in the medieval period before farmers' fields were commonly walled or fenced, the pound was the place where livestock which had strayed into crops would be imprisoned for retrieval by their rightful owners in exchange for a fee. The word 'impounded' derives from this usage. There is even a 'keeper's cottage' opposite the tiny field.

Part of the fun of a project like The Long Run is unravelling these little details after the event. I had no time to read information boards or use search engines while running. One of the things that most impressed me running though endless small towns and villages in Scotland and England is the near-universality of 'civic pride'. For the most part, people take care of the places in which they live. As a lifelong dweller in cities, where there are always forgotten corners ruined by inhumane town-planning, social problems and concomitant visual blight, it did impress me how small communities tend to pull together to ensure their environments are pleasing. Efforts to replicate this small town community spirit meet with mixed effects in cities, where transience and constant change work against community cohesion. Nevertheless, the best bits of cities do have a 'village' feel – in London you can see this in areas as diverse as Hampstead, Bethnal Green,

Brixton, Camden, Wimbledon and Soho. People identify themselves with their local areas – we are naturally tribal, after all, and despite our best efforts to be global citizens, we are parochial too.

On the evening of the 9th October, we had a bit of unusual luck with our accommodation. Sorrell had booked the Cannard's Well Inn in Shepton Mallet online for two nights. However, when calling to double-check the booking, she found there had been a glitch and the hotel could only provide us with one night's accommodation, due to there being a large local event that week. The manager was thoroughly apologetic and, once Sorrell had explained what The Long Run was about and had mentioned the two charities, he offered a phenomenal deal – one night's free accommodation, dinner and breakfast for two. We were staggered, having not managed to secure much in the way of discount accommodation so far and nothing at all for free. The owner even donated some money to my causes. Well-fed and grateful, we departed the following morning revitalised and ready for the big push west. The leg of Devon and Cornwall pushed out into the Atlantic and we were at its stocking top. From now on, no injury, weakness of will, inclement weather or anything short of the end of the world would stop me completing the project.

There were two mini missions in the days ahead – firstly, to reach the sea and stare out across the blue Atlantic Ocean, knowing that if I kept it on my right and headed south, I'd inevitably hit Land's End (the second and final mission). Things were simplifying – all I had to do was remain focused and (somewhat harder to control) not get seriously injured.

A little way outside Chaffcombe, Chard Reservoir added a bucolic lift to my morning. No longer used for water provision, it is now a nature reserve. Well stocked with carp, even on this midweek morning, it had attracted several groups of anglers. A couple of boats floated placidly on the gently rippling water as ducks, grebes, herons and other water birds went about their business. The idyll was slightly spoilt by the retort of distant rifles; somewhere something feathered was being shot at.

I stretched out along the flat roads towards Chard and tried to ignore the fatigue filling up my limbs like a sluggish liquid metal, making me scuff my shoes along the roadway. Looking back, I'd had four days of thirty or more miles per day and it was taking its toll.

A little west of the town of Chard I did a quick appraisal of how my body was coping. Apart from a turn of speed that, frankly, your granny could better, I wasn't aching anywhere specific enough to worry about. A clicking in my knees didn't really constitute pain and the twanging of a tendon in my left calf would have to be monitored. I just had to drag one foot in front of another for another five or six miles to lunch and then hopefully the fuel I'd ingest would do a bit of emergency repair and I'd make it through the afternoon. My body's ability to process food with admirable efficiency and direct that energy where it was urgently required was one of the revelations that most impressed me. I think this process had definitely improved as the run had continued, as if my body had now adapted to a life spent running. For this I was grateful – I would have given up long ago if every step had become an agony.

A brief word about blisters: I didn't get any. I know ... it's mysterious and inexplicable. Almost every ultramarathon video on YouTube features a horrific blister-lancing sequence. It seems compulsory. And yet, apart from one small hard spot on my longest right toe around day four, this common ailment of distance runners did not bother me for the whole of the adventure. I suppose I'm just lucky but I'd also suggest it is strong evidence for two-ply socks. Towards the end of the run, when my heels were getting rubbed away by my shoes, I'd wear a second pair of socks over my running ankle socks, to protect the plasters covering my wounds. In effect, I was wearing three pairs of socks for the last few weeks. You'll get no stories of nightmarish foot trauma from me.

Between Chard and a place called Stockland, the flatness of the Somerset plains began to give way to hills once more – this was an encouraging sign. Exeter and Dartmoor were within the scope of a good day's running and Dartmoor is largely at an elevation between 400 and 600 metres so I should expect to start climbing. There would be a lot of hills between me and the moors and inclines would predominate; that was just a fact I'd have to deal with. One 12 per cent slope gave me a chance to stretch out the calf with a longer walking gait as well as catch my breath. You do learn to accentuate the positive side of any problem during an experience like The Long Run!

Somewhere that morning I officially left Somerset and entered Devon, a fact which made me think immediately of cream teas and that thought kept me going until lunch, for which we drove to Honiton. Scones were not forthcoming but I did enjoy some Scottish pancakes and found to my relief that another bout of 'rocket legs' descended in the early afternoon, propelling me along rollercoaster lanes and single-track roads.

Honiton was where the A30 began – the major artery through the centre of Devon and Cornwall. I'd be looping around this road all the way to Bodmin and I was grateful for the way it left the more obscure and tangled B-road relatively traffic-free. I found myself running along long, wide peaceful B-roads lined with trees. Occasionally a Land Rover would pass or I'd see a sign for a local business or autumn fair, or horses grazing in sloping fields of lush grass but the pervading atmosphere was one of uninterrupted calm. The metronomic percussion of my feet on the tarmac kept time more meaningfully than the ticking of any wristwatch. I wondered how many steps I'd taken so far, how many repetitions of the near-miraculous balancing act of lifting my body weight off one foot and throwing myself through the air only to arrest the motion, coil the springs and push off again. My post-lunch burst of energy carried me along at sub-8-minute miles. What a contrast from the morning's pathetic shuffling!

The low afternoon sun illuminated a quilt-patterned sky as I collected another type of cloud formation for my photographic record. Altocumulus, its peculiar patterning causing a corona to appear around the sun as it struggled to shine through – a red and blue ring forming like a serpentine eye above me. The valley below lay swathed in layers of mist, each successive hill paler and less substantial than the one in front. Everything felt considerably more epic.

My fleet-footedness carried me on to Honiton, whose suburban reaches were deceptively spread out, making me feel I'd never reach the town centre. I think I'd have been tempted to stop there if the energy left in my legs hadn't driven me into town, along the pretty main street with its cobblestones and brightly coloured shop-fronts. It was good to pass the café where we'd earlier had lunch and just keep on running. I wouldn't have predicted that outcome in the early morning when my legs had felt rigid and leaden.

Soon I was standing on a road bridge watching traffic whizzing along the A30 beneath me, feeling almost transfixed by the buzzing energy below and the contrasting quietude of the countryside beginning to bed down for the evening.

For the first couple of miles after hitting the A30, I jogged along an old and almost forgotten roadway which ran in tandem to the main road. Tall hedges prevented me from seeing the parallel A30 and yet I could hear its traffic almost as if I was running along its hard shoulder. I dubbed the route I was on The Ghost Road and enjoyed the eerie juxtaposition of traffic noise and emptiness. I have to admit, at this point, I had no real idea where I'd be stopping for the afternoon. Either I'd chance upon Sorrell or pick a place at random. I saw the name Whimple on signs and that became a likely candidate. Once again, I'd run close to thirty miles and had that 'lap of honour' feeling of having completed the day's allocation of miles. Anything else now would constitute a bonus.

The rather beautiful thatched exterior of The Greyhound Inn near Feniton caught my eye and made me salivate and fantasise about pints of foaming ale but I pressed on. Then my eagerness got the better of me a little later when I spontaneously decided to take to a footpath that led me under the A30 and into some fields and stranded me there. After considering climbing the embankment, I thought better of it, backtracked and took this as a sign that I should probably stop running. At least until tomorrow's slice of Blighty.[5]

MILES RUN: 1,005; MILES REMAINING: 95

---

1. Yes, I know you can make apple juice from them too but really, why bother?

2. Caused by the bending of light through many layers of mist, so that the viewer is seeing a reflection of the sky, although looking at the base of the tower.

3. But then nor was Haight-Asbury when I visited San Francisco in the mid-2000s and London's Carnaby Street is now a shadow of its former self.

4. Scots for – you've guessed it – 'leaped'

5. For the benefit of non-British readers, Blighty is an English slang term for Britain, based upon the Hindustani word vilâyatî.

Section Four

THE LAST LEG

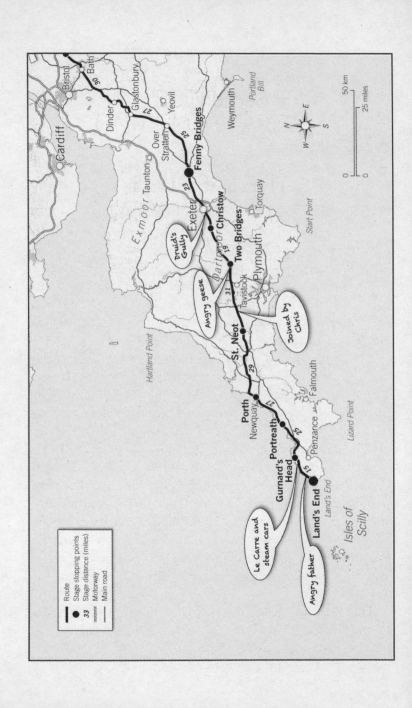

FENNY BRIDGES TO MORETONHAMPSTEAD

Two fleeting memories of running from childhood.

The first was an unusual PE (Physical Education) session in which we were taken out on a cross-country run, the one and only time this occurred. I must have been twelve or thirteen years old and I still have a powerful memory of this experience because, unusually for PE, I both enjoyed it and was good at it. I've never been much into team sports, as either a participant or spectator.

This was different – all I was being asked to do was run and that seemed both easy and fairly pleasurable. It was a crisp autumn day in Edinburgh and our route took us through various playing fields in Oxgangs before looping back into Firrhill High School's grounds. I didn't really understand why many of the other kids seemed to think this was a form of punishment or torture, why so many of them bunked off to smoke cigarettes behind bushes rather than participate. At that time the school didn't have a particularly stellar academic or sporting record and even though I came second in this non-race, I don't remember ever receiving any encouragement to take up running competitively. This is especially puzzling as I was showing little or no aptitude for any other sport.

That said, my second memory is of somehow being asked to participate in an Inter-scholastic games event which, remarkably, was taking place at Murrayfield Stadium, Edinburgh's most prestigious athletics venue. I wonder now if the school's participation was sprung upon them at the last minute since I can remember no selection process nor any training whatsoever. Nevertheless, I was asked to run third position in a 400 metre relay race.

I remember a stadium full of spectators and dozens of school teams taking part. I can't remember much about the race itself except I think I fumbled the baton and ran as fast as my legs would carry me. Despite my best efforts, I dropped a place. I think we finished halfway down the field in that event. Nothing much remains sharp in memory bar the actual feeling of running along that gently curving track between those white lines. The relay race was also to prove a one-off. I think I received a certificate of some sort. Perhaps Mum has it in the bottom of a cupboard somewhere.

I'm mentioning these two experiential fragments to illustrate that my upbringing was as un-sporty and non-competitive as it's possible to be, despite the fact that there was at least one activity I might have excelled at. Such regrets are pointless. At best I might have managed a sub-3-marathon if I'd started in my youth. Perhaps a 15–16 minute 5K would have been possible. I doubt I'd have troubled any leader boards.

Two of the great things about running is the accessibility of the sport and the fact that you need not compete against anybody but yourself if you so choose. The latter factor makes it appeal to me more than any one-on-one or team sport ever could. The pressure of contributing to a team performance caused me absurd levels of stress. Even the pressure of competing against myself and my expectations reduces me to a quivering jelly before the start gun goes off at any marathon.

The Long Run was different. Given its extraordinarily duration – six weeks of running – and the fact that nobody else was doing it with me and very few people have ever attempted it, there was no possibility for stomach-churning worry or competitive stress to develop. Instead, the only negative emotions I ever felt were the occasional trough of self-doubt and perhaps a creeping disappointment that I wasn't quite the forty-miles-a-day super-athlete that, for some unknown reason, I'd thought I could be.

That said, after five consecutive days of 30-plus miles, on the brilliantly sunny, crystal clear morning of the 12th October 2015, I was feeling pretty good about myself. I had five or six days left as I skimmed alongside the manicured hedges of Devon heading towards Exeter and Dartmoor. It was perfect running weather, my legs were magically renewed, somehow, and all was right with the world.

Forty minutes into the day's running I'd already managed to take the wrong turning but the complex web of small roads between Fenny Bridges, Talaton and Whimple meant I could just alter course a little and I'd find my way back to the desired route without too much difficulty. Most of my small roads skirted the aforementioned villages rather than passing through them but I would briefly visit the town of Broadclyst, (also known by the rather odd name of 'Dog Village'), which turned out to be a rather pretty parish once put to flame by the invading Danes in 1001AD. Its canine nomenclature refers to a village square where the Black Dog pub once stood (now converted to housing). The English do love their pubs.

Exeter lay five miles to the west as I walked and jogged up a steep leafy lane pursued timidly by two sheepdogs, whose unseen owner was presumably round the corner. I hoped they weren't strays and, in any case, I had no food to offer them. Perhaps they were just on a pilgrimage to Dog Village. The roads were utterly quiet, brilliantly sunlit and heavily wooded, all of which suited me just fine.

Getting closer to the city, I passed more and more cyclists, hikers and even one or two runners. Seeing others exercising in the fresh air helped me feel a sense of connection, a kinship I'd not felt since the Pennine Way's busier stretches. Running for forty odd days straight by oneself can be lonely at times; we may be our own best reserves but those reserves aren't boundless. I was missing the pub conversations, nights out and even the interactions I'd had in the office before giving up my job to pursue this craziness.

The task ahead seemed eminently achievable – get into Dartmoor by the end of the day, cross the wild moors by the end of the 13th, hit the coast by the end of the 14th or 15th and then run along the shoreline to the end of Britain. Meanwhile, I found myself passing an endless array of almost painfully cute thatched and whitewashed stone cottages, brightly berried hawthorn hedges, burgeoning apple trees and leaf canopies full of birdsong. The climate this far south felt markedly different from anywhere else I'd been, milder, less capable of threatening and sudden shifts. Was it really going to be this easy for the remainder of my running challenge?

This late in autumn, the sides of the road were deep with sun-crisped leaves, the peace punctuated by the plop of falling acorns and the whirring of sycamore seeds as they spiralled to the ground. A light breeze rustled the hedges on the higher roads. My optimism began to fight the erosion of a growing fatigue and the nagging calf pain that had returned after eight miles. I found myself oscillating between hopeful-ness and a kind of despairing awareness of every dragging footstep. Leaden legs and deep fatigue are habitually my worst enemies. Jolts of pain can perversely spur me on – I'd fight their occasional interruptions; all-pervasive exhaustion that builds and builds proved a more formidable foe.

When I hit the main road into Exeter, gratefully hopping onto its pavement, it couldn't have come a moment too soon. My animal self was nagging me to stop now with every step, refusing to submit to my will. I had to trick it by promising it an excellent meal – surely a city the size of Exeter, with its huge student population, would offer every kind of food available to mankind. Let me run there, I promised, and I will sate your desires. As outskirts gave way to suburbs and then to the city centre, my willpower reasserted itself and I raced past student pubs, red-brick office buildings and public parks.

There's a shot I'm particularly proud of in the film heading through the shopping precincts of Exeter city centre. In my delirious hunger I'm running purely on autopilot and I've thrown shyness and caution to the winds and am actually running down the middle of the main street, weaving in and out of students and office workers making their way to lunch and shoppers on the prowl for a bargain. Magically, everyone just seems to avoid me at the last possible moment, and without irritation – I glide through them like an unseen spirit. Somehow there is busy foot-traffic but very few vehicles. I feel secure in stepping off the pavement into the main thoroughfare when I need to. The soundtrack to this shot mingles music, fragments of conversation, the engines of hybrid buses and the clatter of distant building work. I'd not seen so many people in one place since leaving Edinburgh. I felt oddly superhuman – nobody but me was deranged enough to jog down the main shopping streets.

My pre-lunch mission was to locate Exeter cathedral and stop there; it would be an easy rendezvous point for Sorrell. At first, I took a back alley and got a little lost. After a bit of investigation I located the lane leading to the front of the cathedral and ran out into a large public square. Dozens of people were picnicking on the lawns in front of the twelfth-century cathedral, whose impressive west front dominated the square. A ring of cafes and shops circled the space in which workers rested and ate or, in the case of one group of teenagers, played table tennis. I flopped to the grass, at long last able to stretch out, and made the necessary phone call.

Lunch was unusually healthy – we ate in a vegan café overlooking the square and, having not had much in the way of 'greens' over the last couple of weeks, my body drank it all in avidly. I had some sort of vegetable tart with various side salads – grated carrot, couscous, beetroot then a piece of vegan cake with tea. It proved just what I needed to get over the mysterious slump I had been experiencing. Perhaps Mr Jurek and Mr Roll[1] had the right idea after all in ditching meat and dairy.

The sun continued to blaze down as I navigated my way out of the city, past remains of the old Roman wall and the medieval bridge, under a brightly painted subway, over the river Exe and on through the city limits. Next stop would be the village of Ide, just beyond the A30, then on to Dunchideock (a place name that sparked many conversations about pronunciation and I'm still not clear how to say it). Green tunnels of narrow lanes enshrouded by high hedges and trees soon dominated. The traffic was still relatively heavy this close to Exeter and there were occasional cyclists and pedestrians. My mood lightened as the energy from lunch flooded my system. Things were back on track.

Until they weren't. As is my prerogative, I got lost as soon as humanly possible, missing the correct turning after Ide and trying an alternative route only to find the way I wanted to take didn't form a crossroads with the one I was running along. Instead, the desired route was on a high ridge of some sort, a tunnel allowing my current road to pass under it but nothing connecting the two at the point of crossing. My choices seemed to be trespassing into a field or burrowing through the underbrush and up to the higher road. Or turning back to look for an alternative way. At the moment my Garmin told me I was heading north, clearly a bad idea. Continuing on this wrong road would get me nowhere. Should I take the sensible third option and double back? As you'll have noticed by now, I am not sensible.

Looking more closely at the vegetation by the tunnel entrance I saw what looked like the mouth of a footpath of some sort. It wasn't marked as such but by now I'd developed something of a sixth sense for finding unmarked ways – not necessarily a helpful trait. I decided it was worth exploring. Perhaps some locals had forged a path up to the high road.

Fighting through briars and nettles, I pushed through into a tiny pathway that climbed a dozen metres or so before resolving into something less like an animal track and more like a proper trail – there was even a stile over a small fence, which reassured me that I was at least heading along something created by humans, rather than badgers or deer. Nevertheless, it felt like this trail was very much on its way to becoming forgotten. It didn't quickly veer to the right and up to the high road, as I'd been hoping it would. I pressed on regardless, heading roughly north-east now (which no doubt would confuse Sorrell). As usual in these situations, I had only intermittent phone coverage. I think curiosity began to get the better of my common sense, and old memories of exploring forest trails as a kid flooded back.

As I pushed my way through trailing creepers (creepers, in England?) and long, looping strands of briar, the path resolved into a kind of gully, the sides of which were steep, impenetrably wooded and about fifteen feet high. There was a jungle feeling to the enormous runnel I was passing through, which began to seem man-made. Could it be a remainder of some Roman earthworks? There were definite signs of recent human habitation – a couple of hanging creepers had been tied in knots and woven branch 'fences' held back leaf-falls at the side of the trail.

After about a quarter of a mile, the centre of the path held a large round stone, about the size of a bathtub, which would be perfect for animal sacrifices. I'm sure my school friend

Richard and I would have invented a complex mythology involving druids or Satanists and worked ourselves into that pleasurable thrill of manageable fear that accompanies childhood exploration.

I had almost scared myself into that childlike state of not knowing by the time I found the road again, which intensified when even the blue dot of Google Maps couldn't locate me. Was this some sinister region where ley lines intersected or a magnetic anomaly affected GPS devices? My imagination was running riot as, not without further difficulty, I found the right way out of the narrow, busy main road at Ide and headed out towards Dartmoor. When I could, I called Sorrell and filled her in on some of the oddity of my afternoon. I'd lost at least an hour in my aimless meanderings and now it was time to get back on course.

Halfway up the hill out of Ide, I stopped briefly to sit on a bench that seemed to be positioned purely for my gratification, giving a great view down to Exeter. I figured out that I was about six miles from Dunchideock and vowed to at least reach there before calling it a day. As I pressed on, the irrepressible sunshine and cloudless blue sky warmed and motivated me. More than ever, I was chasing down that sun, since I would be heading due west until I hit the coast.

I developed an arbitrary goal to reach the green section on the map that delineated the edge of Dartmoor proper. My fatigue had returned with a vengeance and I knew I was only good for about twenty-four to twenty-six miles today. Given the mileage I'd been scoring over the last week, I thought I could justify having a light day. I used a large-scale version of a coping strategy used by many long-distance runners. If the scale of the whole race feels too impossible, break it down – just get to that next mile marker, or the next landmark, then worry about the next one. Incremental progress builds overall success. The important thing is just to keep going.

Another great technique in long-distance running, when you are following a self-set goal rather than an official race, is to pause and look back – literally, not metaphorically. You'll often see that you've run further than the horizon – the curvature of the earth prevents you from seeing your point of origin and this gives you a sense of what you've achieved. Whenever the landscape opened up and the hedgerows fell away to reveal a view north and east, I would avail myself of this confidence-boosting trick.

I'd worked myself into one of those almost trancelike states of low-energy running, the sun now like a giant beacon directly in front of me, when a small deer stepped gingerly across my path and into the underbrush. It was quite a magical moment and made me hold my breath for a second. The animal was silhouetted against the sun, entirely in its element and unflustered – either it hadn't seen me or it wasn't the least bit concerned. The lane I'd been running along was utterly devoid of traffic and this unexpected encounter gave me the lift I needed at that point to keep going. I'm not at all religious but encounters like these can make me feel more interconnected with nature. It's a blindingly obvious truth – we were both animals at home in our respective environments, both warm-blooded mammals just going about our day.

We do need to remind ourselves of this truism from time to time, however. Humans are not apart from nature, they are a part of nature, a simple truth that should underpin all environmental policies. Our ascendancy is arbitrary – were a meteorite strike or nuclear Armageddon to wipe us out tomorrow, most probably the insects would inherit the earth. Come back to post-apocalyptic Britain in ten million years and you might be talking to the first cockroach prime minister of the UK. I find the chance element in our evolution a humbling thought. As a species, we simply got lucky and that, amongst other humane considerations, should motivate us to look after the place we call home, Carl Sagan's 'pale blue dot'.[2]

While mayflies danced in pools of early-evening sunlight, I reached a road junction where a handwritten sign pointed to the impressively-named village of Doddiscombsleigh. I knew that meant I was close to where I'd be able to stop – my legs were crying out for respite and I was simply focusing on putting one foot in front of another. Oddly, I was making good pace though – up to 9-minute miles once more. A narrow farm road above steeply sloping fields brought me over a hill and down into a valley where, I hoped, I'd soon hit the B3193 and meet up with Sorrell and stop.

The road got steeper and steeper, descending sharply and really challenging my quads and knees. Out of nowhere a tall, whitewashed stone house, renovated with a modern finish, reflected the sunlight and brought me to a halt at a junction. A wrong turning would finish my spirit now – I was in that slightly fragile, delirious zone where the body's entreaties are affecting the mind's ability to focus. I'd find that a squirrel clinging to a tree trunk or a sign advertising an idyllic-looking footpath would suddenly pull all of my attention away from the task in hand. I forced myself to stop, focus, and consult the maps.

Minutes later I staggered down to the B-road and found that Sorrell had parked in a pub car park directly opposite (I always seemed to end the day near a public house). This was extremely good news – my mind and body had reached their daily limit. I staggered into the car, having only done twenty-four miles, but secure in the knowledge that, that day at least, I had nothing left to give.

The following day was a little chillier but just as bright and sunny as I reached Bridford and had to jump up onto a wall to get around a lorry that had misjudged a narrow bend and got stuck. That my legs allowed me to do this came as a pleasant surprise after the fatigue of the previous day. I'd bought a Dartmoor map a few days before and, although I'd not yet worked out a walking route, my plan was still to find a way of off-roading through the moor as much as possible. The first task was simply to find the beginning of a trail that would lead me out of the maze of high-hedged lanes. We'd started fairly early that day and, as I ran, the low sun at my back threw my shadow before me, allowing me to see my gait. I'm sure this helped impel me on at a greater speed than I'd have otherwise managed.

Bridford Wood was where I'd hoped to exchange tarmac for leaves, mud and stones. Unfortunately, it didn't seem to be especially close to the town of Bridford and took much finding. A National Trust maintained forest, the wood would take me close to Doccombe, avoiding sections of the busy B3212. That said, I didn't have anything as clearly marked out as the Pennine Way (at its best) to follow so I was very much playing it by ear. A mile or so of running back north from the town took me along a very quiet leafy lane with the familiar 'grass Mohican' running up its centre.

Eventually I reached the mouth of a trail with Steps Bridge and Burnicombe engraved into handmade wooden signs. A grass and gravel path led me to a bridleway which wound around some farms. Steps Bridge was where I'd begin to head properly west once more, with the aim of hitting North Bovey or Moretonhampstead by mid-morning. The bridleway began to ramp steeply downhill, leaf-strewn and treacherous to the unwary foot. Sunlight flashed through the trees. I was enjoying myself immensely, in my element on this forest trail. I felt myself speeding up, running close to my usual training pace of around 8-minute miles, having to make a conscious effort to break when approaching gates and stiles.

Next came a wider gravel and dirt path heading me up through the forest proper. Signs made it clear that I was now on National Trust property and it was well maintained and easy to run. I think I'd expected my off-roading on Dartmoor to be a little more exposed and moor-like but I was perfectly happy for now to run pain-free and fast in my favourite environment. A clearing opened up with a finger sign pointing me between two large piles of cut logs. Although there were other paths leading away, this one seemed so obvious as to be incontrovertibly correct. Some mistakes I seem incapable of learning from.

The forest now seemed far less domesticated and yet I passed a few dog-walkers and hikers, so wasn't put off when the trail narrowed and began to climb alongside a fast-flowing stream. Muddier, wilder and precipitous, the path reduced me to a march. Remarkably it was a bridleway, presumably used by the sturdiest and fittest of ponies. I slowed to a 15-minute pace or worse and headed for Burnicombe farm.

The view from the high fields, looking out across the moors, was spectacular but as clouds began to roll in amidst the blue, I lost my way once more. I made it down to the B-road and then headed along it for a while before locating another bridleway that led me back uphill. Although such diversions might provide picturesque routes for a day's rambling, I was rapidly losing time and not gaining as many miles as I'd liked. From then on, I stuck to the B-road.

The mid-morning traffic wasn't as bad as I'd expected, so I thought it was worth chancing the odd encounter with a speeding motorist to head towards Moretonhampstead as speedily as possible. For personal reasons it would be unfair to go into, I didn't want to run through the town, which lies at a major crossroads in the eastern part of the moors. A close friend of mine had been married there a few years prior and it hadn't worked out (what is it with Devonshire and weddings?) I'd been there for the wedding and met all the locals and the groom's family but, for various reasons, the memories were a little soured now and the thought of reawakening those memories was a little worrisome, even for me. Still, it was the fastest and most logical route to take and I didn't plan to tarry so I bit the bullet and headed down into the valley. The breeze picked up, shaking loose the few remaining leaves in the trees as the sun warmed the fields. Moreton's church stood decorous upon a distant hillside, beckoning me on. I kept an eagle eye out for cars, trucks and even the occasional local bus negotiating the route's many curves.

The first familiar sight was the fifteenth-century almshouses at the eastern edge of town, then the church where my friend had been married (I remember the surreal sight of a swarm of bees escaping from the belfry before the ceremony). I ran through the town of pretty whitewashed buildings, quaint pubs and local shops. There was not a single national chain store in sight. The village retains its intimacy despite being a major traffic thoroughfare, as evidenced by tour buses struggling to negotiate its narrow lanes. I passed through without incident, meeting up with Sorrell briefly for a confab about the route ahead. Whatever doubts I'd had about coming this way now seemed ridiculous. However, I was glad to get some of those tainted memories behind me, along with some of the attendant guilt.

MILES RUN: 1,047; MILES REMAINING: 53[3]

---

1. Rich Roll, ultra-runner, vegan, multiple Ironman and author of the highly recommended *Finding Ultra*, although this man's extraordinary level of physical fitness might make anyone feel inadequate.

2. If you haven't seen this glorious clip from his famous show Cosmos, watch it here: https://www.youtube.com/watch?v=XH7ZRF6zNoc

3. At this point it should be evident that my estimation of the total distance I would run was woefully inadequate – from the next chapter, the corrected remainder will be given.

MORETONHAMPSTEAD TO TAVISTOCK

Running the B-road had proved fairly painless, so we decided to keep the momentum going and make it to Two Bridges at least by the end of the day. I thought I might have it in me to reach Tavistock, or close to it but I knew from yesterday's experiences that the exhaustion was now rising and falling in unpredictable waves. I couldn't count on anything but forward motion. However far I got, if I stuck to the main road, I could never get lost and Sorrell could always find me.

I had dinner with my parents to look forward to – my father was due to take over the reins once more and this time Mum had come with him. Obviously the drive down from Edinburgh now was a rather epic one so they'd decided to make something of a holiday of it and stay in Cornwall for a couple of weeks. The simplest thing had been to book one self-catering apartment on the coast and they had based their choice of location on the overambitious estimate I'd made of where I'd be by the end of the day (the far side of Dartmoor). Perranporth would be my home from home each night until the end of The Long Run. It would entail a lot of driving but, on the other hand, having our own base made all other aspects of organising the journey's final chapter much easier. We could stock up with whatever food I required, start each day whenever we wanted, not worry about making last-minute hotel bookings and save money on dinners by eating in most nights. It would grow to feel almost too comfortable, since I'd been used to a peripatetic existence with my head hitting a new pillow almost every night but, all things being equal, it was still the best way of providing for all our needs.

The road from Moretonhampstead took me past the entrance to the rather grand Bovey Castle, now a hotel where the aforementioned friend had stayed during her nuptials, then on towards Dartmoor proper, where side roads would give way to small semicircular car parks for picnicking and gazing across the land. I rounded one tight corner and a few hundred yards later was almost knocked down, irony of ironies, by two disability charity minibuses (fortunately belonging to neither of the charities I was supporting). I didn't waste my breath cursing them. I didn't want anything to spoil my growing spirit of optimism or reduce the focus of my newfound 'finishing line' mindset.

A much more endearing encounter lay ahead at the Miniature Pony Centre.[1] Given that I have a pony fanatic sister, Katy (she owns and rides an Icelandic called Glennur) I had to stop and film a shot or two of these impossibly cute animals, hard at work reducing the grass in their paddock to a military crop. Later in my run I'd have specific reason to be grateful for these creatures' insatiable appetites; for now they were just a distraction from the endless fatigue I was feeling on day 43.

For seven weeks now I'd become used to being so tired at the end of each day (and often at the start) that I had to use handrails to ascend flights of steps or exercise extra caution going downstairs in case my quads gave way; so exhausted that when sleep came, it came as a total annihilation of consciousness. No more restless nights for me – sleep now switched me off like a light as the body began its overnight emergency repairs.

In the planning stages, I'd mapped out a complex series of B-roads and farm tracks to make it to Two Bridges and Tavistock, and had included potential off-road sections.

Having abandoned this plan in favour of sticking to the
B-road, I quickly realised that, for once, I'd made the right
decision. The B3212 and B3357 both run right through the
middle of the moor in an unbroken rollercoaster and are
as direct as you might reasonably expect. Even better, they
are not more than moderately busy with day trippers and
coaches, since the A30 and A38, which flank the moors to
the north and south respectively, carry most of the through
traffic. To help maintain the relative quietude and to protect
the local livestock roaming freely across the moors, there is
a forty miles per hour limit imposed on Dartmoor's wildest
section. The groan-inducing motto 'Take Moor Care'
hammers the point home. It's not always properly observed
but I did see at least one parked police car, presumably
poised to catch the unwary speeder.

A better deterrent are the herds of unconcerned cows
and insouciant sheep that wander freely across the roads.
They do seem to affect an almost belligerent lack of concern
for their own well-being with last-minute sashays between
coaches and cars. This indeed is their right – this was really
their landscape more than it was mine. There is evidence of
Dartmoor having been widely farmed for over 5,000 years;
even now, over 90 per cent of its land is given over to this
purpose.[2] During my run I saw the remains of many ancient
walls and corrals, as well as 'reaves' or regular banks of earth
used to subdivide parcels of land, some of these earthworks
dating back to 1200BC. There are seventy-six prehistoric
stone rows and fourteen stone circles on Dartmoor – it is
an ancient yet living landscape. Tourism is a recent incur-
sion onto the moors and is, quite rightly, kept in check. One
of my only regrets in taking to the 'high road' through the
moor was that I couldn't photograph the view from one of
the high tors. Nevertheless, there were sufficient layers of
visible history alongside the B-roads to keep my imagination
active as I ran.

Speeding there must be tempting if you're not much of an animal lover or law-abiding citizen; the roads curve gently but impressively up to 600 metres above sea level, with fantastic views all round – perfect for an open-topped sports car and indeed, I saw several such during my run. On the 13th October 2015 the weather remained spectacularly warm, sunny and dry, with the sun a vivid beacon in the sky above me. Visibility was good but not perfect. I've read that from some of the high tors you can sometimes make out the sea to the west or south. I had no such luck but just knowing that this was, in theory, possible, made me feel I was getting close to my goal.

Despite the beauty of the day, I got the sense that, on a stormy, windy evening this could be an extremely wild and unforgiving landscape. There was little or no tree cover over much of the high moors, which presented me with something of a difficulty when it came to taking a pee stop. I had to become content with the minimal privacy offered by simply striding out into the moor and facing away from the road. On the other hand, the actual running surface itself was amazingly conducive to good pace, once I left the tarmac and took to the closely cropped verges. These provided around three feet of clearance from the edge of the road on both sides, intermittently broken by drainage trenches narrow enough to hop over. The soft springy grass and peaty soil was perfect at absorbing the impact of my footfalls and most of the hills were lengthy and gradual, so I was able to keep running. I was just another mammal by the side of the road, dodging tour buses and constellations of dried-out sheep dung.

That said, the distances were deceptive. An ancient mile marker informing me I was five miles out from Moreton-hampstead must have been laid long before Ordnance Survey maps or GPS technology; surely I had run further than that? And yet I didn't feel like I was in a hurry or rather, although there was a growing need to refuel, I had no specific need to stop running. I'd finally become completely habituated to running being a normal mode of transport.

We lunched in a whitewashed stone pub with surely one of the best views in England – the Warren Inn, at 434 metres above sea level it's one of the highest pubs in the country and sits entirely isolated from other buildings since the local tin mines closed in 1930. Subsisting now on passing trade and tourism, the Inn is something of a legend amongst Dartmoor's hikers. Its gleaming frontage is visible from miles away and certainly drove me on at a faster pace as I approached.

Reinvigorated, I vowed at least to reach Two Bridges by the end of the day. My legs did not hurt at all now, pain and fatigue diminished by the sheer pleasure of being in such a beautiful environment on this unexpectedly glorious day. I began to feel that rare thing, a 'runners' high'. The afternoon got as close as almost any stretch of The Long Run to being perfect. My pace was good, my legs didn't hurt and I felt free from worry, regret or fear for the future. I was just running, enjoying the heightened sense of all of my body's systems working in unison. I felt an almost evangelical zeal and had I been running with any newcomers to the activity, I'm sure I would have bored them with my insistence that *this* was what it was all about.

I also began to realise just what I was about to achieve. It's a bit of an obvious point but it struck me quite vividly that day – I had almost run 1,000 miles in six weeks. Where I'd started today's running was 131 miles, by my calculations, from Land's End.[3] Tomorrow I would top the landmark four figures in mileage. That thought spurred me on even faster. Even mistaking the distant group of houses for Two Bridges (it was in fact Postbridge) didn't put a dampener on my mood. The exhaustion I'd been feeling, camouflaged under that top layer of renewed enthusiasm, began to reassert itself towards mid-afternoon but this time it didn't trouble me. I knew I'd earned it.

Soon enough my route began to progressively dip towards the confluence of two roads that marks Two Bridges. The high opens moors gave way to wetter grasslands and the road was flanked by trees on one side as the white walls of the Two Bridges Hotel appeared in the valley below me. I knew my parents would be waiting for me there, along with Sorrell, ready to do the final handover of support responsibility.

Another jolt of memory presented itself when I reached the hotel, with its old stone bridge over the river[4] and flock of unruly white geese who patrolled the car park like a gang of hoodlums. The same once-married friend who had warned me against passing through Moretonhampstead had had her wedding reception in the Two Bridges Hotel. Once again, I was defying her wishes but really, this was the only building or car park for miles and I couldn't help it if I'd reached my energy limit for the day. She would just have to close her eyes in this section of the film if the memories proved too troubling. My urge for a cream tea and a sit-down on a comfortable sofa was just too important! For my own part, I remember being photographed in my kilt by the ancient stone bridge, dodging the feral gaggle of geese and drunkenly lifting a petite Filipina friend off the ground for a photo – for me it is only a happy memory, now joined by a new one.

Starting off at Two Bridges with my father filming the following day seemed fitting – we would finish as we began, supporting one another, both trying out new skills and learning by trial and (frequent) error. The weather was just as idyllic as the previous day and, although I was far from as nimble as I'd felt the day before, I hobbled up the road towards the last section of moorland with the same renewed feeling of hope.

By now I knew that this 'nothing in the tank' early morning feeling was an illusion and that my body would find hidden reserves to see me through the first chunk of the day. Dramatic rocky tors stood out on the horizon and my eyes drank in a harmonious colour palette of green grass, brown bracken, whitewashed farmhouses and azure blue sky. The views continued to take my breath away as I climbed to the heights of the tiny hamlet of Merrivale, at around 450 metres above sea level. I stopped to say hello to someone's pet goat, tethered by the local pub; it would not be distracted from its breakfast. I knew the feeling.

As the moors began to descend towards Tavistock, the breeze built up and a few clouds scudded across the blue expanse of sky overhead. I'd seen signs by the side of the road advertising the Tavistock Goose Fair and suggesting a road diversion for motorists. I didn't know what the fair signified or what to expect as I headed down towards the city. I passed over a cattle grid marking the end of the protected zone and, less than a mile later was back to negotiating narrow lanes with fast-moving traffic, high hedges and sharp corners. I moved up a gear, tearing around blind corners and rejoicing at a strip of pavement that inevitably frittered out after thirty yards. A nearby horse listened to my grumbled complaints but remained unimpressed. I soldiered on.

Finally, the town's sign appeared, announcing Tavistock as both a market and 'stannary' town. This latter term required a bit of googling – apparently white lead was once refined, assessed and sold here in what was known as a stannary.

One final push around dangerous corners and I could see the town proper ahead, a church tower standing out on the hillside, a scattering of buildings hidden amongst trees down below. I jogged past grey stone and whitewashed brick buildings, ran alongside a well-maintained graveyard and riverside park and headed for the town centre where the pounding of amplified music could already be heard.

Dartmoor's solitude would soon be a fading memory.

MILES RUN: 1,078; MILES REMAINING: 96

---

1. http://www.miniatureponycentre.com/ – worth a visit, unless you are under doctor's orders to avoid the excessive cuteness of dwarf or baby animals.

2. http://www.dartmoor.gov.uk/learningabout/lab-printableresources/lab-factsheetshome/lab-farming_history

3. Not entirely accurate, as it turned out.

4. Most visitors assume the old stone bridge over the river and the newer road bridge give the place its name. In fact, in the eighteenth century there was another bridge further upstream – the current modern bridge has nothing to do with its nomenclature.

TAVISTOCK TO MAWGAN PORTH

Thousands of people – a sight I'd not experienced since, well, for as long as I could remember. Birmingham had been rather too spread out to feel like a city of millions and, in any case, I'd sneaked through it by means of the canal. Bath and Chipping Campden had been more about omnipresent traffic than pedestrians. Even Exeter's lunchtime crowds had been rarefied enough to run through at speed. This was something else entirely. It seemed like half of Devon was thronging a couple of long market streets that morning in Tavistock.

Stalls sold an odd mix of the local and the mundane. For every stall of local farm produce there seemed to be one selling branded clothing knock-offs or mobile phone cases. Far from being a modern creation though, the Goose Fair dates back to the Michaelmas markets of the twelfth century, when geese were sold in time for fattening for Christmas (our current obsession with seasonal turkey is comparatively modern[1]). Now it has to juggle tradition with practicality – market stalls are expensive to run and keenly sought-after.

I didn't tarry as I weaved through the shopping crowds to the strains of James Brown and The Jackson Five blasting over the PA system. There were waltzers and a small Ferris wheel. Candyfloss and ice cream. Tiger print throws, an old-fashioned hall of mirrors, chocolate-coated marshmallows, a guy playing a didgeridoo. I hoisted my gimbal over my head for a better view as I sought out a narrow alleyway that short cut me through to the high street. I had my own mundane shopping to do and needed a bank – this would be my last chance to pass through a major town until Newquay. Parents found and chores completed, I decided to run on. We'd have lunch somewhere a little less frantic.

Minutes later, the contrast couldn't have been more marked. The tiny back roads west of Tavistock were quiet, narrow and afforded great views back to the bustling town. I think I had been conditioned to solitude by this point in The Long Run and I could feel the relief of being away from all those people as a palpable release.

I have, since my early teens, experienced some species of social anxiety, though it has never troubled me to the point of wanting to have it diagnosed by a professional. At school it manifested in a severe level of shyness. I couldn't talk to my much cooler (or so it seemed) classmates. Walking past a group of girls on the street would reduce me to a blushing mess (I assumed, without any evidence to that effect, that they were laughing at me). I was academically high-performing but socially inept and didn't have a girlfriend until I was in my mid-twenties. My parents and sisters weren't aware of me having a problem because, when I was at home, it simply never manifested. I was comfortable in the home environment and knew where I stood.

At school, at university, at work, I behaved quite differently. This is not to say that my condition was crippling – I functioned well enough in these difficult places to make the progress my ambitions required of me – but I was seldom truly happy until I hit my mid-twenties. It was during the nineties that I learned coping mechanisms such as simply excusing myself if things became too uncomfortable, rather than trying to press on through a growing sense of social failure or alienation.

At times what might these days be identified as 'Social

Anxiety Disorder'[2] drove me to suicidal thoughts and even to one banal, almost comical 'cry for help' involving a lot of paracetamol that led to a night in the overdose ward of an Edinburgh hospital. That trough of despair proved a sort of 'aversion therapy' – I had felt utterly out of place amongst the serious manic-depressives and drug addicts who filled the ward. I realised how ridiculous allowing myself to feel so down was (and that night it was a girl's disdain that pushed me over the edge) and vowed never again to sink to such depths, a vow I have managed to keep until this day.[3]

It might not come as a surprise to you therefore to hear that I dislike crowds. This is partly because they slow me down (I habitually walk unusually fast, even when I'm relaxed) and partly for reasons I can't entirely reconcile. They just make me feel more exposed than I'm comfortable with, even though the opposite is probably true – it's easier to hide amongst a throng. I still don't much like going to house parties (although I sometimes force myself to do so and usually find sympathetic people to talk to). I'll do almost anything to escape a dinner party unless I know the majority of attendees. Even something as simple as getting a haircut causes anxiety – I feel I have no small talk and also that I'm obliged to try to make it. A cycle of self-consciousness can occur in these situations which is occasionally so awful that I have to quietly absent myself. It's seldom a significant problem but it's always there, waiting to pounce.

Perhaps all of this in part explains why I'm so predisposed to long, solo runs – I need a lot more 'me time' than most people and running is one of the healthiest and best ways of obtaining that regular fix. I feel mentally cleansed by running – it's like a brain reboot. Anxieties slip away as I focus on simple, physical rhythms. Long runs also prove hugely creative and inspiring experiences for me – more of the problems in my screenplays are solved during my Thames-side excursions than by sitting, rigidly staring at a flashing cursor on an unforgivingly white screen. Don't just take my word for it – try it. Take your problems for a run (or a cycle or a swim or a walk). Get in the right frame of mind and, although they may not be solved, your problems will at least return thoroughly examined.

Damerel, Horsebridge, Venterdon, Bray Shop. The expressive, mysterious village names continued as I exchanged the moors for tiny local roads and farm lanes once more. I'd soon be sharing the run for the third and final time – author and keen (but relatively new) forty-something runner Chris Thrall would be joining me on the morning of the 14th October for a little while, keen to share his newfound enthusiasm for ultra-running.

Chris has had an eventful life, to say the least. A former Royal Marine, Chris's life spiralled out of control when he moved to Hong Kong at the end of his ten-year tenure with the military to work on a marketing business he'd developed. For complex reasons outlined in his book *Eating Smoke*,[4] his career foundered and he ended up being introduced to the dangerously addictive world of crystal meth, becoming heavily dependent on the drug and ending up paranoid and isolated by culture clash, working as a doorman for a club owned by a local Triad gang. To say his story is bizarre and chaotic is to do it an injustice and condemn it by understatement.

Now, however, having published a bestselling memoir, Chris is in control of his life and, like me, found great release in the simple act of repeatedly putting one foot in front of the other. Cheerful and enthusiastic, still sporting a military 'number one' crop, Chris proved something of an unexpected acolyte, since he too had an ambition to run the length of the country. We'd met in the summer during the 24-hour race I described in the foreword and had shared a few difficult Sunday morning laps near the end of our respective reserves of stamina. At that point, after twenty hours of running, even finding the energy to hold a civil conversation proved something of a challenge, yet Chris proved an amiable companion during our shared hours of madness.

We met at a place with the unlikely name of Chipshop. Perhaps it was just as well as a chip shop was not in evidence anywhere in the tiny settlement. There was, however, a pub (the Copper Penny Inn). Its name derives from the way that local copper and arsenic miners were sometimes paid in scrip – tokens often called 'chips', to defray the effects of the regularly tardy cash payments from the mine owners. These chips could be exchanged for local goods at places including the Inn. The Copper Penny still sells local farm produce, maintaining a tradition dating back to the 1800s.

Chris and I headed out at a fairly easy 10-minute mile pace, weaving our way through fairly quiet and rather nondescript farm roads. I was glad of the company, given the anonymity of these local roads, which were flanked with high hedgerows on both sides. Chris hails from Plymouth, so he was comparatively local – a fact that might stand him in good stead for his own JOGLE run, since he will be getting nearer and nearer to his home right up until the last day or two.

As we ran, we talked about subjects as diverse as land access laws, training techniques and how to deal with injuries. On the first subject, as Chris pointed out 'I was gobsmacked to learn that it's illegal to camp in the UK [...] The fact that you can't camp anywhere in England, even if you abide by the rules of the countryside is quite a sad thing.' He acknowledged that, in Scotland, different rules apply. Chris's ambition includes camping throughout his run, which will enable him to run for longer per day but without the creature comforts I (usually) enjoyed at the end of each arduous session. I'm sure his own tale will include many stories about where and how he pitched his tent each night. Since I was filming so much of my journey myself, I didn't have the liberty of doing this, without farming out all the technical stuff to my support crew, which would almost certainly have entailed hiring a second person to focus on that aspect of the task. Perhaps if I attempt a similar project in the future I will try to delegate a bit more of the non-running chores.

I was glad to be able to pass on the insights I'd picked up along the way regarding dealing with injuries by reducing speed, increasing walking breaks and, in some cases, by selectively ignoring them, the key thing being knowing what sort of injuries *can* safely be ignored. I was also able to recommend the Velo Champion calf compression supports I was using when my calves were protesting too much. Designed for cyclists, they work excellently at promoting blood-flow and forcing the muscles to work with maximal efficiency. I'd also used knee supports at times, which worked to limit unhelpful lateral motion.

Chris talked about his newfound enthusiasm for 'barefoot running,' which can be interpreted literally or slightly more cautiously as a recommendation to wear minimal shoes, rather than the heavy-soled running shoes that promote unhealthy heel-striking.[5] I don't think I'm ready for running Britain's roads in bare feet but I remember the legendary South African middle-distance runner Zola Budd competing barefoot in the 1980s and, less famously, I recall seeing a cross-country runner tearing through a muddy forest in bare feet during one west London winter race. Perhaps I'll try the famous, albeit peculiar-looking Vibram Five Fingers, a 'shoe' that acts as a sort of rubber sheath for the foot. Many runners swear by them; I remain sceptical.

Chris informed me what one of the distant chimneys was – the remains of an old tin mine. We were clearly nearing the border with Cornwall, something of a milestone as that would be the last county boundary until Land's End. As we played leapfrog with the support car I was glad to be able to advise Chris in turn not to take the route I'd chosen for my first two days, and thereby avoid the vehicular horrors of the A9.

We also talked about the huge increase in ultra-running, obstacle races and triathlons. As Chris said 'It's like the nation's having one big midlife crisis together'. I replied that 'Part of my film, my run, is to prove that an ordinary, middle-aged runner can do these things'. In talking to Chris I was, I realised, retrospectively clarifying my purpose. You don't have to be superhuman to do an extraordinary thing – this is as close to a moral as my story has, I suppose.

'If you invest just twenty minutes into running round the block in the evening, your evening's so much more fun,' said Chris, in explaining his general motivation for running. We agreed that running increases our appreciation for food, allows us to deal with worries better and even becomes a kind of benign addiction (particularly useful if, like Chris, you've struggled with the horrors of a real addiction).

We continued towards Stoke Climsland and over the mirror-smooth Tamar River at Horsebridge into Cornwall, chatting about the merits of vegan pasties, continental breakfasts and cider. Clearly, lunch was beginning to prey on our minds. We located our supporters – my parents and Chris's wife and child and headed to a fairly basic café in Bray Shop for baked potatoes and home-made soup, where our discussions continued at some length. All in all, Chris and I had very similar experiences of ultra-running and the same sorts of reasons for doing it. I'm sure we will run together again, probably in some ludicrously lengthy race along a brutal bit of coastline. And I wish him well for his JOGLE experience – I am certain he is up to the challenge.

Not far out of Bray, I hit and crossed the B3257 and the road's endless stream of traffic reminded me why I had taken to the farm lanes rather than running the B-roads. I'd managed about sixteen miles to Bray and felt like I should have another fourteen in me, which would take me as far as Bodmin by the end of the day. Of course, this assessment, as ever, assumed that none of my historic injuries would return to tax me or be joined by new and exciting ones. My run was made a little more challenging by the fact that I'd accidentally spilt most of my water on my feet while trying to drop electrolyte tablets into my Camelbak. I met up with Dad eventually and restocked, knowing too well how disastrous dehydration can be.

Linkinhorne, Rilla Mill, Upton . . . the villages I'd planned to run through would always take longer to appear than I'd imagined – a sure sign that fatigue was returning. The previous evening Dad and I had thrown out the original plan to go off-road over Bodmin Moor and head for the famous Jamaica Inn. I'd done a bit of research into the setting of Daphne Du Maurier's novel and had discovered that it was considered something of a tourist trap. The managers had also proven intractable in terms of offering any sort of discount and seemed unimpressed by my project; it's quite possible that the Inn is a regular haunt of JOGLE cyclists, which might well make them a bit blasé about the whole endeavour. I'd reminded myself that I was not a tourist and that my mission now was to finish as quickly as possible so that I could proceed with the rest of my life.

Furthermore, with the whole of the Cornish Coastal Path from Newquay to Land's End ahead of me, there would be plenty of off-roading. I'd still cross the southern extent of the moor but I'd do it by road. At Rilla Mill I started cutting south-west, following the dotted line my father and I had marked on our identical maps with Sharpies. The B-road junction had featured a sign pointing to Bodmin and claiming it was twenty-two miles away (rather than the fourteen I'd somehow calculated) so I began to doubt that I'd make it to the town before the sun went down. I lost time incrementally at every crossroads making sure I was heading the right way.

I'd been a little disappointed during The Long Run not to be able to run through the villages of California or Tiddleywink, which my route had skimmed. Here in Cornwall, however, I did unexpectedly pass through Minions. As any fan of the *Despicable Me* animated films knows, the enthusiastic, yellow, pill-shaped blobs called minions were the true stars of the movies (and deservedly got their own spin-off).[6] Apparently not everyone was amused, however, when the entrepreneurial town council replaced the old sign with images of the cartoon creatures. Universal Pictures had supported this bit of reverse-engineered opportunism by paying for the new sign to celebrate the release of their new Minions film. However, as one local told it, Minions' grumpy neighbouring villages demanded the sign be removed.[7] The official Cornwall Council line cited safety concerns, as families would stop along the admittedly narrow road to take photos. The truth may lie somewhere in between. The sign had only apparently been removed thirteen days before I passed through the village. I took photos of the standard sign for my nephews and niece anyway.

A little while later, peering through a gap in the hawthorn hedge, I saw my first glimpse of Bodmin Moor. It looked dark, tangled, thick with bracken and very exposed. I'd probably made the right decision in opting not to try to run across it. Outside Minions, lower hedges let me see the moor and its tin-mining remnants, which stood starkly silhouetted against the low, fading sun. Minutes later, the road crossed flat, brown expanses of moorland, dotted with the gnarly dwarf trees and gorse bushes particular to the area. As in Dartmoor, I was able to run along a grass verge but this place felt considerably bleaker and spookier.

A strand of thick cumulonimbus cloud covered the sun,

darkening the land as I ran up to a solitary standing stone
by the edge of the road. Rather phallic in aspect, this stone
pointed crudely into the air, echoed by the chimney of a
distant tin mine and by a needle-like mobile phone mast
on the horizon. Properly called a *menhir*,[8] the monument's
erection (no sniggering at the back please) may date to
as far back as 5000–6000 BC. The just-evident Christian
detailing would have been added in a much later era in an
attempt to co-opt some of the stone's mythic power. Very
little is known about the lives of the people who made these
menhirs but they can be found all over Europe, including a
particular concentration in Brittany, which is why we use
an old Breton word to describe them. At some stage, I'd like
to visit more of the ancient stones, dolmens, barrows and
brochs of megalithic Britain. They connect us with a history
of man and landscape far more ancient than many of us dare
to imagine.

As the sun began to flirt with the horizon, I looked out
across a dramatic and wild landscape and enjoyed the inti-
mations of an impressive sunset. A few flashes of leg pain
slowed me and I occasionally had to return to the tarmac,
the grass verge more humped and heavily vegetated than
on Dartmoor. As the sun sank low, long evening shadows
revealed hidden contours in a deceptively bumpy plain.
Long fingers of shadow accentuating the crooked trees from
which they fell. I took photos, filmed the impressive skies
and ran on.

Bodmin became an increasingly unlikely target, so as the
time closed in on six pm and I realised I'd managed at least
thirty miles, St Neot seemed more realistic. That would still
make hitting the coast quite possible the following day. I
veered off the busier road across the moors and started
passing whitewashed houses as the incidence of villages and
hamlets increased. Bathed in golden hour light, I now ached
all over but it was a good ache, the sort that comes from

honest toil. As usual, with the day's finish line approaching, I found myself speeding up, digging into deep reserves (and, it has to be said, thinking of beer). The hamlet of Draynes appeared first as I dashed down a steep hill past rhododendron bushes and mullion-windowed homes. The scenery was becoming that odd mix of the wild and the domestic that I associate with Cornwall from my previous visits. You'd run along a narrow lane of torturously twisted trees only to come across a pretty cottage or a thoroughbred stallion standing decorously in a field. Nothing was straight any more – all lanes curved, dipped and ascended, making the judgement of elapsed distance very difficult. I would feel quite lost, even if I knew exactly which road I was on. I recall telling myself 'As beautiful as this road is, it does need to lead somewhere eventually'.

The last stretch to St Neot, via a tiny lane just wide enough for a single vehicle, taxed all my energy reserves. The position of the sun made seeing the end of the road impossible – it was right in the centre of my field of vision and I had to press myself against the hedges once more to allow local farm vehicles to pass. I fell into that exhausted trance where sheer willpower and the repetition of footfalls and breathing drives the runner on. I began to talk to persons unknown, saying 'Come on, guys, give me a sign'. By 'sign' I didn't mean something miraculous or metaphorical; I meant a mile marker. When 'St Neot ¾ miles' appeared I almost kissed the signpost.

A little while later, the sky assuming a peachy orange hue I could almost taste (it would have been a refreshing and very sweet sorbet), St Neot's church appeared high on the hillside and I raced down into the village (past a pub oddly called the London Inn) and located, not my support car, but a Social Club where I sat and sipped my long-desired pint while awaiting my pick-up. I didn't really mind the wait – the friendly locals who raised eyebrows at my exploits, equipment and peculiar garb and the delicious local ale put the perfect cap on another good day's running.

'The third last day of The Long Run' – as the words left my mouth in a piece to camera, I realised once more just how close I was getting to the end of my epic journey. I also noted just how comfortable I'd become with chatting to a tiny camera on a stick. I'd been quite self-conscious about this aspect of the project at the start of September and my monologues had been a little too formal and composed. Now, in contrast, it felt like having an (admittedly rather one-sided) conversation with a friend. Perhaps I would miss my GoPro when it was all over.

Predictably, the start of the 15th October was rather slow and stiff-legged but, as ever, this didn't last. As the sun warmed my limbs and the blood began to pump at its regular running volume, the aches eased off and there was every chance of another great day's running. Perhaps not a thirty-plus day of mileage, but a good day nonetheless.

It had cooled considerably overnight and the dew had turned to a thin frosting over the fields that now began to melt into a hazy mist. I made it to Mount and beyond on a quiet, relatively flat road between fields of thick brown bracken and gorse. The last slice of moorland would take me to the town of Bodmin itself, which formed a kind of gateway between the wilderness and the more tame and inhabited west Cornwall. I could look forward to an overall dip in the land now as I descended to sea level. As the frost and mist lifted, gaps in the hedgerows afforded glimpses of a lush green quilt of fields and villages below. A cyclist passed, legs and lungs pumping, too tired to return my hello with more than a curt nod. I took deep lungfuls of oxygenated air as I felt my speed increase with the severity of the incline.

A little later, I hit a major road and took to a pavement

that, once again, seemed to peter out after a little while. There was nothing for it but to dash, as fast as possible, along the white line at the edge of the road while cars whizzed by at seventy miles per hour. A little later, an insanely busy stretch one mile out of Bodmin reduced me to a cautious walk along a ragged verge as I ranted to the camera about the lack of provision for pedestrians. A lot of swearing and nettle stings later I hit pavement and gratefully followed it down into Bodmin.

The town, twinned with towns in Germany, France and the USA,[9] proved larger and busier than I had expected, although looking at the map, it was something of a hub for traffic heading towards all points of the compass. I left the main road for a picturesque pedestrian precinct lined with shops and cafes and emerged onto the High Street. I seemed to be ahead of my support car once again as I ran uphill and looked for a spot to rest. A flight of steps outside a church proved too tempting and I took a short mid-morning break. I'd managed nine miles with another twenty or so to go, which I felt boded well. Too early to stop for lunch, I got back on my feet after five minutes and ran down a leafy avenue leading out of town to the northwest. A road sign I'd passed told me that Newquay was eighteen miles away by the A-roads. I could expect a few more miles on top of that by the back lanes.

I felt optimistic that Newquay would at least be reach-able today, if not Perranporth, although it would be nice to be able to stop for the day outside the self-catering apartment where we were staying. That would of course require a day free from injury, from getting lost and from slowing down or stopping for too long. I already knew by now that such days were few and far between.

The prettiness of the Cornish roads kept me going. Although you might think they were indistinguishable from the many small lanes I'd taken throughout England,

I was fast becoming a connoisseur by the time I headed through Nanstallon, Ruthernbridge and Rosenannon. The differences were small but telling. Cornish farm roads just feel less fraught – traffic is less common and slower-moving with more sightseers and holidaymakers hunting down remote B&Bs. The roads curve a lot more, the fields are smaller, the villages closer together and the signposts more prevalent and helpful. You can get lost in Cornwall, but only if you don't pay attention to the signs.

I began to feel something compelling my tired legs towards a greater turn of speed – the urge to glimpse the Atlantic. Each hill ahead of me felt like it must surely be the last, and it never was. I longed to run along a beach for the first time since the Scottish Highlands, which felt like a lifetime ago. The flashing hazard lights of Dad's car encouraged me too, as he leapfrogged me as he had at the very start of this journey. Village by village, mile by mile I would pick away the centimetres on my map, following a dotted line of my own making. Cockerels crowing in a field near Ruthernbridge woke me from what was beginning to feel like a delirious stupor as the morning progressed.

I'd weighed myself several times during the run, whenever a guesthouse or hotel had a set of bathroom scales. My normal weight of 70kg had been reduced to nearly 63kg – a loss of 10 per cent of my body weight. Looking in the mirror I couldn't quite decide whether I was gaunt or nicely lean. What was certain was that I'd not been so skinny since I was in my early twenties. Most gratifying was the sight of a set of abdominal muscles I'm sure I'd never seen before. I wouldn't be troubling any 'after' photos in muscle-building protein ads but I was happy to see that you don't have to lift weights to see the muscle groups become more defined. All you have to do is run every day, all day. Okay – perhaps it's easier to hit the weights!

I was also going a very strange colour both for a Scotsman and, to be honest, for a human being. I've never tanned – pale Scots tend not to. We redden and peel. As a twenty-year-old, I'd once taken an Italian backpacking holiday and fallen asleep on the beach. My friend Grant and I had each downed a very nice bottle of a local white wine. When we woke up, around two hours later, our backs were lobster-red and lividly painful. A week later I was sitting on a train whose windows were open to let in the breeze. I noticed strange white flakes floating down the carriage, like snow. They were pieces of my skin. I'll never forget the pain of shouldering my three-stone backpack on top of this epic sunburn.

My Long Run tan was a sort of 'Essex orange' and I had pronounced 'tide marks' where the sleeves of my shirt and legs of my shorts ended. My face and neck too had that peachy glow that more usually accompanies the start of a spectacular sunset. It was hard to decide if this too was an improvement from my usual peely-wally[10] hue.

Fourteen miles into the morning, I paused by a signpost indicating many different villages, including Rosenannon. By now, I'd learned the value of checking my route-finding assumptions against at least two maps. Fortuitously, my mum and dad pulled up in the car and we consulted. It was decided we'd do lunch at Rosenannon. We could head for the big coastal towns to eat but I wanted to see the sea for the first time while running – I didn't want to pre-empt that moment with a seaside lunch. Google Maps informed me that, to my delight, I was only around five or six miles from the coast so the epiphany, if there was to be one, would come sooner than expected.

On the last leg prior to lunch I passed some very attractive converted farm buildings and what seemed to be a garden shed in the style of a miniature Baptist church (or perhaps hunger was causing hallucinations) but there were no restaurants or pubs in evidence and my stomach was protesting. I'm fairly certain I saw my mum duck into a hedge to avoid spoiling my dad's shot as I rounded one leafy corner (she failed) but no restaurants or pubs were in evidence and Rosenannon seemed determined not to materialise. My food cravings were becoming unbearable and sheep in nearby fields almost became legs of lamb under my desperate gaze the way they once did in Tom and Jerry cartoons.

Sadly, the town had nothing to offer me in the way of eateries. A Methodist church, a dog-grooming parlour and a house selling free-range eggs could not satisfy my cravings, pretty though they all were. After much driving around we found St Columb, a neighbouring town which boasted just one pub open for food and we caught the kitchen just minutes before it closed. The place was offering half-price meals to seniors between 12 pm and 1 pm and my parents both qualified – I think I would have cried if I had not persuaded the bartender to serve us. I've rarely enjoyed a meal more.

After lunch I encountered a very strange roadside sight – a tree by a little stream had been decorated with cut-out fairies, possibly to enchant local kids. The sight reminded me of the famous Cottingley fairy[11] photographs, a hoax perpetrated by two young sisters in 1917 using their father's camera, fooling many photographic experts and even the great writer Sir Arthur Conan Doyle (perhaps not such a surprise as this famous exponent of deductive reasoning was later in life seduced by such tawdry spectacles as séances and spiritualism). There was nothing to indicate who had placed the fairies I found in their green arbour, or why. I rather liked the mystery of it – these strange encounters were part of the fun of The Long Run. Every corner could potentially hold a little secret waiting to be discovered only by those progressing with the patience of a pedestrian.

After lunch I started at 12-minute miles, accelerated to

ten minutes per mile, hoping to get yet faster as the carbs kicked in. The sky was beginning to grey over and I began to feel like my knees were a little weak and annoyingly hypermobile (possibly not aided by my Ehlers-Danlos syndrome). I vowed to try one of my knee supports if things didn't improve. Still, there was no explicit pain as such and hadn't been for days.

St Venn, Talskiddy and Mawgan were the notable villages along my afternoon route but, with the quest for lunch having taken longer than I'd hoped, it would probably now prove impossible to run much of the coastal path. Just getting to the seashore would be enough. It was tantalisingly close now. As Jacob's ladders began to break out through the clouds to the west, I could almost smell the briny sea air. A wind farm on the horizon encouraged me – the wind would be stronger by the seaside. I'd actually drawn out a map of all the turnings to make sure I didn't waste too much time at crossroads. Nothing would get between me and the Atlantic that wasn't on my master plan.

Frustration began to build as St Mawgan and Mawgan Porth approached – high hedges on both sides of the roads prevented me from seeing the blue line of water that was achingly close now. Hills rose up from nowhere to defer the moment yet further. Everything spurred me on until at last I crested a slope and stood on tiptoes to peer over a hedge where a tiny V-shape of brilliantly azure water between distant headlands rewarded me. I sped up immediately in my desperation to get my toes on the sand.

Mawgan Porth appeared, a winding road leading me past holiday chalets and rhododendrons in bloom. Under one hedge, remarkably, a family of guinea pigs scurried, their brown fur bisected by a white stripe. A little googling reveals they belong to the Sun Haven Valley caravan park and roam semi-wild there. An unexpected animal to add to my list of sightings. The road teased me by taking its time to wind down the valley to the beach but eventually I was faced with an expanding slice of sea, brilliantly illuminated under patchy cloud turning pink in the late afternoon. I felt a real delight and, once more, remembered that I would soon be returning to 'normality' and would have to find a new routine to get me through the days.

Endless small holiday flats and bungalows lined the road, many with balconies or verandas that, in the comparatively balmy Cornish climate, probably got a lot of use. I began to see a small wedge of beach dotted with streamlets carving the sand into slices. The tide was fairly far out and, on the headland to my left, I spotted a winding path – the Coastal Trail. Having told my parents I'd meet them at Newquay and relishing the chance to move from tarmac to sand and dirt, I lost no time in heading up the path.

As I rose above the beach, the sea spread out before me, impressive breakers drawing white lines across the silvery shore. My knees and calves protested as I climbed, reduced to a walk now but delighting in the view spread out below. The blue water looked deceptively inviting and there were even a couple of surfers bobbing about, waiting for the next good wave. Further along the sandy strip of path, I saw the craggy coastline take its first bite out of the Atlantic as the sky turned salmon-pink. I looked at my watch and was surprised to see that it was barely 5 pm. The sun should not be setting for another ninety minutes.

I'm not entirely sure why the Cornish sunsets seemed to last so long. My theory is that, with nothing but the horizon line of the sea between me and the sun, I could savour every last second of the sun setting from the sky taking on its first golden glow in late afternoon to the burnt umber preceding twilight when the sun first dipped beneath the sea. This unimpeded view gave the impression that the sunsets were drawn-out and epic. It may also have something to do with atmospheric perspective and weather conditions at the time of year – I'm no meteorologist. I was simply glad of the light show – it would allow me to end each day with something so beautiful that it could distract me from any amount of pain.

MILES RUN: 1,107; MILES REMAINING: 67

---

1. A boar's head was a common Yuletide centrepiece in medieval times (with peacock or swan not unknown amongst the landed gentry) – goose was an affordable alternative right up to the eighteenth century.

2. If you feel you may suffer from this condition, a useful resource can be found here: http://www.social-anxiety.org.uk/

3. I also felt guilty because, having downed nineteen paracetamol and gone to bed, I awoke the next day feeling sprightly and generally better and went to work in my local arthouse cinema, where my sister Fiona was ushering. It was only at around eight pm that I began to feel a little light-headed and informed my sister what I had done. This was during the Edinburgh Film Festival, where Jarvis Cocker was a guest of honour, having made his first documentary film. Both I and my sister were big Pulp fans and Jarvis was being approachable and friendly – various cinema staff even joined him for drinks. Fiona did not, since she had to take me to A&E at the Royal Infirmary instead (ironically the hospital where I was born). I still feel bad about ruining her evening.

4. *Eating Smoke* by Chris Thrall (John Blake Publishing, London, 2014).

5. For a lengthy and in-depth discussion of this subject, check out Christopher McDougall's *Born to Run*, possibly the best book ever written about ultra-running.

6. *Despicable Me* (2010), *Despicable Me 2* (2013) and *Minions* (2015), all from Universal Pictures.

7. http://www.bbc.co.uk/news/uk-england-cornwall-34410847 – BBC report on the story.

8. Old Breton for 'long stone'.

9. Those towns would be Bederkesa, Le Relecq and Grass Valley, California, respectively.

10. A great Scots term for 'unhealthily pale' or any skin tone that my granny would have described as looking 'like the inside of a banana'.

11. https://en.wikipedia.org/wiki/Cottingley_Fairies

MAWGAN PORTH TO PORTREATH

My first sunset run south along the coastal path was slow-going for the best of all possible reasons – I kept stopping to photograph and film everything. Each time I came to a dramatic rocky bay or sheer cliff-face, I presumed that this must be the most photogenic section of coastline, but each time I discovered something even more impressive around the corner.

The trail between Mawgan Porth and Newquay was easy to follow – a well-trodden path wound its way around the very edge of the headlands. It was even visible on Google Earth's satellite view and marked out on Mapmyrun.com as a runnable route. The distance from Mawgan Porth to Newquay is about six miles but that's a deceptive distance – each inlet where a stream finds its way to the sea requires a descent and then an ascent. If the descents were especially steep I'd be walking or slowly jogging them as well as the worst of the climbs. The path would wiggle around rocky sections or weave its way around gorse bushes, adding a few additional feet each time. My ambitious plan to make it all the way to Perranporth quickly seemed absurd – getting to Newquay proper before the light faded would be ambitious enough.

Ending the day with the most challenging terrain was also something of a miscalculation. My legs felt wobbly and unsteady and I was deeply fatigued as I followed the winding sand and gravel trail but somehow none of that mattered – I was just blissfully happy to be there. Suddenly it struck me – I could no longer get lost (or so I assumed). So long as I kept the sea to my right and followed the trail, I'd get to where I was going. No traffic would spoil my day either. All of the obstacles I'd become grudgingly used to were rendered irrelevant. Surely nothing could stop me now?

A hiker kept leapfrogging me as I stopped to take photos for my Instagram account or film shots of surging surf quietly roaring down below. I'd start running and overtake, only for him to saunter past me as I filmed everything. I ran by him one last time and apologised in passing; he just laughed, as happy to be out here on the cliffs as I was. To prevent this embarrassing scenario happening again, I ran a fast couple of miles without stopping.

The clifftop path was, as times, not for the faint-hearted. In places the trail took me within ten feet of the edge of a hundred foot high cliff-face. I liked the way safety had not yet won out over the sublime. Should you wish to stride right to the edge, you could. Even in this comparatively still evening, I kept a safe distance and slowed down whenever things got a little too daredevil. Plunging from a cliff into the Atlantic, just days from the end of my adventure, would just be too bathetic.

I took a call from my father, who had found a surfer's beach but wasn't sure if it was the right one. I'd suggested they head for Fistral Bay as, from previous visits, I knew it was one of the better-known and accessible beaches near Newquay. I hadn't counted on (hadn't remembered) there being five beaches between me and Fistral,[1] the latter being the final beach to the south of Newquay. I told him to locate the coastal path and I'd run to Fistral and stop there – if I hadn't seen him, I'd call again to tell him I'd finished. It seemed a sensible plan. Except for the fact that if you measure the coastal path from, say Porth to Fistral it is one mile as the crow flies but two and three-quarter miles as the Boyter[2] runs!

I have been to Newquay twice, both times for the surfing. The first, visit, in around 2007, was with my news producer friend Sam and a couple of her friends. I remember being struck by just how devoted the town is to surfing and, more generally, to the young. As well as being a popular destination for hen nights, stag nights and assorted drunken away-days, it boast numerous surf hire shops, surf clothing stores, surf schools, dormitory-styled hostels, bars and nightclubs. It's probably easier to buy a boogie board[3] than an ironing board in Newquay.

That said, I also found it a friendly and decidedly-laid back town, full of leonine, bronzed young men and sylph-like young women in wetsuits, flapping barefooted down to the shore while optimistic house music pumped ceaselessly from waterfront bars staffed by surf tutor/DJ/bartenders whose multiple streams of meagre income sustained a life-style predicated on chilling out and avoiding the nine-to-five like it was a living death (which it often is). While able to keep all this at an ironic distance, I couldn't help but feel a certain degree of admiration and envy for these 'alternative' lifestyles. Watching a group of surfers lying on their boards, waiting for the perfect wave, chatting as the sun performed a peacock display of evening colour overhead, I got it. If only my overweening ambition would relax enough to permit me to chill out like these kids effortlessly could. I've never had the gift of relaxation; I usually feel there's something more important I should be doing, which is of course missing the point entirely. I suppose I've also got to that stage in my life where I'm beginning to envy the young their very youth – again, wholly pointless and illogical.

I suppose I could console myself by remembering that here was I, forty-four years old and running 1,100 miles without a break (or very nearly).[4] I wasn't exactly an enfeebled old man just yet.

On my second visit to Newquay, with Canadian musician

friend Selena, we befriended a couple of fellow travellers, quite a bit younger than ourselves, and went surfing. I'd been before and had enjoyed it, and even managed to stand up a couple of times. Still condemned to the yellow 'banana boards' of beginners, we paddled out into the cold but refreshing Atlantic breakers and I discovered a secret. Surfing (unless you're a semi-pro) is not really about those rare instances when you catch a wave at just the right moment, stand up and get that feeling of impossible velocity as the water carries you towards the shore. Those moments are remarkable, for sure. However, given their comparative rarity, you'd be crazy to focus too assiduously on those transcendent achievements.

Most of surfing as a social activity is floating out beyond the breakers, where the water is often fairly calm, broken intermittently by surges as waves pass under you, lifting and dropping the board, just lying on the water, talking to your friends and enjoying the unusual and deeply relaxing sensation of being effortlessly carried by an unending tide. That's what surfing really means to me and there's a kind of lesson there. It's not for nothing that lifelong surfers tend to be quite spiritual, meditative types. There's definitely a kind of Zen lesson in just being in the moment and not worrying too much about anything but the simple act of floating and waiting.[5]

Another lesson from surfing – my first training session on the board, with about twenty other holidaymakers, on Fistral Bay on an early September afternoon. We've had the safety preamble and tips on technique. We've practised flipping ourselves from a prone position to a crouch and we're now ready to try surfing for real, our huge foam boards tied to our ankles in case of 'wipe-outs' (you fall off the board or the wave throws you off and you tumble in the surf like a shirt in a washing machine). We wade out in our wetsuits, flop onto our boards and paddle through the breakers, closing our eyes against the sting of saltwater as we push through the foam. I feel quite proud of being able to catch a wave and stand up, albeit very briefly, within the first ten minutes. Then I hop off the board in the shallows to bring it back to the circle of fellow students, who are receiving more wisdom from the handsome, forty-something teacher who, I can already tell, several of the girls and perhaps one or two of the guys have developed a crush on.

As my foot hits the wet sand, a sharp stabbing pain flares up my ankle. It feels like I've stepped on a sliver of glass. Perhaps I have? I inspect the sole of my foot and find nothing but a tiny, red pinprick. The pain now fills my whole lower leg. I limp back to the group and the surf tutor asks me what's wrong. I explain my symptoms and he shakes his head with something like wonder. 'Weaver fish. Like a tiny stingray. They lie in wait, camouflaged under the sand. I've been surfing here for 19 years and I've never stood on one. Stings like hell doesn't it?' I struggled not to show just how much it stung like hell and nodded instead.

'Well, there's two things you can do about it,' the sage opined. 'You can return to your hotel and put your foot in a bucket of warm water, leach out the poison. Or . . . ' He left a dramatic pause. 'You can just deal with it.'

Of course, I did the latter. Masculinity demands that losing face in such situations is unacceptable. And so I limped back into the water a little later, treading warily, and kept on surfing. Actually, the saltwater made the pain fade away and probably the fun of surfing did too. Lesson two: you're in pain? Just deal with it.[6]

I began to deal with my pain once more as six o'clock came round. I'd started running early that morning, at 8 am. With an hour for lunch and a brief tea break mid-afternoon, I'd been on my feet for eight and a half hours. Wondering what the signposted and protected corn buntings[7] were and gazing at the sunset could only distract me so much from a deep-set ache and a numbing feeling of utter exhaustion.

Fortunately, Newquay appeared over a headland just past the hour – brightly coloured apartment buildings looking out over the bay, the black flecks of evening surfers bobbing on the blue-grey sea and a beach. I didn't recognise it – it wasn't Fistral – but it would have to do.

I followed the trail round the headland, rather too pedantically as it happened, since it led me out to a rocky promontory of slate-grey volcanic-looking rocks battered into dramatic shapes by the surf. I took some more photos and looked for the route back towards the beach – it led to a fence, industrial-sized bags of gravel and signs warning of trail renovation works. I confess that I was so exhausted that I ignored them, squeezed past a gap in the temporary fencing and trotted along the new-laid white gravel. It was getting dark enough for a head torch but I didn't bother trying mine. The strip of gravel led me to another fence, which I breached, and onto legitimate trail again. Moments later the path gave way to tarmac and I ran down a pavement past holiday homes and hotels to a sandy beach signposted as Porth.

The sunset was in its last gasp, livid red giving way to a brown-blue darkening along the horizon line. Even the most ardent surfers had left the water. Dogs and their walkers owned the beach now – scampering in and out of the small stream that cut across the sand, racing for thrown sticks, silhouettes of normality set against the drama of the sky. I phoned my father and explained that Fistral would have to wait. Then, while waiting for my pick-up, I took yet more photographs and walked out the ache on forgiving sand.

The morning of the 16th punished me for the excesses of the day before. Throbbing pain in both calves reminded me that there were limits to what my legs were capable of. I pulled on my calf supports, downed my usual paracetamol and ibuprofen cocktail and hobbled out around Porth bay and round to the next bit of headland.

Newquay proper appeared with its own array of hotels

and holiday homes, balconies facing the sea like the mouths of devotional caves. Seaside-dwellers worship the waves; there is definitely something aquatic buried deep in the human make-up, despite the sea's dangers. In evolutionary terms at least, it wasn't so very long since our distant ancestors swam in warm primordial oceans – a mere 400 million years ago in around 3.5 billion years of life on Earth.[8] I began to recognise some of Newquay's streets and buildings, including the huge Victorian red-brick edifice that is the Headland Hotel. Cutting round the streets closest to the water, I ran through a small park to get a good view of one of the town's more remarkable architectural follies – the House in the Sea.

Sitting atop the tiny Towan Island, the 1930s house is connected to the mainland by a private 100-foot-long suspension bridge which hangs 90 feet above the surging waves. Sleeping six, it can be rented for a mere £1,950 per week off-season or £4,500 in the height of summer. It is a fabulously bonkers place to build a house (but perfect for surviving a zombie apocalypse).

Running through Newquay awoke some strong memories, not all of them idyllic. I was more than a little troubled during my first visit there, as ever pining for an unattainable woman. However, I soon found myself pleasantly distracted from morose remembrances by the approach of Fistral Beach, which happened to be playing host to a surf competition. Hundreds of surfers dotted the breakers, which were moderately impressive (though hardly of Hawaiian quality). I got my gimbal and GoPro out and filmed a tracking shot of the competitors and photographers as I ran along the sand. I wondered if I'd have the energy left to surf after completing The Long Run. It seemed unlikely.

A little later, I'd left the familiar behind and had hit a tricky and fairly non-negotiable obstacle – the long wide throat of the River Gannel estuary. At low tide, this might be passable with a bit of deep wading or a short swim. Given my recent experience crossing rivers and the fact that it was around 90 minutes after high tide and the water was deep, I opted for a slightly more sensible option. I say 'slightly' advisedly.

I consulted a local cutting his hedge and was directed to a lane leading down to the water. The estuary was around fifty feet wide, small yachts floating placidly on its calm surface. A curve of black granite cliffs carried round the headland, with what looked like a strip of sand to run along. I took my chances, hoping the tide was going out rather than in, and ran along the water's edge. Every so often I'd reach what looked like an impassable section but each time found I could clamber around a wall of rock and there would be more dark sand and granite rock pools to pick my way between. Eventually, I came to a section of shore along which many yachts were beached and found a trail leading through twisty, stunted trees. Sand and muddy grassland carried me to a small bridge as the land pinched in once more.

On the southern side of the inlet, I located a public footpath (though not the Coastal Trail proper) which led along a grassy, forested edge down by the water. A hiker, also heading south, asked me if she was going the right way. I said I hoped so and pointed out a party of infants and their teachers a little way ahead. If this route was safe enough for five-year-olds, it was safe enough for us. On the way back round to the headland I enjoyed jumping over puddles and splashing through muddy streamlets, waving hello to the kids as I passed. I was glad of my trail shoes – they could handle anything except flat, wet stone, and there wouldn't be much of that ahead.

Minutes later I stood staring at a ten-feet-wide stream about a foot deep, beyond which I could see the coastal trail heading up a rocky stair set into the cliff. Steeling myself against the shock of icy water, I waded through. Actually, the experience was pleasantly soothing, although it meant my shoes squelched audibly and embarrassingly for the rest of the day. Back on the coastal path, I looked down to the Gannel as the dwindling tide shrank it down to something I could have crossed in a minute with a rubber dinghy. I kept in mind another of the 'lessons of The Long Run' – you can only run where the trail takes you.

I picked and ate a few wild brambles and drank some water as the path rollercoastered its way south. Two large beaches would appear soon – Holywell Bay and Perranporth. It was becoming easier to mark progress in terms of beaches and headlands, rather than miles. Because of the variable terrain, estimating mileage and pace would be extremely difficult and my dad would have his work cut out for him in keeping up with me and getting the shots we needed. I hoped there would be a chance in the next day or two to fly the quadcopter once more and capture the amazing granite cliffs and rocky islets, which over the centuries had proven so dangerous to shipping (the north coast of Cornwall is quite famous for its shipwrecks).[9]

The overambitious plan for the day was to make it to St Ives, some forty miles away, making the following day the big push for Land's End. Could today be my penultimate day on The Long Run? I quickly realised that there was no point in assuming anything and forty miles was a big ask on an ordinary day, let alone an off-road one. Still, long-distance runners thrive on unrealistic hopes. Another life lesson from The Long Run: have goals but be prepared to move the goalposts. Given that the whole project was going to take at least forty-seven days, nearly three weeks more than I'd originally planned, what difference would an additional day make?

Holywell's sand dunes provided a bit of variety, reminding me of family holidays – leaping down the epic dunes at quiet

Scottish beaches like Gairloch was something of a tradition as I was growing up. As was roasting sausages on sticks over an open fire and building impromptu rafts. I do hope parents still do these things with their digitally obsessed children. At Holywell I began by following the subtle posts marked with the National Trails acorn logo, then abandoned the trail and took to the beach instead.

Beach running looks idyllic but can be tough. I quickly realised that not all sand is equal. Some sand is as solid and runnable as hard-packed earth. Another type, visibly identical, seems to have a hard crust, under which lies a softer layer. Perhaps this crust is sand which has dried to the point where salt crystals are holding the grains together, whereas the layer beneath remains just moist enough to be pliable. Whatever the scientific explanation, the crusty sand is tough to run on – with each step, there's a tiny delay as the foot sinks when it ought to push off, wasting energy. It's almost like running on snow which has refrozen overnight. Do this for half an hour and it can be exhausting.

Holywell's sands were only moderately difficult to run, fortunately, and less than a mile long. I nearly had the beach to myself – there were only another three people out and about at this early hour and I could almost mistake it for a Scottish beach. Almost.

On the next bit of headland I passed something strange – an array of lollipop-shaped aerials arranged in a circle, resembling a mixture of fairground ride and abstract sculpture. This proved to be a high frequency radio antennae once used by the military on what is now a retired Ministry of Defence training camp. Still used, the transmitter and receiver is part of the DHFCS (Defence High Frequency Communications Service) and is one of six sites in the UK. Next door to the array is a windowless bunker that is presumably an operations centre. I'm always on the look-out for filming locations and this would be a wonderful place to locate a cold war scene.

The headland had risen fairly high now and the cliffs were precipitous. Looking down from one fearful edge, I noticed a strange door-like hole in the side of one promontory, carved out by collapsing rock in conjunction with the ever-restless waves. My stops to take photos of such sights provided much-needed respite. Each incline I tried to run up now brought awful lactic acid build-up in my calves, reducing me to a walk with a debilitating headache-like discomfort. On the other hand, the continuous muscular torment of the early morning had dimmed a little and what residual pain remained was manageable.

I knew my parents and support car were waiting somewhere ahead to take me to lunch but I simply couldn't work up a decent pace. Each brief spurt along a flattish section was inevitably interrupted by yet another descent and ascent as the coastline's complex topology proceeded fjord-like to the south. I kept seeing distant headlands and imagined them to be Land's End, although I knew this couldn't be possible. Atmospheric perspective made everything seem much further away than it could be – I was probably only seeing about ten miles down the coastline at each transitory 'summit'.

Eventually a huge beach spread itself out before me – Perranporth – almost two miles of white sand sparkling under a sun that threatened to emerge from veils of gauzy cloud. The coastal path had all but vanished amongst the dunes and I thought it was pointless to stick to the trail with this flat expanse of sand tempting me. Our apartment was close to the beach and it felt like a logical place to have lunch, if I could locate my parents (who had the only keys). I thought Dad had probably found a vantage point on the headland beyond Perranporth, although it was also possible he was behind me. The problem was that, aside from the small towns strung along the way, one bit of headland looked pretty indistinguishable from another and it was proving hard to pinpoint where I or my parents were.

Another difficulty was the sheer magnitude of Perranporth beach. The old problem of beach perspective pertained here more than anywhere else I'd run. I just couldn't tell how much of it I'd crossed at any given moment. Dog-walkers and families strolled past me as I ran down to the water's edge for a low angle shot of the bubbling surf caressing the sand. Seagulls took to the air as I panicked them, their insouciant elegance mirrored in pools of standing brine through which I splashed. The sea's perpetual white noise, which had proved conducive to sleep the last few days, now formed a backdrop to my rapid breaths and the continuous squelching of my shoes. Standing lakes of seawater acted as giant mirrors, reflecting banks of stringy cirrus and cotton-like cumulous clouds through which the sun peeped. I knew I was making good speed, however exhausting it was proving, running much faster than I would have managed amongst the maze-like dunes.

Although I was enjoying the endlessness of it, I was enduring it as well. I decided that two miles on a beach feel subjectively like four on tarmac and realised that, by the time I reached the shorefront café that marked the start of the town proper, I would have run two beach miles and about sixteen miles in total. I looked around for my father and his tripod to no avail – perhaps he was still south of my position. However, all thoughts of continuing without eating fell away once I reached the busiest section of beach, with its lifeguard station and school. The lure of lunch drew me inland to the apartment, where I found my mother coping with a bit of a crisis.

An emergency indicator on the support car's dashboard was signalling an engine fault and the car was juddering a little as it moved. If the fault developed, the car might simply conk out and I would have no means of getting a pick-up at the end of the day, or transport to my starting point the following morning, not to mention all three of us getting to our respective homes when I was finished running. This could spell disaster. A local breakdown service was called out to supply a replacement part.

Unhelpfully, while this was going on, all of our phones were getting intermittent signals at best and my dad's had run out of power. He had walked north up the coastal path and had been waiting at a vantage point overlooking Perranporth wondering, with great frustration, why I was not appearing. My mother finally got a message to him and he returned to help her sort out the car situation as I grabbed a guilty lunch and set off once more, fingers crossed.

A finger sign indicated it was three miles to a place called Trevellas and I thought I'd probably manage no more than ten miles after that, which would take me somewhere like Porthowen or Portreath. In a worst-case scenario, I could call a taxi (reception allowing) to get back to the apartment. Fortunately, an engineer arrived while I was running and replaced the coil. We assumed this would fix the problem. As we would later discover, there was actually nothing wrong with the coil, per se, and the warning light persisted with the new part in place. A few days later a faulty spark plug was identified as the real culprit and replaced. Until we received the correct diagnosis, however, the replaced coil at least acted as a mild placebo. Yes, the warning light was still on, but at least we'd consulted an expert, however illusory the first 'fix' later proved. Fate, it appeared, was trying to throw obstacles our way but we'd all invested too much effort over the last month and a half to be defeated by a mere mechanical malfunction.

The sand and dry mud of the coastal trail gave way to a dry white clay-like gravel as I neared Trevellas – possibly the spoils from one of the many defunct mines the region had once boasted.[10] There are the remains of silver mines dating back to the thirteenth century in Cornwall. I'd already encountered a cliff dotted with rectangular holes where sections of rock had fallen away into the sea exposing open mine shafts now accessible only to seabirds.

The crumbly gravel trail veered dangerously close to the edge of the cliff in places and I slowed my pace accordingly. At one point, I hit a flat summit flanked by walls of diagonally striated white rock, the area looking exactly like an other-worldly set from the original Star Trek – I imagined Captain Kirk wrestling an unconvincing lizard-like alien amongst the rock formations. Beyond stood the foundations of demolished mine buildings. Distracted, I all but plunged down a steep gravelly slope, stopping myself at the edge at the last moment.

I reflected on the day's mishaps, problems, obstacles and mistakes and realised that none of it bothered me in the slightest. I was learning how to let go of accumulated stress, which I would say is one of the most powerful things I learned from The Long Run. Most problems can and will be overcome with the right effort and no amount of fruitless fretting or deconstruction after the fact will help. You simply let go and move on. I think having the dark memories of the 5th September still in mind made every current glitch in the plan seem utterly trivial in comparison.

I know this attitude frustrated my parents a little, since it looked like I wasn't taking their concerns (about the car, the non-functioning phones, locating me) seriously. In fact, I was troubled by all of the above, but only at the level of a background hum of irritation or worry. One man's blasé is another man's controlled, in other words. I'd previously been the type of person to hold onto unhelpful feelings about the past and future – shame, regret, worry, fear were constant companions in my twenties and thirties. In my forties I've learned to let go of a lot of that and live a little more in the moment. This attitude is especially helpful in long-distance running but it's a pragmatic attitude to adopt to life's endless vicissitudes too.

Nearing St Agnes, I passed several standing chimneys and open shafts covered with a sort of conical hat-shaped frame-work, possibly to allow bats and birds in but keep humans out. Some of the cliffs here were composed of a reddish and softer rock, rich with metal ore. A long flat section followed, which I described to camera as 'trail-running at its best'.

Steps led down to St Agnes, where the houses were painted in vivid pastel shades. I stopped to film a child's toy wind-mill left propped up by a bench, spinning wildly in a strong, cooling breeze. The by now familiar but occasional runner's euphoria took over and the run became fast and effortless. The sky remained a brightly backlit blanket of white and grey already taking on a peachy hue at four o'clock in the afternoon. Far out at sea, gaps in the cloud cover allowed shafts of light to spotlight silvery patches of ocean.

Beyond St Agnes stood a near-complete mine structure – Wheal Coates – with its tall, rectangular pump-engine housing and red-brick chimney proud and intact only a dozen feet from the cliff. An observatory of some sort could be seen in the distance – stargazing is a popular pastime this far south, away from the haze of cities to mar the view on a clear night. Further south and east of where I was running stands Goonhilly, an array of sixty large satellite dishes, featuring 'Arthur', the world's first parabolic communica-tions antenna, aimed at 1962's Telstar satellite. Twenty-five of those dishes are still in use. Cornwall, often associated with antiquity, was once at the forefront of futuristic science and space exploration. I was quickly learning that it is a fascinating place, full of contrasts and associations. For a comparatively tiny corner of Britain, it punches well above its cultural weight.

As I ran on, the sky began to blush vividly. I knew I

had to make it to somewhere my parents could easily find. Portreath, the next village, was six miles north of St Ives but I knew those miles could be deceptive; it might not be possible to finish the following day. What I wanted to avoid was getting to Land's End in failing light. The film deserved a finish the audience could actually see!

I gave my parents the postcode of a pub at the next town, so that this could be input into the satnav. I'd certainly have run close to thirty miles, I calculated. Running constantly all day had become something I could just do without excessive suffering. I finally understood what drove people like Scott Jurek and Dean Karnazes – this was probably how they felt all the time. For now, I enjoyed a boundless burst of energy that propelled me endlessly on. At the end of a long day, I had more energy and speed than I'd had in the early morning. I felt that, had I done The Long Run in August, I'd have managed another couple of hours of running that day. I'd simply run out of daylight.

The final push took me past a large military enclosure, sinister black pill boxes lurking behind tall fences emblazoned with stern anti-trespassing notices. The trail hit a road north of Portreath and I took to the tarmac, wanting to end with a fast finish. Coming down to the town, I segued out of running mode and into support car locating mode. For once, I did not have long to wait and was grateful to slide into the back seat, and switch off. It was only then that the fatigue caught up with me, as we began the complicated drive back to Perranporth.

If all went well, I was now a day and a half, at most, from the end of The Long Run.

MILES RUN: 1,134; MILES REMAINING: 40

1. From north to south: Porth, Lusty Glaze, Great Western, Towan, Newquay Harbour and Fistral.

2. Apropos of very little, I once located 'Boyter' in an ancient 20-volume Oxford English Dictionary – it's an archaic term for a kind of buzzard; Gavin comes from Gawain (of green knight fame) which means 'white hawk'. I really ought to be able to fly – or at the very least to run a lot faster.

3. A short, lighter kind of surfboard to be used lying down, for the *really* relaxed (or hungover) surfer.

4. And at this point I was beginning to suspect that 1,100 miles was something of an underestimation.

5. Just type 'surfing and Zen' into a search engine if you think this is a stretch. When I did it, it threw back over 1.1 million results. Alternatively, watch John Milius' classic 1978 film *Big Wednesday*.

6. Obviously I'm not claiming that all chronic pain can be quashed with a 'mind over matter' approach. There is for everyone a threshold where increasing pain (mental or physical) becomes so present that it starts to push out all other thought processes. Below this threshold, however, it might just be possible to divert attention away from the source of pain and thereby, perhaps just temporarily, escape from it.

7. *Emberiza calandra*: An endangered ground-nesting bird, stout and nondescript of plumage but with a distinctive jangling call and a fluttering flight, often seen around crops or scrubby low vegetation.

8. Although a rather daffy 'aquatic ape' theory favoured by, amongst others, Sir David Attenborough, has been fairly comprehensively debunked by the scientific community.

9. A Wikipedia page claims around 6,000 shipwrecks since 1200 over a coastline 250 miles long, more than any other stretch of UK coastline. https://en.wikipedia.org/wiki/List_of_shipwrecks_of_Cornwall

10. Amongst the metals once mined in the region were Tin, Silver, Copper, Arsenic and Lead. Visit https://www.cornish-mining.org.uk/ to understand why this region is designated a World Heritage Site.

PORTREATH to LAND'S END

October 17th: in the dim light of the hours just after dawn, on a sleepy Sunday morning I stood in front of Dad's camera, outlining at cumbersome length the developing issue involving the support car. The replacement part had done nothing to alleviate the potential problem of the warning light on the dashboard and the engine was now rattling in an odd way. There was the possibility of me being completely stranded in a remote region with a critical injury and only a local taxi service to fall back on. Despite this calamity in the making, that morning, exhausted as I felt, optimism reigned. I had awoken with a new determination to try to finish the run. It would be a tall order with almost forty miles of Coastal Path remaining but not beyond the realms of possibility. I clicked on my head-worn GoPro one more time, said goodbye to my dad and trotted off back down the street at Portreath towards the ever-present Atlantic.

Running through the streets as Portreath's inhabitants slept, showered or prepared their breakfasts, I found a finger-post pointing up a steep hill behind some modern houses and indicating 'Gwithian 6½ miles'. The place names on these signposts seemed seldom to relate to anything on my map, whose scale was too large to list anything other than the main coastal towns but it didn't really matter. The map now rarely made it out of my backpack. Choice had been eradicated from the task in hand – I would run the coastal path and that was all I needed to know. Or so I thought.

As I rounded the top of the hill, I was passed by another

runner (one of the few times this occurred during the whole project). He tore off around the ragged headland at a pace considerably faster than my own. I resisted the (surprisingly still present) urge to compete. What a wonderful resource that runner had at his disposal though – hundreds of miles of coastal path to explore at will. This landlocked Londoner felt a hint of envy as I watched him quickly diminish to a dot on the horizon. Rather than chase him down, I preferred to pause and film some other early risers, a small herd of Shetland ponies employed by the National Trust[1] to keep the grass on this headland nice and well-cropped. Their breakfast (or 'conservation grazing' as it's officially known) made the ground underfoot fast and easy-going. I didn't tarry too long – there were many miles of unknown terrain still ahead.

The morning was cold enough to require the thin gloves I'd bought and the land up ahead was blanketed in a fine mist, adding to the mystery of whatever lay ahead. When I reached the highest point on my current plateau, I could see a nested set of headlands arcing out into the Atlantic, the mist gradually hiding each successive slice of land behind a thicker veil. Here and there, chunks of land had broken off the jagged coastline to form pointed miniature islands. This was very much an active geology. In the not too distant future many sections of this clifftop trail would have to be diverted as the sea eroded yet more of the coastline. For now I was able to enjoy the sensation of being close enough to the sea to smell the salt spray.

Once again, I returned to the question of why I was undertaking this epic journey. To summarise it in a simple premise, I thought that if I could complete this sort of challenge, if I could rise above whatever obstacles fate and an ailing body threw my way, then I could attack the other challenges in my life with a similar degree of determination. The battles I yet had to look forward to included meeting a life partner, raising a family, sorting out my creative career and growing old, all but the last of which I'd deferred as much as was realistically possible. There could be no more procrastination – when I got back to London it would have to be full steam ahead with the overarching project of making my life work. The confidence The Long Run had built, tempered with a very real sense of what my limits were, could not be underestimated. Now I would have to put that confidence to work.

There was scarcely a breeze to break the solitude that morning, the calm underscored by the distant white noise of the breakers pounding the rocks below. On such a day it would be easy to get morosely introspective; instead I distracted myself with arithmetic. I was about twelve miles from St Ives and could run, on average, 9-minute miles, which meant I should allow two hours to get there, adding a little for stopping to rest and take photographs. It ought to be possible to finish today, providing. . . well, providing a lot of things. Injuries, terrain, inclement weather and exhaustion could all conclude my day early. I didn't really allow for weakness of will – I seemed within touching distance of the end of my journey now and I'd get there if I had literally to crawl the last mile.

While I was making these mental calculations I saw a posy of flowers had been placed by the cliff edge a few feet away; presumably someone had met their end here. It was a beautifully forlorn sight. I decided not to take this as a bad omen and ran on.

At one stage I had the odd sensation of seeing the sea appear to the left and right of me – the promontory at Godrevy, its contours oddly reminiscent of a section of famous fractal the Mandlebrot Set. I elected to cut off its head, darting west along an alternate trail through the low heather down towards St Ives Bay. Drizzly rain began to spit down as I descended a regular slope towards the sea, with the crescent-shaped beach and dotting of whitewashed buildings on the distant headland spurring me on. My eagerness to reach what would be the last town of any real size made me run even faster. Looking at my Garmin, I realised that I was managing almost seven and a half-minute miles. Probably it would be wise to slow down but one of the other lessons I'd learned on my run was not to question the 'adrenalin muse' – when my legs felt like going that fast, so long as I wasn't in too much pain, I'd let them.

Nearing St Ives I passed a few more walkers and hikers and even a lone runner, forging up the hill towards me with a smile on her face as I ran gleefully down at unreasonable speed, holding a camera. The rain faded away as quickly as it arrived but as I made it down to the road at Gwithian the wind picked up a little and I was grateful for the shelter of some sand dunes, while a surf school convened on the beach below. A narrow boardwalk carried me like a conveyor belt amongst the golden dunes until I could stand it no more. I headed over a band of granite pebbles towards the beach. I hoped to make it all the way to St Ives by means of the sand, hoping the tide would let me wade across the estuary at Hayle.

The sands continued for an exhausting three miles, much of it a little damp – deep rivulets of sand blown by the wind had filled with seawater and proved tricky to run across. I had to splash through ankle-deep bands of seawater but I was beyond caring. I passed many walkers, runners and dogs amongst the impressive blocks of layered, many-coloured rock which had broken away from the mainland. Disappointingly, the mouth of the river at the western end of the beach didn't apparently warrant a footbridge, despite all these pedestrians. The tide was pretty far out but a channel of water about thirty feet across remained. It looked waist-deep at least. As I had with the River Gannel, I decided to be sensible and avoid getting thoroughly soaked or swept out to sea. Maybe there would be a bridge just a little further inland.

Seemingly not, for after running along soft sand for about twenty minutes, I arrived at a small harbour and a road leading up to a lifeguard station, pubs and shops and a major B-road. Hayle is a town in its own right, the first of several before you reach St Ives proper. This necklace of towns creates a kind of mini-conurbation through which flows the last heavy traffic before the end of Britain.

In exactly the way I said wouldn't happen again, I found myself running alongside a dual carriageway once more. This time the road ran through the middle of a wetland nature reserve. A group of keen twitchers[2] were in evidence, binoculars and notebooks at the ready, leaning against a wall together and scouring the mudflats and sandbanks for teals, widgeons, lapwings and waders. I left them to it and sprinted between cars, up a peaceful side street, finally heading towards the town of many artists.

When I'd been heading inland along the beach I'd seen a church tower high on the headland opposite and heard the unmistakable clangour of bells ringing in a seemingly endless, ever-changing sequence. Now that I was approaching that church on the other side of the channel, I could hear the ringing louder and clearer than ever. Some keen Sunday campanologists were 'ringing the changes', a painstaking activity involving sounding every possible sequence of a series of bells, a task that becomes logarithmically more complex with each additional bell. I think there is something wonderfully and dementedly English about this activity, combining extreme pedantry with devotional music. The painstaking nature of it mirrored my own determination to tread absolutely every step of a route across Britain. Sadly, the tintinnabulation faded away as I skirted the church grounds. Perhaps one day someone will arrange a race between bell-ringers and runners, the latter setting off with the first clang and trying to reach the church before the final round.

A manicured golf course appeared, fringed by a narrow and overgrown section of trail, briars and nettles slashing at my legs as I raced the mile and a half to Carbis Bay, just south of St Ives. Despite my impressive turn of speed, everything seemed to be taking longer than I'd expected. In part, I blame something called the 'coastline paradox',[3] which states that no coastline has a well-defined length since this is dependent on the scale of approximation you use. In other words, laying a virtual ruler 100 kilometres long around Britain's coastline gives a total estimate of 2,800 kilometres whereas halving this unit of measurement makes it 3,400 kilometres, a not inconsiderable difference when you're on foot. For this reason, it would be difficult to properly measure any chunk of coastline or estimate how long it'd take to run. Or so I tried to explain to my frustrated parents who found me as hard to spot as the birdwatchers' elusive golden oriole.

The path met Carbis Bay at a suburban knoll of modern houses and hotels overlooking golden sands. There the trail rather unexpectedly veered through the car park and grounds of the Carbis Bay Hotel, where a temporary diversion past the sunloungers and swimming pool provided a surreal moment. The whitewashed buildings and semi-tropical foliage felt utterly alien to everything I knew about rain-drenched Britain but then, here in the toe of the country, life seemed quite different from my shivery Scottish upbringing. It felt like a place where the sun might not be an especially rare visitor, which I suppose is why the area had long attracted artists of the calibre of Barbara Hepworth, Ben Nicholson and Frances Hodgkins.

I was looking forward to seeing St Ives. I'd heard much about its galleries and creative heritage and had not been able to fit in a visit on my last two trips to Cornwall.

Eschewing the art, I was content to dash down a leafy track
to the sands of the bay and sit by a seaside café looking out
at the blue ocean and the oddly named Island promontory
(it isn't an island) and eat my slightly flabby strawberry jam
sandwiches.[4] Twenty minutes later I climbed some rocky
stairs stained with rust from long-corroded handrails and
clambered up to the town proper, finding there a maze of
tiny streets, a throng of tourists of an artistic bent and many,
many tiny galleries. Strangely it wasn't difficult to weave
my way up and through the town and out to the other side,
although it did feel a shame to bypass its charms so peremp-
torily.

The scenery changed dramatically south of St Ives – I
had been warned that it would. My parents had met a local
RSPB conservationist who had told them that the coast got a
lot more barren and rocky and the trail conspicuously more
challenging south of the town. At first, all I noticed was
a profusion of sharper rocks sticking up out of the grassy
plateaus and a more finger-like aspect to the rocky headlands. After a while, however, large misshapen boulders
began to accumulate, many of them in the middle of the now
noticeably muddier trail. I would get up a bit of pace and
then have to brake sharply to leap over or sidestep a rock.
Tripping hazards were rife and I stumbled a few times as my
post-lunch legs warmed up.

There were fewer walkers and the trail definitely began
to present more of a challenge. The gullies were steeper and
more frequent, necessitating controlled descents and calf-
straining climbs. Nevertheless I enjoyed the challenge and it
brought out a family memory of rock-hopping along Burn-
tisland beach once again. This kind of highly focused, very
present running was mentally taxing as well as exhausting.
I'd read Catalan distance runner Kilian Jornet's eye-opening
book about his obsession with running mountainous ultras,
Run or Die[5] and it was a sobering thought to realise that this

terrain would just be par for the course for him. Then again, Mr Jornet is twenty-eight years old and was brought up in the French-Andorran Pyrenees.

By 2 pm I'd run about twenty miles according to my Garmin, which I trusted more than any map. I knew my support car was waiting for me at Treen, near Porthmeor, my father hoping to get a quadcopter shot in on a beautiful and quiet headland he'd identified. I was probably at least an hour away from there, however, and that meant that continuing much further south could prove unwise. As I'd suspected, there would be no way of knowing if I'd still have enough light to see, or for my cameras to film, when I reached Land's End. It looked like there would be one more day's running after all.

My father surprised me by telling me that the pub where he and mum had enjoyed lunch (and where they were still waiting for me) had a rather famous patron – John le Carré. My dad is a massive fan of Mr Le Carré and I urged him to politely, tactfully, introduce himself. No writer objects to being told his work has enriched a reader's life, especially if the fan pays the compliment and leaves, without insisting on photos or autographs. I have inherited my father's shyness though and I wasn't surprised to learn later than he was simply content to eat and drink in the same pub as the great man and then buy a couple of signed copies of his books from the publican before leaving, which is probably what I would do were Haruki Murakami[6] (to give one example) dining there.

I was now feeling spates of extreme fatigue although my muscles felt paradoxically strong and springy. Regular pauses to look out at the sea and increasingly craggy coastline reinvigorated me. It was getting warmer and I was perspiring heavily and drinking frequently as I ran. I didn't strip off though – instinctively I wanted to keep my muscles and joints warm. The trail was clearly defined, although rocky, steep and muddy in places. At times I found myself goat-stepping in tiny, frequent paces, rather than running.

Gushing streams flowed between shattered rocks – at one such miniature waterfall I downed a few handfuls of the sharply mineral-tasting water. The trail seemed determined to round every last messy contour – I paused by a National Trust place-marker telling me I had reached Tregerthen but this meant little to me. I passed a family climbing between large rocks that studded a hillside then walked up a back-breaking and muddy slope to a comparatively high ridge blanketed in bracken. The wind grew a little more persistent. I could now see no sign of human habitation whatsoever. That said, half an hour later I passed a group of around twenty middle-aged hikers who must have started somewhere civilised. An unexpected sprouting of pampas grass at the next gully made me think I must be near some houses – the ornamental feather-duster like reeds are far from native to Cornwall. In a bit of a delirious state at this point in the day, I was literally clutching at straws.

Some peculiar rock towers, like cubist or futurist sculptures appeared around the bend, guarding a rugged spur of coastline. The granite blocks looked like they had been sliced into chunks by a giant cheese-wire and then balanced on top of one another. A little way further on, a marker post announced that I'd almost reached Gurnard's Head. Ruins of old buildings protruded from the bracken and the rocks. There were still no signs of human habitation but I knew Le Carré's local was close by and that there must be a road or path up to it. I'd find it and head in the direction of warmth, pints and a comfy chair.

Remarkably I had not a single ache or pain in my legs, just an overall coating of fatigue which made it difficult even to move my lips to talk to the camera. I found a wooden bridge over a large stream and then a junction where a track headed off inland up the side of a gully. The blue dot on my smartphone told me that some sort of road near here led up past a group of houses to the pub. The 'road' turned out to be a neatly paved and steep row of flagstones suitable for only the most confident motorist (with a fully-functional handbrake). I passed a ruin of something truly ancient and ivy-covered but unidentifiable (possibly another tin mine), then a lone cottage and a quarter of a mile after that, farm buildings, cows and sheep and a brightly orange-painted building that turned out to be the Gurnard's Head. Although I was now heading away from the coastal path, I ran as much of the last mile as I could, eager for the rest that would come at the end of it. I almost wept with joy as I saw my dad standing outside the pub, watching a car pulling out of the car park. Amusingly, as he stretched out his arm to point, I mistook this for an uncharacteristically tactile gesture and moved in for a hug. We glossed over the very Scottish embarrassment this caused as he said, 'You just missed him – that was John Le Carré.'

What I didn't miss was the spectacle of two steam cars parked outside the gaily coloured Gurnard's Head, its owners trying to instil some life into the spluttering engine of one of the beautiful but temperamental vehicles.[7] Apparently the famous author had offered a tow.

As was their wont, my parents had told the Gurnard's manager what we were all up to in Cornwall and he had vowed to buy me a pint 'on the house'. I had a local beer and it was utterly delicious. Even more generously, the Gurnard's Head offered us all a free breakfast the following day. Of course we accepted and took full advantage on the morning of the 18th October. I did not rush my repast. By my calculations, which were admittedly prone to various kinds of error, I had about sixteen miles to run to reach Land's End. Given that I'd managed close to thirty over the last two days, it seemed quite achievable.

Before I could properly set off, however, there was

film-making business to attend to. I'd stopped a little early the previous evening (around 4 pm) and we'd tried and failed to get a good quadcopter shot down on the coastal path due to high winds and the appearance of a friendly camper who called himself Jesse James 'O', whom we didn't want to accidentally decapitate (I would meet him again a little later on my journey). Both my dad and I were determined to get the shot, so we returned the following morning. This time the weather and solitude were on our side and we secured some usable footage. There's an incredibly abstract bit I like – the shot reveals a roiling, dark blue canvas flecked with white, which is mysterious until a seagull flies across the frame and you realise the camera is pointing directly down from about 200 metres above the waves. There is also a shot of me eagerly racing off to make personal history – today would be the day I complete The Long Run (or die trying).

Everything seemed set for a lunchtime finish at Land's End so long as there were no more calamities. I devoutly hoped there would be somewhere to eat but as usual had done no research. I felt full of energy, aided by the natural adrenalin produced by the excitement of being so close to journey's end. When I thought back to the various things I'd seen and experienced, those images were still vivid but seemed to belong to an earlier age. I had definitely changed now, both physically and mentally – paradoxically I had discovered that I was capable of both more and less than I'd thought.

I should explain that one. Less in the sense of having planned and hoped to run forty miles a day and finish within four weeks. More in the sense of being able to run a marathon per day, every day, changing and adapting as required, coping with injuries and exhaustion and weakness of will and seeing the project through to its conclusion. Very simply, I'd discovered the truth of a simple assertion – you can do a lot more than you think you can.

Porthmeor Cove approached, a green haven with a calm

ultramarine inlet and a trickling stream, a perfect smugglers' bay. As well as mining, the less salubrious economic activities of smuggling and deliberate shipwrecking followed by looting were once rife on this wild coastline. There is even a smugglers' museum at the Jamaica Inn,[8] containing many artefacts from a more lawless age.

The further south I got, the more remarkable the views, ragged shards of granite forming outcrops overlooking hidden coves disturbed only by the relatively gentle breeze, the calls of seabirds and the lapping of waves far below. I absorbed it avidly, not wanting to let go of these scenic views. Meanwhile, as I ran an intricate dance between rocks, gorse and heather, the sky began to brighten, a thick pillowy mass of cumulous clouds beginning to thin out overhead.

Then, at a place I later identified as Bosigran, a ruined cottage stood in the middle of a small plain, just a few walls open to the sky, a small stream running alongside. A group of teens were meandering nearby dressed, as kids will, in anything but hiking gear. There must have been a road somewhere inland but I couldn't see it. Nearby stood the strangest rock formation I'd yet encountered – several knife-like pinnacles, their faces striated in triangular patterns, pointing at the sky like something evil. I briefly lost the path and headed for these rocks out of curiosity. Midway up one vertical face a plaque was set into the rock. It read: 'Commando Ridge: On this ridge commando soldiers were trained in rock-climbing in the years 1940–1945'. I found an old wartime public information film on the internet which shows them doing just that.[9] Bosigran is still a popular site for climbers, with or without ropes. In fact, while I was there, I could just make out a couple of climbers embarking on a roped route on the cliff-face opposite me.

Climbing is something that has always terrified me. When I consider trying it, my imagination tends to run riot and I see my mangled corpse sprawled at the bottom of a cliff. But it has always thrilled me too. As a child, I was forever halfway up a tree (climbing up was always much easier than coming down) and I'd been known to scramble up short cliff-faces too. Looking up from my perch at Bosigran, I fought a brief inner struggle. I really wanted to climb a steeply sloped channel between the rocks and reach the top, just thirty or so feet overhead. It was either that or backtrack towards the teenagers and find the path. Plus, it might be fun.

I'd nearly decided upon the common-sense option when I found myself, almost without willing it, reaching for the first handhold. It was easier than I'd imagined, even in my running gloves and trail shoes. I found solid holds and climbed steadily between the planes of rock. The learned routines of childhood did not let me down. I also remembered a few words of training I'd received on a couple of indoor 'bouldering' sessions. I kept my arms as straight as possible whenever they took my weight, making sure I had three good grips before moving one. Of course, here, hanging high on a Cornish cliff-face, there would be no crash mat to break my fall, just the sea.

A few minutes later, the rock levelled out and grass appeared – I'd made it. The sense of relief was palpable. From now on, I'd not be risking my life, there would just be running. The trail continued along a level section studded with granite pieces like broken toffee. Occasionally a rocky protuberance would conceal a sharp drop in the land and I'd brake sharply as my hands were called into service to keep me from plunging into the sea. This unforgiving landscape really did feel like the end of a land – rugged, lonely and wild. I filmed as much of it as I could, preparing for the film's conclusion as much as the run's.

Shortly, accelerating ever faster, I passed a couple of fifty-something hikers who laughed good-naturedly at my attempts to run through a muddy bog they were picking their way around. I doubt they suspected just how far I'd come and how little a mere pool of mud would bother me. The lighthouse at Pendeen gave me my bearings, letting me know I was now in the toenail of the big toe of the foot of the leg of Cornwall. Less than ten miles stood between me and Land's End. I began to pass groups of walkers making their way north and shared a cheery greeting.

The chimneys of Geevor Tin Mine could be seen from a couple of miles away; a living museum of a dead industry, the rocks around it red with iron ore spoil. I liked the way it had been left partially intact and accessible. There were even underground tours on offer, plus the ubiquitous shop and café, but my sightseeing had to be of the peripatetic and accelerated variety. Support columns for a derelict building stood out against the sky like a Roman ruin, reminding me of my visit to the Forum as a twenty-year-old. Piles of colourful slag added to the end of the world feel.

Approaching Botallack, the path edged around more rocky pillars and shattered spurs of granite. Hands were once again pressed into service. This was hopefully as wild as it was going to get – the man from the RSPB had been correct in his assessment. Still more chimneys added perspective to the headlands that remained – somewhere out there was the final beach before Land's End, Sennen Cove. Then, unexpectedly, appeared an oasis of partly cultivated land, a stream, a garden and a horse grazing on the lawn before the wilderness reasserted itself once more.

Cape Cornwall jutted out into the sea – a green pasture and hill topped with the chimney of a mine that subsequently became a monument to the H. J. Heinz Company,[10] who bought the headland in 1979 and returned it to the nation. Containing remnants of an iron-age fort and St Helen's Oratory, a medieval chapel as well as the nineteenth-century mine, it was an important bequest.

Remarkably, a few hardy houses stood by the shore, gazing out at the offshore islets and the vast Atlantic Ocean. You would have to love solitude and the sea to reside here, although the village of St Just was accessible a little way inland. I ran on dusty paths past whitewashed cottages and saw a slab of engraved stone informing me I was just five and a half miles from Land's End. I'd estimated that I had around nine miles to go, so this came as something of a surprise. When I'd stopped yesterday, it had seemed like I'd have to run twenty miles to finish. In fact, it was a little more than a half-marathon between the Gurnard's Head and the symbolic southern tip of Britain. I called my parents to adjust my estimate – I should be finishing within the hour.

Minutes later, I climbed a slope to a long, flat grassy pathway and there ahead of me was a sliver of beach, beyond that a finger of headland, beyond that just the ocean. In under an hour I would run out of country entirely. A brief loop of road led down to a sheltered beach at Porth Nanven, sometimes known as 'dinosaur egg beach' due to its peculiar ovoid rock formations. I pressed on along a rocky ledge and uphill to yet more granite vistas – the trail seemed to be teasing me with endless headlands but now I had a distant crescent of yellow sand to motivate me.

Lactic acid was building painfully on every uphill slope, necessitating small pauses for recovery before I raced off again through colourful swathes of heather and gorse. Just as colourful were the cliffs, whose rocks took on the hues of the various ores they contained – ochre, rust red, even a coppery green in places. I started feeling a real euphoria build as I began to race faster and faster, approaching Sennen. One more triangularly cracked rock ridge stood between me and the beach now. I stopped to drink, then heaved my way across its boulders.

I thought about the vast store of footage I'd filmed and the huge trove of memories I'd built up. I felt I'd gained a little more insight into the scale of the country. Britain is not unmanageably large – it was quite possible to pass the whole of it under one's feet in a matter of weeks. It had been tough, but not unmanageably so. I felt quite surprised, thinking back, by how much of my run had been pure enjoyment.

That said, the coastal trail wasn't going to relinquish without a fight. Still fatigued from yesterday's exertions, I tried to maintain a decent pace but my progress, limited by the tidal pain in my calves, remained rather stop-start. However, as I approached Sennen Cove, the weather gods smiled in encouragement. The sun glanced out for the first time that day through a tear in a bank of cirrus cloud, illuminating the silvery waves and golden sand. The air grew warmer and I persevered: clambering, scrambling, advancing metre by metre towards the beach. Soon a flood of sunlight fell over the land and cloud gave way to a cerulean blue sky, the shallows taking on an aquamarine hue.

I crossed the loose sand of a miniature cove north of Sennen and inadvertently kicked up gouts of loose sand which got into my heels, rubbing the raw wounds that had formed there over the last few days. For the last three weeks I'd taken to putting plasters on my heels and then stretching KT tape (usually used for supporting strained muscles) over the plasters to help them stay on. The sand found its way under both layers of protection, adding a spice of discomfort to my growing feeling of elation.

I remembered disappointing my father the previous day by taking to the beach at Holywell while he was waiting for me at the coastal trail. He'd set up a spectacular quadcopter shot and then watched in disbelief through his binoculars as I deviated from the path and took to the sand. He later told me his cursing had turned the air as blue as the azure sea below him. That in mind, when I reached Sennen, despite the inviting crescent of sand before me, I decided to stick to the marked trail through the high dunes, so as to avoid my dad's disapprobation. Hidden by hedges and tall grasses, I could no longer see the sands as I made it to the small scattering of shops and cafes that marked out the last place of human habitation before journey's end.

I'd fully expected to pass my parents and I wanted to stop and talk to them about the plans for filming at Land's End. There was no sign of them. There was, however, a familiar car parked outside the beachfront restaurant. I realised that my parents must be down on the sands. What I didn't quite appreciate was that my father had been there for two hours, having set up a perfect shot. I ran down to the beach and caught them both making their own tired way back to the car.

Through some miscommunication, Dad had expected me to take to the beach this time. Mum had spotted me through binoculars running through the dunes and then they'd watched in perplexity and frustration as I made the seemingly perverse choice of avoiding the beach and their perfect shot. There's a wonderful (and it has to be said, hilarious) take of my father stepping in front of his own lens to berate me in colourful Anglo-Saxon. Twice.

I mollified Dad this time by suggesting we get the shot anyway. It would be an acceptable 'cheat' since it would actually mean me running half a mile *more* than was necessary. After some negotiation, we did just that. I backtracked half a mile then weaved my way across the sandy expanse, dodging dogs and strolling families and leaping a stream. The shot was in the can and I was grudgingly forgiven.

Now we had a minor problem though. Sennen is only just over a mile from Land's End but it's a 2.6-mile drive. It was just conceivable that I'd get to Sennen before my parents. I had to give my dad time to set up a good shot of me arriving at the finish line. I hadn't done a whole lot of research into exactly what to expect but I knew there would be the iconic signpost to John O'Groats and that would be where I would finally stop. There would be no second takes this time. We decided that, absurd as it seemed so close to finishing, I'd have to wait fifteen to twenty minutes at Sennen to give my parents a head start.

So I sat down, a mile or so from my goal and had a cup of tea and a scone at a beachfront café. Was this a betrayal of the ultra-runner's creed? I hoped not. After all, I was merely taking on fuel for the final big push. To salve any guilty feelings from sitting in the sunshine sipping tea, I decided that I'd run the last mile like a maniac, in as close to six minutes as possible. I'd push myself to the edge. The clock ticked, I finished my repast and, after some encouragement from a group of locals who applauded my departure, I raced away up the hillside to enjoy the last of many long, painful miles.

Getting the gimbal and GoPro out one final time, I decided to film one continuous shot as I ran. Coupled with my sudden speed as I raced over rocks, bounded up stone steps and darted around tourists, this no doubt made me appear quite demented. Probably a few folk guessed what I was about to do and I heard a few whistles and cheers as I passed people. I do love the shot I filmed as I ran. You can hear the surging wind off the Atlantic and my feet's percussive sound growing faster over the salty gravel.

A deep calm happiness suffused me, along with a feeling of near-invincibility. Running as close as I could to 5K pace, I felt unstoppable. Only a heart attack could finish me now and I felt fairly confident that wouldn't happen, despite how violently that vital organ was pounding in my chest.

I tore up a steep, irregularly paved track, my breath like a steam train struggling up a mountainside and saw the group of buildings that make up the Land's End Visitor Centre appear over the summit.

Then one last bit of confusion, a fork in the pathway – three possible routes. I took a wild guess and headed the middle way, vindicated a few moments later when I saw the gleaming white post pointing at the sky and my mother running too, trying to get back to the finish line in time, having been out scouting for me with binoculars.

I ran up to the signpost and leapt over the chain-link fence, not knowing what the protocol was. My mother hugged me and the man in the photographic booth laid out plastic letters spelling 'The Long Run' and took my photo standing by the famous landmark. My father stood nearby, filming with the Panasonic and proudly telling anyone who would listen who I was and what I had just done.

'I think I might sit down,' I said, more profound words failing me. I had prepared nothing to say and all I wanted was a beer. Fortunately, the nearby restaurant was able to supply that. I had a few photos taken, chatted with some visitors and even signed an autograph book. The intrepid hiker Jesse James 'O',[11] himself a multiple JOGLEr (albeit at a more leisurely pace) came up to congratulate me. He had left his camping place several hours before I started that morning and had managed to beat me. I didn't mind at all. Jesse was tall, bald as a coot and had the leathery tan of a seasoned outdoorsman. We compared notes on our experiences. He began to tell me his own tales of crossing the Australian outback on foot.

I was only able to lend half an ear to anything anyone said, I'm afraid, as I sipped my Cornish lager and looked out at the silvery-grey Atlantic. The ocean seemed in that moment to be the most beautiful sight I'd ever seen. The realisation of what I'd achieved filled me with a pride I instinctively tried to quash with an outward show of modesty. My inner feelings were quite different. Inside I thought – that was *something*.

Half an hour later, I wandered a few hundred yards further along the knobbly coast, to deposit my threadbare running shoes on a rock with a spectacular view of the sea.

As is my tradition, I left them there as a kind of devotional offering to the sun. Those shoes had served me well.

I took a few photos before letting them go. For all I know, they're still there.

MILES RUN: 1,174; MILES REMAINING: NONE

---

1. Working together with the Dartmoor Pony Heritage Trust: http://www. dpht.co.uk/

2. A slightly derogatory term amongst birdwatchers for completists for whom quantity of species sighted is preferred over a more painstaking approach.

3. See https://en.wikipedia.org/wiki/Coastline_paradox for a useful elucidation of this.

4. In Scots parlance 'a piece and jam'.

5. *Run or Die* by Kilian Jornet (Penguin, London, 2013): A joyful memoir, heartily recommended, it will make you want to run up and down mountains. Honestly.

6. Another book recommendation and one that definitely fed my own obsession – Murakami's quirky memoir *What I Talk About When I Talk About Running* (Harvill Secker, London, 2008). I return to it frequently and always find inspiration there, although it is by no means a technical running guide.

7. I'm no car enthusiast but these were splendid vehicles, at least 95 years old and in pristine condition. Which is how I expected to feel at the end of The Long Run.

8. http://www.jamaicainn.co.uk/cornwall-museum and, regarding shipwrecking, see, for instance: http://www.telegraph.co.uk/travel/723860/ Cornwall-The-shipwreck-coast.html

9. It is here: https://youtu.be/F11UABufuos

10. Yes, of baked beans fame. During its centenary, the company bought the privately owned land and returned it to National Trust ownership. Yet another reason why I enjoy their fifty-seven varieties.

11. At least that's what my parents and I think he said. Jesse was amiably odd and we did get the feeling he might just have made this name up on the spot for the hell of it.

AFTERWORD

I'm writing this three weeks after reaching Land's End and it still feels like I'm in a process of readjustment. Physically, the experience has certainly taken a toll. I've run four times since the 18th October and each time, although it's generally been possible to run a fairly steady 8 to 9-minute mile pace for 10 miles or so, the legs keep reminding me what I put them through. The back of my thighs[1] are aching, oddly, since they gave me little trouble during the challenge itself. My knees now seem to bend in a multiplicity of directions, rather than just back and forward, and ache perpetually, albeit at the low pain threshold I've long learned to ignore. The front of my left shin begins to catch fire around seven or eight miles into any run. All of these aches and pains are diminishing, certainly, but it is taking a lot longer than I'd anticipated.

It's as if my body is reluctant to run again, as if it fears I will return to tormenting it daily. I wish I could somehow calm its fears and reassure it that four runs a week (around twenty-five miles) will be perfectly adequate for a while. Until I book my next ultra.

I've resisted doing that so far. I'd like to test what my body can do in its new shape before I inevitably begin to gain weight and lose tone but I'm reluctant to commit. I know this is an understandable slump from which I must pull myself. The trouble is, there is so much to do. I have 8.2 terabytes of data to sift through to put together some sort of assembly edit of the film together. It's taking my poor laptop six days of continuous processing just to make a backup copy of the drive containing the rushes. I'm logging the clips (writing a summary of what each shot contains) and am up to 620 clips and I'm only on day eight.

The book, itself an unknown and epic challenge, is gestating in my head as I write this (I'm writing the afterword before chapter one so that these thoughts remain vivid, since I have no film of the last three weeks to jog my memory). And finally, there's the small matter of obtaining gainful employment. I'd like to think that when *Sparks and Embers* is released, film work will come my way, under the auspices of an agent perhaps, but I can neither rely upon nor wait for that. London remains a fascinating place but also a massive whirlpool, sucking in one's resources and time.

Time for training must be eked out of this schedule, somehow. I did not intend The Long Run to be any kind of full stop to my running but it's a rather hard act to follow! The lunatic part of my brain wonders what it might be like to attempt something like the Appalachian Way, in the footsteps of Scott Jurek and Jennifer Davis.[2] Or even try a 'Longer Run' from, say, the northern tip of Alaska to the most southerly point of South America (Point Barrow to Cape Froward, Chile). But I reckon it will be years before anything that extreme is possible.

Instead, I'm thinking a few hundred miles or similarly extreme ultras, in the UK and abroad might now be the goal. Use what I've learned on The Long Run to maintain effort for a day or more, rather than a month and a half. The famous American races appeal – Western States, Leadville, Hardrock, even Badwater (even the names are daunting, let alone the terrifying statistics I've read concerning their elevation, distance, terrain and temperature). I suspect I'll start a bit closer to home, however.

If some part of me thought that perhaps The Long Run would 'cure' this perverse desire to run endless distances, it hasn't worked. Instead it has renewed my appetite, dormant for a decade and a half of London-dwelling, for the wild places in the UK. There's a West Highland Way Ultra, a Cape Wrath Ultra and several ultras around the South-West Coastal Path. Perhaps I'll revisit a section of The Long Run in the company of several hundred other people, perhaps I'll find a new trail in Wales or Ireland, since those two countries were necessarily absent from my recent adventure. Wherever I find it, the next challenge will come with its own surprises and trials. Will I approach it a different way than I would have before The Long Run? Perhaps. This begs the larger question – how exactly has running from John O'Groats to Land's End changed me?

Firstly, it's made me realise just how strong my willpower can be, if I crank it up properly. In everyday life it's all too easy to succumb to sloth, gluttony, doubt. I've been there myself. Even in the last few weeks I've rested a little more than perhaps I should have, eaten rather more than is wise (my body still doesn't seem to realise I don't need 6,000 calories a day anymore). However, when it's really needed, I now know that I have a huge supply of willpower and determination to draw upon. It just needs to be usefully directed.

My horizons have opened up a lot. I've seen just how many different environments and styles of living are available. I don't need to remain cooped up in a basement studio in West London if I don't need to. I don't have to endure the daily struggle just to keep my head above water if I decide instead to opt out, move to a small town, go and live by the coast, return to my birthplace perhaps. Those are options open to me. This was always true, of course, and you might think, rather obviously so. In a place like London you can get city-blind though, as if the place conspires to throw enough obstacles in your path to keep you from thinking of escape plans. Somehow seeing so many people seemingly living acceptable, even desirable lives, in towns, villages and other cities has opened the country up for me. I think I'm probably stuck in the capital for another year, at most. After that – well, who knows? And that uncertainty is oddly comforting. It's the uncertainty that comes with boundless possibilities.

Finally, but not insignificantly, I feel less fear. Although the future is not just unwritten, it's not even conceived yet, that doesn't really bother me anymore. I can and will get through whatever life throws at me. The Long Run has proven that we *homo sapiens* are resilient and adaptable creatures. The road ahead might be difficult, the trail may be un-signposted with steep climbs and sudden, unexpected descents or seemingly impossible terrain. It can all be overcome. There's no need to be afraid.

Endurance. That's not just what ultra-runners do at the weekend; that's what we humans do, every day.

---

1. The vastus lateralis muscle group, anatomy fans.
2. At time of going to press, Scott Jurek holds the record for running this 2,200 mile course (an incredible 46 days, eight hours and seven minutes, beating Jennifer Davis's record by a mere three hours.

APPENDIX I:
The Fuckity Fuck Song

To be sung only at times of great stress, to a tune of your own devising.

Fucking hell. Fucking hell.
Fuck fuck fuck. Fucking hell.
Fucking hell. Fuck fuck fuck.
Fucking hell. Fucky fuck fuck fuck.

Fuck fuckity fucking hell.
Fuckity fucking hell.
Fuck fuck fuck fucking hell.
Fuck fuck fuckity fuck.

Fuck fuck fucking hell.
Fuck fuck fucking hell.
Fuckity fucking hell.
Fucky fuck fuck fuck.

Fuck fuck fucking hell
Fuck fuck fucking hell
Fuck fuck fuckity fuck.

Fuck fuck fucking hell
Fuck fuck fucking hell
Fuck fuck fucking hell
Fuckity fuck

Fuck fuck fucking hell
Fuck fuck fucking hell
Fuck fuck fucking hell
Fuck fuck fuck
Fuckity fuck.

APPENDIX II:
Equipment List for the Support Vehicle

FOOD:
- NutriBullet blender
- Fruit, nuts and seeds for NutriBullet blender
- Carbohydrate and protein snacks

DRINK:
- At least a dozen litre bottles of tap water
- At least six Lucozade Sport drinks
- Vacuum flask containing tea/coffee

CLOTHING:
- Quick-Change Bag – one outfit for post-run
- Warm recovery coat
- Comfortable post-run boots
- Emergency changes of running clothing
- Bath towel

FIRST AID:
- Full First Aid Kit
- Ice-packs and slings – swelling reduction

CAMERA:
- Panasonic G7 compact-system camera[1]
- DJI Phantom Quadcopter in backpack
- Full range of GoPro Accessories

- Spare Panasonic Batteries and charger
- GoPro Battery Chargers
- GoPro wrist-worn monitor
- Tripod
- Umbrella and bungee ropes
- Protective tarpaulins/blankets
- Waterproof camera cover
- Stick – to gaffer tape umbrella to
- Tiffen variable ND filter
- Canon Ixus compact camera
- Panasonic Camcorder
- Fold-Up Bike or 21-gear Ridgeback bike
- iPad

SOUND:
- Zoom H3 Recorder
- Roland Edirol R-09HR Recorder
- Sennheiser radio mic kit
- Rode hot-shoe mic for G7
- 2 Rode radio smartphone mics

DRIVES / COMPUTER:
- HP Pavilion 15.5 inch laptop
- Lacie Rugged 2TB USB3 Drive
- Seagate 8TB Backup Drive
- SD Card readers
- Multiple 32GB and 128GB SD cards
- Multiple 32GB MicroSD cards

MISCELLANEOUS:
- Toolbox containing screwdrivers, gaffer tape, pliers, blades, adhesives, cable ties, chalk etc.
- Satnav and route maps

---

1. Fitted with a 14-140 Panasonic zoom lens.

APPENDIX III:
My Ultra-Running Kit List

On my person:

Technical T-shirt

Windproof zip-up jacket

Lycra cycling shorts

Over-shorts

Trail or road shoes

2 ply socks (with optional second pair)

Running cap

iPhone on armband

'Vanilla' phone in 'bum bag'

Garmin GPS watch

GoPro on FeiYu Gimbal

Gimbal shoulder-sling (home-made)

GoPro in plastic cover on headband

Camelback Mule running pack

In my backpack:

2 litre Camelbak reservoir (3/4 full of water)

Electrolyte tablets

Glucose Gels

Flapjacks or fudge or mixed nuts/fruit

Factor 30 Sunblock

Running sunglasses

Ibuprofen / Paracetamol

Plasters

Cash – notes and change

Foldable small-scale trail maps

Laminated map-book of whole route

Thermal survival bag

Spare technical T-shirt

Running gloves

Chalk to write emergency messages

Ballpoint pen

GoPro batteries

Gimbal batteries

Smartphone backup USB charger

Smartphone wall charger

iPod shuffle and headphones

SD cards in protective wallet

APPENDIX IV:
Six Life Lessons from The Long Run

Never assume. Or, if you must, accept that your assumptions may be challenged and overthrown.

Try as much as possible to appreciate the moment. The past is gone, the future as yet unwritten.

There are times when you just have to ignore the pain and keep going.[1] Find distractions where and when you can. Take help when it is offered.

You can only run where the trail takes you. Don't fight the inevitable, find another way around the seemingly insurmountable obstacle.

Goals are not immutable. Sometimes circumstances may force a change. Accept this, revise your plan and move on.

Never second-guess the muse. Take advantage of whatever opportunities come your way and give everything as much energy as you have.

---

1. My favourite quote from Murakami's *What I Talk About When I Talk About Running,* from a mantra he recounts as used by a fellow runner: 'Pain is inevitable. Suffering is optional.'